Travel and Exploration

The history of travel writing dates back to the Bible, Caesar, the Vikings and the Crusaders, and its many themes include war, trade, science and recreation. Explorers from Columbus to Cook charted lands not previously visited by Western travellers, and were followed by merchants, missionaries, and colonists, who wrote accounts of their experiences. The development of steam power in the nineteenth century provided opportunities for increasing numbers of 'ordinary' people to travel further, more economically, and more safely, and resulted in great enthusiasm for travel writing among the reading public. Works included in this series range from first-hand descriptions of previously unrecorded places, to literary accounts of the strange habits of foreigners, to examples of the burgeoning numbers of guidebooks produced to satisfy the needs of a new kind of traveller - the tourist.

Notes on the United States of North America during a Phrenological Visit in 1838-39-40

George Combe (1788–1858) rose from humble origins to tour widely in Europe and the United States, lecturing on phrenology, the popular Victorian belief that character traits were determined by the configuration of the skull. He founded Britain's first Phrenological Society in 1820 in Edinburgh, and was considered the foremost phrenologist of the nineteenth century. These volumes, first published in 1841 contain Combe's account of a phrenological lecture tour he undertook in the United States between 1838 and 1840. In the form of a journal, Combe describes the social and political institutions of the United States, and provides vivid descriptions of American society and customs. He also provides accounts of phrenological practice and the lectures he presented. These volumes provide a wealth of information on nineteenth-century society in America, and invaluable details concerning the practice of phrenology. Volume 2 covers his stay in Philadelphia and Maine.

Cambridge University Press has long been a pioneer in the reissuing of out-of-print titles from its own backlist, producing digital reprints of books that are still sought after by scholars and students but could not be reprinted economically using traditional technology. The Cambridge Library Collection extends this activity to a wider range of books which are still of importance to researchers and professionals, either for the source material they contain, or as landmarks in the history of their academic discipline.

Drawing from the world-renowned collections in the Cambridge University Library, and guided by the advice of experts in each subject area, Cambridge University Press is using state-of-the-art scanning machines in its own Printing House to capture the content of each book selected for inclusion. The files are processed to give a consistently clear, crisp image, and the books finished to the high quality standard for which the Press is recognised around the world. The latest print-on-demand technology ensures that the books will remain available indefinitely, and that orders for single or multiple copies can quickly be supplied.

The Cambridge Library Collection will bring back to life books of enduring scholarly value (including out-of-copyright works originally issued by other publishers) across a wide range of disciplines in the humanities and social sciences and in science and technology.

Notes on the United States of North America during a Phrenological Visit in 1838-39-40

VOLUME 2

GEORGE COMBE

CAMBRIDGE
UNIVERSITY PRESS

CAMBRIDGE UNIVERSITY PRESS

Cambridge, New York, Melbourne, Madrid, Cape Town, Singapore,
São Paolo, Delhi, Dubai, Tokyo

Published in the United States of America by Cambridge University Press, New York

www.cambridge.org
Information on this title: www.cambridge.org/9781108021562

© in this compilation Cambridge University Press 2010

This edition first published 1841
This digitally printed version 2010

ISBN 978-1-108-02156-2 Paperback

NOTES

ON THE

UNITED STATES OF NORTH AMERICA,

DURING

A PHRENOLOGICAL VISIT

IN 1838–39–40.

BY

GEORGE COMBE.

VOL. II.

EDINBURGH,

MACLACHLAN, STEWART, & COMPANY:

LONDON, LONGMAN & COMPANY; SIMPKIN,
MARSHALL, & COMPANY; AND
W. S. ORR & COMPANY.

MDCCCXLI.

PRINTED BY NEILL & CO. OLD FISHMARKET, EDINBURGH.

ERRATA.

t. means from the top; b from the bottom.

Page 22 line 5 t. *for* conveying *read* converging
... 47 ... 16 t. *for* fast *read* past
... 109 ... 4 t. *for* Assembly *read* Representatives
... 115 ... 5 b. *for* established *read* abolished
... 136 ... 10 b. *for* $\frac{1}{844}$ *read* $\frac{1}{148}$
... ... 6 b. *for* foot *read* root
... 144 ... 14 b. *delete* few
... 272 ... 1 b. *after* year *insert* , *and delete* 18

The text is printed from a report in an American periodical, but apparently there are some inaccuracies in the figures, which I have no means of correcting.

... 287 ... 6 b. *for* two *read* a
... 337 ... 13 t. *read* This village is the
... 364 ... 3 b. *after* notch, *insert* a

ADDENDA ET CORRIGENDA.

The printed sheets of this volume have been read in New York, Boston, and Philadelphia, and I have been favoured with lists of additions and corrections, of which I gladly avail myself.

Page 117 lines 8 and 3 b —A friend in the United States who has read this volume in sheets, and who is intimately acquainted with the state of education in Massachusetts, corrects the text by the following remarks :—" I do not think the history of our country forms the staple of our instruction at school. It is by our 4th of July orations, our toasts at militia musters, our patriotic songs, and a few histories of Indian wars, none of which are read in school, that the combative and martial feeling is fostered, and it is kept alive also by traditions handed down from generation to generation." I, however, saw " histories" in many of the schools in various States of the Union.—G. C.

Page 259 line 1 and 2 b. A friend in New York writing in January 1841, says, " A comfortable two-storey house, in a medium situation, can be readily obtained for $500 or $600. For such houses, I think, few rents exceed the latter sum." The rents mentioned in the text were actually paid in the cross streets, as high up as Washington Square, in May 1839. Those who paid them informed me of the fact.

Page 286 lines 12 and 13 t.—Many of the judges of the courts also are Unitarians.

CHAPTER I.

1839.

Philadelphia, Jan. 21. Ther 33° *The Climate* —
There is far less moisture in the air of Philadelphia
than in that of British cities in winter, and more
electricity. The climate is so stimulating, that wine
is unnecessary, and to many persons disagreeable.
On 11th January, I mentioned the circumstance of
my collection of drawings and casts being on board
of a schooner which was then frozen up in the Delaware. The ice-boat has succeeded in cutting a clear
way in the river, and the vessel has arrived. I find
that the boxes have been on deck all the voyage,
and these not waterproof : Nevertheless there is
scarcely any damage done even to the drawings. A
small portion of water has entered and been frozen
after reaching the first layer. In Dr Franklin's
days, the English considered the climate of America

A

more damp than that of their own country, and he, with his usual sagacity, expresses doubts whether the opinion be correct, at least in regard to Philadelphia. Whatever may have been the state of matters then, the air is now certainly drier in the American city : But much of the forest has been cleared since that time.

Godliness profitable unto all things.—The Boston newspapers contain a circular, dated 19th December 1838, addressed by the Commissioners appointed by the Western Railroad Corporation, to the clergy of Massachusetts, pointing out to them " the moral effects of rail-roads," and earnestly requesting them " to take an early opportunity to deliver a discourse before your congregation, on the moral effect of rail-roads on our wide extended country." A Philadelphia newspaper, in copying this circular, remarks that it is an improvement on the text, " Religion (Godliness) is profitable unto all things."

John Quincy Adams and Slavery.—Mr Adams has encountered great obloquy for presenting to Congress petitions praying for the abolition of Negro Slavery: He is reported to have mentioned in his place in the House of Representatives on the 21st January current, that he had received many letters, all postmarked, threatening him with assassination, while others were direct challenges to fight duels, in consequence of his presenting resolutions for inquiring into the conduct of Mr Stephenson in England, and petitions for the abolition of slavery and the slave trade, and for the recognition of Hayti. He explained that he would vote against the *slave trade*, but " he would now distinctly tell the house that if the question was put for abolishing slavery in the district of Columbia, he would vote against it." He hoped that the writers of these letters did not really mean to kill him, but only to intimidate him. In this, however, they should not succeed. Mr Adams deserves praise for having publicly announced that such disgraceful communications had been sent to him. They shew, in the individuals who could pen them, a mean, dastardly, and ferocious spirit ; which nothing but a strong expression of public indignation can check.

January 22. Ther 23° *The Eastern Peniten-tiary* *—This day we visited the Eastern Peniten-tiary, of which Mr S. R. Wood, one of the Society of Friends, is the warden. It is a state prison, situated on high ground north-west of the city, and is built in the Gothic style. It covers about ten acres of ground, and the ranges of cells radiate from a central tower to the high walls which surround the whole. It owes its origin to " the Philadelphia Society for alleviating the miseries of public prisons," who, from 1801 to 1821, addressed several petitions and me-

* I am aware that the Report of Mr Crawford to the British Go-vernment, and the works of De Tocqueville, Miss Martineau, and other travellers, have deprived this subject of all pretensions to no-velty ; but I perceive a great deficiency of information concerning criminals still existing in the public mind ; and as important altera-tions in the Prisons System of Scotland are now in progress, it ap-pears to me to be useful to present once more, even at the risk of repetition, a view of the Eastern Penitentiary.

morials to the Legislature, praying for the more effectual employment and separation of prisoners, and " for proving the efficacy of solitude on the morals of those unhappy objects." On 20th March 1821, the Legislature authorized its construction on the principle of " separate and solitary confinement at labour," and provided funds for its erection. It is said to have cost $772,600.* It has attracted great attention not only in America but in Europe, in consequence of the experiment which has been tried in it of the effects of solitary confinement with labour on the health and morals of offenders. It was opened on 1st July 1829.

When a prisoner arrives, he is examined by the warden, and is then taken to the " preparing room." " Here he is divested of his usual garments, his hair is closely trimmed, and he undergoes the process of ablution. He is then clothed in the uniform of the prison, a hood or cap is drawn over his face, and he is conducted to his cell. The bandage is removed from his eyes, and he is interrogated as to his former life, which, as a matter of course, is seldom accurately related." The consequences of his crime, the object in view in his punishment, and the rules of the prison, are next explained to him. He is then locked up in solitude without employment. After enduring this state of existence for some days, and feeling its discomforts, he supplicates for the means of employment; which are granted to him, not as a punishment, but as a favour. He is also furnished with a

* " A Concise History of the Eastern Penitentiary." 1835.

Bible, some religious tracts, and occasionally other works calculated to imbue his mind with moral and religious impressions. In every cell there is a pipe supplying pure water, a kind of water-closet, a bed, a chair, and the implements of the convict's labour. The apartment is heated in winter by pipes filled with hot water, and there is an aperture for ventilation, which is at the command of the convict. Every convict is obliged to keep his cell perfectly clean, and great attention is paid to the cleanliness of his clothing and person. The men receive a towel, a razor, and shaving apparatus. The clothing is comfortable, and adapted to the season. Their food consists, for breakfast, of one pint of coffee or cocoa, made from the cocoa nut, or mush. Dinner three-quarters of a pound of boiled beef without bone, or half a pound of pork, one pint of soup, and an ample supply of potatoes. Occasionally boiled rice instead of potatoes. Supper, Mush (made of the flour of Indian corn boiled) *ad libitum,* one-half gallon of molasses per month, salt whenever asked for, and vinegar as a favour occasionally. Turnips and cabbage in the form of crout are sometimes distributed. The daily allowance of bread is one pound, made of wheat or rye.*

---

* The allowance of food in the Glasgow Bridewell, one of the best managed prisons in Scotland, is as follows: Breakfast, eight ounces of oatmeal made into porridge, with a pint of butter milk. Dinner, two pints of broth (soup), containing four ounces of barley, and one ounce of bone, with vegetables; also eight ounces of bread. Supper, five ounces of oatmeal, made into porridge, with half a pint of butter milk. Cost of the whole, including cooking, 3¼d. " *Fifth Report of Inspectors of Prisons,*" p. 10.

Each convict on his reception receives a number in the books, which is marked over his cell-door, and on his clothes. This is his prison name, and his proper name is kept concealed. This rule prevents one convict from learning the name of another. The convicts on the ground-floor are allowed to walk one hour a-day, in a very small yard which is attached to each cell, and the hours are arranged so that no two contiguous yards are occupied at the same time. The cells on the upper floor do not admit of this exercise being enjoyed, but we were told that the inmates of them are equally healthy with those who inhabit the cells below. Divine service is performed on Sundays, by pastors who serve gratuitously. The chaplain takes his station at one end of a corridor, the prisoners approach their doors, open a small wicket in them, and listen. A curtain is let down in the centre of the corridor, to prevent the convicts from seeing each other across it. Religious books are supplied, but there is no library of miscellaneous publications.

The punishments inflicted for breach of discipline are deprivation of exercise, diminution of the quantity of food, and confinement in a dark cell. No flogging is allowed, and very little punishment of any kind is required. A Board of Inspectors appointed by the Legislature, exercises a general superintendence over the prison, and reports annually to the Legislature. Their reports are accompanied by reports also from the warden and physician; the whole forming authentic and interesting records of the numbers and condition of the convicts, and of the effects of the Penitentiary System for each successive year.

I have perused the Reports for the years 1832 and 1838, and all the intermediate years, and find the following topics touched on in them, worthy of general attention.

In all the Reports, the complaint is repeated, of the want " of the services of an experienced, intelligent, and pious man, who shall be the instructor of the convicts, and visit them frequently in their cells, inculcating day by day the principles of temperance and religion." The Inspectors " do most respectfully and urgently solicit the Legislature to grant them authority to obtain the services of a moral and religious instructor at a compensation adequate to his labour." The moral and religious instruction hitherto communicated has been furnished gratuitously, and the imperfection of its supply is strongly felt.

No single circumstance in the history of Pennsylvania indicates the low state of general information among her people more strongly than the extraordinary fact here brought to light, that, after erecting this Penitentiary at a vast expense, and providing it with all the physical requisites for accomplishing the objects for which it was instituted, the Legislature continues insensible to every entreaty of its legal guardians, urged in the most forcible language for six successive years, to be furnished with adequate means of moral and religious instruction for the prisoners. An enlightened people would as

soon have built a palace without a roof, as have instituted a Penitentiary (a house for moral reformation), without a moral and religious instructor ! One
such teacher is not sufficient. If the intention of
improving the minds of the convicts be seriously entertained, labour must be bestowed in the cultivation
of their moral and intellectual faculties proportionate
to their ignorance and wickedness. If well constituted minds require extensive moral and religious
training and instruction to preserve them in the
paths of virtue, ill constituted minds need much
more. Although we form the highest estimate of
the quantity and quality of this instruction furnished to the convicts, by the excellent persons who labour in the Penitentiary gratuitously, or who are rewarded by benevolent societies, the very fact that
the legal inspectors proclaim it to be insufficient,
leaves the Legislature of Pennsylvania without excuse in denying a further supply. Whenever the
philosophy of mind is generally understood, this
penury of instruction will appear nearly incompre-
hensible. The philanthropists of Europe expect the
American commonwealths to prove, by a liberal ex-
penditure of public money for *moral* objects, the superiority (of which they so loudly boast) of a government emanating from, and responsible to, the people,
over those which depend on the will of an individual
or of a high-born aristocracy. A democracy which
refuses moral and religious instruction to its convicts,
apparently from no consideration except that of saving
the expense, is a greater foe to freedom than the most

ruthless despot of Europe: Such a democracy saps the faith of good men in human virtue; while the tyrant only stifles its outward manifestations, leaving the faith itself to burn the brighter the more he labours to extinguish it.

The warden, in his reports, specifies deficiency in education, as one common cause of crime, and remarks that the convicts in general do not possess the instruction given even in the common free schools of the State.

He repeats again and again, as the result of all his experience, that, " to communicate any material benefit to those who are brought here, their sentences should extend *to two years* or more."

The warden in his seventh report observes, that " a minute inspection of the character of the unhappy inmates of prisons has developed another interesting fact,—that many more of them than was supposed are really irresponsible beings," (p. 8). And the inspectors remark, that " there are no doubt *some criminals who are incorrigible*." The effect of the Penitentiary discipline on them does not generate vindictive feelings, but they leave the establishment with sentiments of regard rather than resentment, towards those who have attempted to alter their vicious habits. Phrenologists have long proclaimed, that the great cause of the incorrigibility of criminals is the excessive predominance of the organs of the animal propensities, over those of the moral and intellectual faculties, and that this class of persons is really composed of moral patients, who should be restrained,

but not otherwise punished, during life. As Nature
is constant in her operations, this truth will in time
force itself on the conviction of society; and after injustice and severity shall have been perpetrated for
ages, by the free and the fortunate towards the ill-
constituted and unhappy, a better system of treatment will probably be adopted. Why are the clergy,
those guardians of the poor, and ministers of mercy,
silent on this subject? Even those of them who are
Phrenologists, and know the truth of what I now
state, have not moral courage sufficient to lift their
voices on behalf of these unfortunate beings.

The *health* of the prisoners is indicated by the following table :

Year.	Average Number in Confinement.	Number of Deaths.	Mortality per cent.
1830,	31	1	3.
1831,	67	4	6.
1832,	91	4	4.4
1833,	123	1	.8
1834,	183	5	2.7
1835,	266	7	2.6
1836,	360	12	3.3
1837,	387	17	4.3
			8) 27.1
			3.4
			Average.

The reports state, that the deaths arise in some
instances from incurable disease affecting the prisoners at their entry, and that the average is greatly
augmented by the sickly inefficient condition of the

coloured prisoners, who, " by self-abuse, become debilitated in mind and body, and diseased, and make up 3-5ths of the whole mortality."

A few convicts labouring under insanity at the time of condemnation, have been sent to the Penitentiary, and the inspectors complain, that in one or two instances they have been convicted, in the full knowledge of their insanity, with a view to get quit of them as troublesome to the county! A committee of the Legislature, in a report read in the Senate on 14th February 1837 states, that " no instance of insanity has, as yet, occurred in the Eastern Penitentiary, which has not been traced to causes wholly independent of, and either anterior or posterior to the confinement. Whatever might be the disturbing and stultifying effects of strict seclusion, without labour, without books, without moral instruction, and without daily intercourse with the keepers, certain it is, that with all these circumstances to relieve the distressing ennui, and the supposed maniacal effects, of absolute isolation, the inmates of our prisons are in no danger of aberration or alienation of mind from the cause supposed." (P. 4.) Again, " A comparison of the bills of mortality of the Eastern Penitentiary, with those of several other institutions, will shew conclusively, that the unbroken solitude of the Pennsylvania discipline, does not injuriously affect the health of the convicts. At the Eastern Penitentiary, the deaths are two and five-tenths per cent;*

* This statement is at variance with the results of the preceding table of mortality, and apparently refers to the mortality of the *white* convicts alone.

at the Sing Sing Prison, four per cent. ; at Auburn, two per cent., and so on, settling the question beyond a possibility of doubt, that as great a measure of health is preserved in the Pennsylvania prisons, as in other similar institutions in the United States, or elsewhere."

In opposition to these statements, several severe attacks have been made on the Eastern Penitentiary system, as leading to excessive suffering, accompanied by loss of health and reason, on the part of the convicts, and the " Concise History," before referred to, contains strong assertions and some evidence in support of this unfavourable view.   But, on the other hand, I found that several highly intelligent professional men in Philadelphia, with whom I conversed on the subject, and who had the means of judging, regarded the official reports as essentially correct and worthy of credit.

We visited a number of the male convicts who had been confined for periods ranging from seventeen months to eight years, and their appearance did not indicate either bad health or mental depression.   We were introduced also into the cells of several female convicts, some of whom had ornamented the walls with pictures and needlework, giving to the apartments an appearance of tidiness and comfort that bespoke a healthy condition of mind in the inmates.

The food appears to be too rich and abundant for solitude, and several of the men had applied to be placed on a tea diet, consisting of tea and bread, which is allowed them when asked for.   Secret vice abounds among the men, particularly the coloured convicts, who have few mental resources ; but one of the white male prisoners had celebrated its pleasures and pains in an ode written with a pencil on the white-washed wall of his cell. In conversing with the prisoners, I found them seemingly resigned and cheerful; but I place little reliance on appearances presented to a casual visitor of a prison, especially when he is ac companied by an officer. He will be shewn only the best cases, while the convicts will be agreeably excited by his visit, and feel little disposition to complain to one who has no power to relieve them, and in presence of a person whose displeasure they dread, and against whom every complaint would be an ac cusation. At the same time, justice requires me to state, that Mr Wood offered to introduce us to any cells we chose to point out ; and gave me the conviction that he had no secrets to conceal. His views of the criminal mind appeared to me to be sound and enlightened, and his principles of action at once just and humane.

In my work on Moral Philosophy, I have discussed the subject of the treatment of criminals, and at page 258 of the Edinburgh edition, have introduced some remarks on the system of solitude and labour, to which I beg leave to refer.

In regard to the effects of the discipline in the Eastern Penitentiary, I observe that the system of entire solitude, even when combined with labour, and the use of books, and an occasional visit from a religious instructor, leaves the moral faculties still in a passive state, and without the means of vi-

gorous active exertion.   According to my view of the
laws of physiology, this discipline reduces the tone of
the *whole* nervous system to the level which is in
harmony with solitude.   The passions are weakened
and subdued, but so are all the moral and intellectual
powers.   The susceptibility of the nervous system is
increased, because organs become susceptible of impressions, in proportion to their feebleness.   A weak
eye is pained by a degree of light which is agreeable
to a sound one.   Hence, it may be quite true, that religious admonitions will be more deeply felt by prisoners living in solitude, than by those enjoying society ; just as such instruction, when addressed to a
patient recovering from a severe and debilitating ill-
ness, makes a more vivid impression than when delivered to the same individual in health ; but the appearances of reformation founded on such impressions
are deceitful.   When the sentence is expired, the
convict will return to society, with all his mental
powers, animal, moral, and intellectual, increased in
susceptibility, but *lowered in strength*.   The excite-
ments that will then assail him, will have their influence doubled, by operating on an enfeebled system.   If he meet old associates and return to drinking and profanity, the animal propensities will be
fearfully excited by the force of these stimulants,
while his enfeebled moral and intellectual powers
will scarcely be capable of offering any resistance.
If he be placed amidst virtuous men, his higher faculties will feel acutely, but be still feeble in executing
their own resolves.   Convicts, after long confinement
in solitude, shudder to encounter the turmoil of the

world; they become excited as the day of liberation approaches, and feel bewildered when set at liberty In short, this system is not founded on, nor in harmony with, a sound knowledge of the physiology of the brain, although it appeared to me to be well administered.

These views are supported by the " report of Doctor James B. Coleman, physician to the New Jersey State Prison (in which solitary confinement with labour is enforced), addressed to the Board of Inspectors, November 1839." The report states, that, "among the prisoners there are many who exhibit a child-like simplicity, which shews them to be less acute than when they entered. In all who have been more than a year in prison, some of these effects have been observed. Continue the confinement for a longer time, and give them no other exercise of the mental faculties than this kind of imprisonment affords, and the most accomplished rogue will lose his capacity for depredating with success upon the community. The same influence that injures the other organs will soften the brain. Withhold its proper exercise, and as surely as the bandaged limb loses its power, will the prisoner's faculties be weakened by solitary confinement." He sums up the effect of the treatment in these words, " While it subdues the evil passions, almost paralyzing them for want of exercise, it leaves the individual, if still a rogue, one who may be easily detected ;" in other words, in reducing the energy of the organs of the propensities, it lowers also that of the organs of the moral and intellectual faculties, or causes the convict to approach more or less towards general idiocy. Dr Coleman does not inform us whether the brain will not recover its vigour after liberation, and thus leave the offender as great a rogue after the close, as he was at the beginning, of his confinement.

The Auburn system of social labour, is better, in my opinion, than that of Pennsylvania, in so far as it allows of a little more stimulus to the social faculties, and does not weaken the nervous system to so great an extent; but it has no superiority in regard to providing efficient means for invigorating and training the moral and intellectual faculties. The Pennsylvania system preserves the convict from contamination by evil communications with his fellow-prisoners, and prevents his associates from knowing the fact of his being in prison. These are advantages that go so far to compensate the evils of solitude, but do not remove them.*

In maintaining that some men are moral patients who should be restrained, but not otherwise punished, I have often been met by the objection, that this doctrine destroys human responsibility. My answer has been, first, that Phrenologists, in urging this view, desire only to extend the class of idiots and the insane, who are by universal consent absolved from responsibility; and, secondly, that men in general, while they reject as dangerous and untrue the proposition in the abstract, adopt it practically, and are unwittingly guilty of the most flagrant inconsistency and pernicious injustice.

I have asked these objectors, if they would receive

* Moral Philosophy, p. 309.

into their families, as domestic servants, or into their employment in stores, convicts who had served out their time in state prisons, supposing them qualified by knowledge for the duties of these stations; and most of them have answered that they would not. On being asked why they would decline, they have generally replied that they had not sufficient confidence in their reformation. There is obviously great inconsistency in such conduct. If they believe that every individual has power to reform himself, and that the prison is wisely framed to effect this reform, it is cruel to assume that the individual in question is not reformed, and to exclude him from social comfort and honour on this assumption. The truth is, they *act* on the principle that some criminals are incorrigible, and that this may be one of the number : and therefore decline placing trust in any. Yet they blame us for teaching the same doctrine, and desiring to found on it a better practice.*

It is satisfactory to find that these views are supported by the experience of the inspectors and warden of the Eastern Penitentiary. They not only express a desire that the incorrigibles should be treated as patients, but strongly urge the necessity of an asylum for discharged convicts intermediate between the prison and common society. In their report for 1838, the inspectors remark, that " the situation and sufferings of discharged convicts have excited our attention and sympathy. We feel that we shall be excused in presenting the subject to the

* Moral Philosophy, p. 307.

consideration of the legislature and our fellow-citizens generally. The small sum of money (*$*5) allowed to a convict on his discharge is often expended whilst he is seeking for employment. But when that is gone, and no employment can be had, what hope is there that he will be able to struggle against poverty and maintain his virtue? This class of men, as well as a large portion of the labouring poor, need advice and assistance to help them along the rugged pathway of life." The warden, in his report for the same year, says, " The unwillingness manifested by most employers to take persons released from prison into their work-shops, makes it difficult for convicts to obtain good situations at any period of the year, but during the winter especially. Out-door work is scarce, and those discharged at this season often find themselves in so very destitute a situation, that we need not be surprised if they should sometimes be tempted to steal rather than starve. I believe much benefit would result from the courts either extending or diminishing in a slight degree the confinement, so as to make it terminate in either the spring, summer, or autumn."

The necessity for an asylum for convicts intermediate between the prison and society, while the present system of treatment is pursued, is obvious. Before a convict can be fitted to re-enter the social circles of his country with a fair prospect of continuing in the paths of virtue, the discipline which he has undergone must have invigorated and enlightened his moral and intellectual powers to such an extent, that he, when liberated, shall be able to restrain his own propensities, amidst the usual temptations presented by the social condition.

There is only one way of strengthening faculties, and that is by exercising them; and all the American prisons which I have seen are lamentably deficient in arrangements for exercising the moral and intellectual faculties of their inmates. During the hours of labour, no advance can be made, beyond learning a trade. This is a valuable addition to a convict's means of reformation; but it is not all-sufficient. After the hours of labour, he is locked up in solitude; and I doubt much if he can read, for want of light; but assuming that he can,—reading is a very imperfect means of strengthening the moral powers. They must be exercised, trained, and habituated to action. My humble opinion is, that in prisons there should be a teacher of high moral and intellectual power, for every eight or ten convicts; that, after the close of labour, these instructors should commence a system of vigorous culture of the superior faculties of the prisoners, excite their moral and religious feelings, and instruct their understandings In proportion as the prisoners give proofs of moral and intellectual advancement, they should be indulged with the liberty of social converse and action, for a certain time on each week-day, and on Sundays, in presence of the teachers; and in these *converzationes*, or evening parties, they should be trained to the *use* of their higher powers, and habituated to restrain their propensities. Every indication of over-active propensity should be visited by a restriction of liberty and enjoyment; while these advantages, and also respectful treatment, and moral consideration, should be increased in exact proportion to the advancement of the convicts in morality and understanding. By such means, if by any, the convicts would be prepared to enter society with their higher faculties so trained and invigorated, as to give them a chance of resisting temptation, and continuing in the paths of virtue.

In no country has the idea yet been carried into effect, that in order to produce moral fruits, it is necessary to put into action moral influences, great and powerful in proportion to the *barrenness* of the soil from which they are expected to spring.*

The convicts whom I saw in this prison presented the usual deficiencies in the organs of the moral sentiments in relation to those of the animal propensities which distinguish criminals in general. One man, in whom the superior organs were very deficient, and Acquisitiveness, Secretiveness, and Destructiveness very large, with a good intellectual development, said, in answer to a question from me, that it would depend on circumstances whether he would steal again after he was liberated.

In the Appendix, No. I., I insert " a Table of the Mental Disorders in the Eastern Penitentiary during 1839," by Dr Darrach, physician to the institution.

Jan. 24. Ther 15° *Phrenology* —Phrenologists estimate the size of the moral organs by the extent

---

* Moral Philosophy, p. 308.

to which the brain rises above a plane passing through the centres of ossification of the frontal and parietal bones, the centres of Causality B, and Cautiousness 12. The correct measurement should be a plane passing through the upper edges of these two organs; but the centres are well marked points, while the upper edge is not so distinctly defined. The line AB in the wood-cut will shew the direction of the former plane.

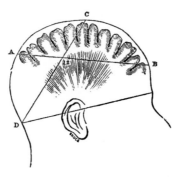

This day Dr Pancoast, at my request, was so obliging as to saw open the skull of a negro woman, aged about fifty, in the plane of A B, the centres of Causality and Cautiousness, and cut the brain, with an amputating knife, across in the same plane, without removing it from the skull, with a view to discover whether the bottom of the convolutions of the moral organs penetrated to that plane. Only a few of the largest did so. On cutting upwards, nearly half an inch of medullary matter was removed before the bottom of the convolutions C, forming the organs of Veneration and Hope, appeared. In repeating the

experiment, the section should be made in a plane corresponding to the *top* of Causality and Cautiousness.
The bottom of the coronal convolutions was found
about the level of this plane.

We examined, in a prepared brain, the conveying
and diverging fibres described by Drs Gall and Spurzheim. In several sections in the upper portion of
the middle lobe, the diverging fibres were distinguishable, crossing the converging, and producing,
when removed by the handle of the scalpel, a broken
surface at the point where the crossing took place.

Jan. 26. Ther 26° *Asylum for the Blind.*—We
visited this asylum, and found it a large, commodious,
well-arranged institution, which receives an appro-
priation from the State. Dr Friedlander, the superintendent, who is greatly esteemed, is at present in
the south, on account of bad health. The pupils labour only three hours a-day, in brush, basket, mat,
and shoe making, needlework and knitting. They
are taught the ordinary branches of school education.
Their books, in raised characters, are printed in the
establishment, and they use the common Roman
capital type. I mentioned Dr Howe's remarks on
the facility with which the blind learn to read letters
of a variety of forms, and the advantage of each
institution printing separate books and interchang-
ing ; but I was told that the pupils here find a difficulty in reading any letters except those to which
they have become accustomed. This seems to me to
be an error founded on an assumption that such will
be the case, rather than on experience that it is so.

Farther, Dr Howe's pupils increase the extent and variety of the exercise which they are enabled to take, by climbing up poles, jumping over beams, and performing other athletic feats. Here it is believed to be dangerous to the blind to do such acts, and the pupils always keep on the ground. It appears to me that Dr Howe has a bold, active, enterprising mind, and that to a certain extent he impresses his own character on the minds of his pupils. He enlarges the practical boundaries of their capacities by encouraging them to believe in the greatness of their natural extent.

Jan. 26. Ther 52° *The Weather* —Yesterday with evening the wind changed to the south-east, and, a high temperature, it rained in torrents all night, and all this day till 4 P. M., when the wind suddenly veered round to the north-west, and blew a gale.*

Dr Benjamin Rush.—We met in society this evening Dr Joseph Parrish, a distinguished and most amiable Quaker physician. He is attending my lectures, and informed me that forty years ago he was a pupil of Dr Benjamin Rush of Philadelphia, and recognised in Phrenology the more complete development of many ideas which Dr Rush had entertained. The same remark had occurred to myself on reading Dr Rush's " Inquiry into the Influence of

---

* In September 1840, in Edinburgh, I heard Mr Espy describe this storm. His facts corresponded with the statement in the text, which was written at the time when the storm occurred, and in ignorance of his views; and his theory appeared to me to account satisfactorily for the phenomena.

Physical Causes on the Moral Faculty," read by him before the American Philosóphical Society on 27th February 1786. That " oration," as it is called in the original, displays great powers of observation, and sagacity in deducing inferences, and approaches more nearly to Dr Gall's discovery than any other work which I have seen.

The Quakers.—Philadelphia was founded by William Penn, who was at once a man of family, and a Quaker ; a fortunate combination for the infant city. In the choice of the situation, the plan of the city, the names of the streets, and in many of his regulations, there are proofs of his cultivated taste ; while the uprightness and simplicity of the Quaker principles, which he and his followers established, strongly and favourably influence society here even in the present day. About eleven years ago, a large section of the Quakers of Pennsylvania became Unitarians, under the influence of Elias Hicks. Some of these, while they have preserved their connection with the sect, have abandoned the costume ; while others have left the Society of Friends entirely. The original Quakers, who have not changed their opinions, are called " the orthodox" friends. In Pennsylvania, the Hicksite Quakers amount to about 20,000, and the orthodox to about 8000. In the United States, the total number of Hicksite Quakers is nearly 80,000.

A man who has produced so great a revolution in the religious tenets of a powerful sect, is an interesting object of observation. A friend kindly presented me with a small engraved portrait of him, which indicates a large development of the moral and intellectual organs; large Firmness, and a high bilious and nervous temperament; the combination usually found in energetic reformers. The base of the brain also seems to have been well developed, but it is more difficult to judge of its size in a picture. The following " Remarks on the character of the late Elias Hicks," were extracted, by the same friend, from several biographical sketches of him :—

" Elias Hicks was born in Long Island in 1748, and died in 1830. When about twenty years of age he embraced the principles of the Society of Friends, in due time became a minister, and for more than fifty years he laboured with unwearied diligence for the instruction and benefit of his fellow-men. He travelled through almost every State in the Union, as well as into Canada several times; scrupulously avoiding any gratuity or reward for his multiplied and protracted labours. The testimonies which his Society held before the world, he bore patiently and fearlessly, urging them on the consciences of his hearers, in a manner which did not permit them to be indifferent, and with a zeal which demanded and secured the attention of those whom he addressed. Large numbers listened and crowded around him to hear the joyful tidings which he had to bear. He was at all times the friend of freedom of conscience, thought, and action, and the able and unceasing advocate of human rights. The African and Indian were never forgotten by him, but were embraced

within the circle of his benevolence. He was in
early life deeply impressed with the injustice and
cruelty of keeping slaves, and was among the first
who brought the subject frequently and forcibly before the members of his religious society. It was
some time before his friends could unite with him,
but where principle was involved, his perseverance
was unabating, and his resolution immoveable.

" He was a man, in the language of Scripture,
' instant in season and out of season' to do good to
his fellow-beings. He was truly a peace-maker; in
all his relations in life kind and affectionate; and his
manners were peculiarly distinguished by a patri-
archal simplicity, and unaffected goodness. Hence
it was not unfrequently the case, that persons who,
from false reports, had contracted strong prejudices
against him, have been completely disarmed by a
short interview.

" The strong and abiding sense of justice and
equality which marked his intercourse with his fellow-men, was exemplified in relation to a circumstance which took place when he was absent from
home. A person to whom he had lent money to
assist him in business, had been unsuccessful, and in
closing his concerns, he secured to Elias Hicks a sufficient amount of his property to indemnify him for
the sum lent. On his return he called together
the creditors, stated to them his unwillingness to retain the amount wholly to himself, and gave directions that it should be divided among them all, in
proportion to the sums respectively due to each per-

son. It was upon these principles that he regulated his conduct throughout his long and valuable life. His kind and benevolent feelings carried him out towards every species of human suffering, and led him to be kind and liberal in supplying the necessities of the poor. He laboured diligently with his own hands, believing it to be the duty of all to be usefully employed in obtaining the necessaries of life.

" In declaring what he believed to be the counsel of God, he was bold and fearless. Possessing an acute and argumentative mind, he assailed the strong holds of superstition and bigotry with great boldness, which alarmed the timid, and aroused the prejudices of many. Yet to the candid inquirer, and sincere seeker after truth, he breathed the language of encouragement, of consolation, and of comfort. His great and primary concern was, to draw the minds of the people to practical righteousness—from all outward dependence, to the sure foundation, the Rock of Ages, the spirit of truth—' Christ within, the hope of glory.' He was an example of Christian humility, and eminently preserved from being elated by the applause of men, or depressed by their censure. He impressed upon the minds of the young, the importance and necessity of early attention to the inward discoveries of Divine light, cautioning them not to rest in the tradition of their fathers, nor to depend upon the teachings of men, for that knowledge which brings life and immortality to light in the soul.

" In times of great trial during the division and

separation in the Society of which he was a member, he experienced the truth of the declaration, ' Thou wilt keep him in perfect peace whose mind is stayed on thee, because he trusteth in thee.' "*

---

* While this work is in the press, Mr James Mott, and his wife, Mrs Lucretia Mott, two of the Society of Friends of Philadelphia, who have adopted the views of Elias Hicks, visited Scotland, and were invited to attend the annual meeting of the Glasgow Emancipation Society on the 1st of August 1840. I became acquainted with them in Philadelphia, and I regard both as among the most estimable persons whom I have met with in any country. Dr Channing, in his Letter to the Honourable Jonathan Phillips, when adverting to the burning by a mob of the Hall of Freedom in that city, writes—" In that crowd was Lucretia Mott, that beautiful example of womanhood. Who that has heard the tones of her voice, and looked on the mild radiance of her benignant and intelligent countenance, can endure the thought, that such a woman was driven by a mob, from a spot to which she had gone, as she religiously believed, on a mission of Christian sympathy." This description falls short of the truth. To the soft delicacy of a refined and accomplished woman, Lucretia Mott adds the clear and forcible intellect of a philosopher. The Meeting of the Glasgow Emancipation Society was held in the Chapel of the Rev. Dr Wardlaw, and the directors of the Society were Orthodox Quakers, and other persons of similar principles. No places on the platform were appointed for Mr and Mrs Mott. No invitation was given to them to address the assembly. " The American friends," says the Christian Pioneer, " bore about them the taint of heresy. This was sufficient to warrant neglect and insult to individuals who had perilled property and life in vindication of the rights of humanity. Dr Wardlaw, in the face of the assembly, could shake hands with a coloured American as a friend and brother; but averted looks were deemed the proper reception for those who dared to think for themselves in theology. Nay, even George Thomson, the declaimer against American slavery, who had received the hospitalities of these true friends of universal humanity, stood by; and no sound was heard to issue from his lips against this desecration of courtesy and Christian justice." On Sunday evening, 9th August, Mr Mott delivered an Address in the Rev. Mr Harris's Chapel, in Glasgow, in which he stated who they were, their object in visiting this country

The Inward Light.—It is a fundamental doctrine with the Society of Friends, that *every* man has received an inward light sufficient to guide him in the discharge of his duty, if he consult it in a right spirit.* My Quaker friends discussed the bearing of

(to attend the great Anti Slavery Meeting held in London in June 1840), their differences in religious views from the Society of Friends in Britain; and he read, in corroboration of his statements, certificates from the Monthly Meeting of Friends in Philadelphia, and of Abolition Societies. Mrs Mott then spoke for nearly two hours, and held a delighted audience in breathless attention. In the course of the following week, a letter, subscribed by " Wm. Smeal, Wm. White, John Maxwell, James Smeal, and Edward White," appeared in the Glasgow newspapers, informing the public, " on behalf of the Society of Friends residing in Glasgow, that we hold no religious fellowship with Lucretia Mott, nor with the body in the United States (called Hicksites) to which she belongs," &c. This is true, but Mr Mott had stated the fact to be so at the meeting, and this appeal to the public was therefore another deliberate insult. The object of the meeting in Dr Wardlaw's Chapel was the promotion of the cause of " Emancipation," and it had no necessary connection with any religious opinions, except those of practical Christianity in which all sects are agreed. The spirit, therefore, which excluded Mr and Mrs Mott on account of their religious opinions, was one of hatred and persecution. When I recall the liberal cordiality with which my Lectures on Phrenology were received in Philadelphia by the Friends of both persuasions, the Orthodox as well as the Hicksites, and the hospitable attentions which I received from *both*, and contrast it with the treatment which Mr and Mrs Mott have met with in Scotland, I blush for the intolerance of my country. These proceedings certainly shew, that the directors of " the Glasgow Emancipation Society," stand in " need of emancipation from more degrading fetters than those even of which they profess the desire to free the negro."

* They affirm that " God hath given to every man a measure of the light of his own Son (John i. 9), and that God, by this light, invites, calls, and strives with every man, in order to serve him; which, as it is received, works the salvation of all, even of those who are ignorant of the death of Christ, and of Adam's fall; but that this light may be resisted; in which case God is said to be resisted and rejected, and Christ to be again crucified; and to those who thus resist and

Phrenology on this doctrine with great acuteness and candour. I hazarded the explanation that the inward light which they spoke of, if it be regarded as natural, probably consisted of the spontaneous dictates of the moral sentiments, which condemn all abuses of the propensities; that apparently George Fox, the founder of their sect, had enjoyed a large development of the organs of these sentiments, particularly of Conscientiousness and Benevolence, and that, judging from his own feelings, and assuming all men to be constituted like himself, he had interpreted certain passages of Scripture in accordance with his individual experience, and thus arrived at the doctrine of the sufficiency of the inward light as universal, while Phrenology shewed that it was limited to men possessing the best constituted brains. This view was new to the Friends; but they told me that it seemed to throw some light on several anomalies which had long remained inexplicable. Some of their body had such a clear and forcible consciousness of the existence of the inward light, that they could not conceive how any person of a sane mind, whether of their society or not, could doubt its existence; while others of their own sect, and numerous individuals who did not belong to them, either doubted the reality of the perception of that light, or regarded it as altogether a phantom of imagination. Phrenology leads us to infer, that the believers in the light probably possess large, and the unbelievers small, or-

refuse him, he becomes their condemnation."—*A Dictionary of all Re ligions by Hannah Adams.* P. 88.

gans of the moral sentiments, and that hence they really differ in their inward experience, and err in assuming their own consciousness as a standard of universal human nature. I expressed the opinion, that individuals who are very deficient in the moral organs, do not possess the inward light sufficiently clear and strong to serve as a guide to their conduct, and that hence arose the need of specific precepts, such as are contained in the Scriptures, commending certain acts, and prohibiting others; and that Phrenology will one day prove useful to all sects in leading them to correct their doctrines, and to bring them into harmony with universal human nature, instead of limiting them to cases of particularly constituted minds.

Jan. 27. Ther 30° The wind still blows strongly from the north-west, with frost.

Catholicism in the United States.—We attended divine service to-day in the Roman Catholic church in Thirteenth Street, and found a large and genteel-looking congregation, with all the usual ceremonials of Catholicism. We were told that the Catholics here are chiefly foreigners, who bring their religion with them; and that they are an inoffensive sect in the United States. The free institutions of the country modify the spirit of their religion, and they are good citizens and estimable neighbours. I mentioned to a Protestant gentleman, whom I afterwards met in society, the great difficulty which I experienced in attaching any meaning to the ringing of bells, burning of candles, and other ceremonies of the Catholic

worship, and he told me that his impressions were
very different. His father (a Protestant) had sent
him, when a boy, to a Roman Catholic monastery in
Canada for the sake of giving him a thorough education in the French language ; the priests initiated
him into the meaning of their ceremonies, and employed him as one of the bell-ringing and train-bear-
ing boys, who serve at the altar ; and so profound an
impression of the sanctity and solemnity of the worship had been made on his mind, that he could not,
to the present day, enter a Roman Catholic chapel
without vivid emotions of veneration, with which his
judgment did not harmonise, for he had not been
converted to their faith. From this, we may infer
that to Catholics these ceremonies are by no means
unmeaning mummeries, as we Protestants are too
prone to imagine them to be.

Legislature of Pennsylvania.—Every one acquainted with the machinery of the British Parliament
knows that for many years nothing could exceed the
profligate dereliction of all principle which characterized the action of the committees of the House of
Commons on private bills. The majority of the
members of these committees often disposed of the
most momentous interests of their constituents without hearing a word of the evidence on which their
decisions were supposed to be founded. Their votes,
governed by motives of private interest, or of political favour or hostility, were secured by solicitation
and influence ; and, in short, they were moved by
every consideration except those of utility and jus-

tice. Even in the present day, when some of these more flagrant abuses have been extinguished, the individual whose rights and interests are in dependence before a parliamentary committee, finds himself degraded into a petitioner for favour, instead of a solicitor for justice. He is still under the necessity of plying the members of the committee with every possible external influence to induce them to attend in their places, that they may hear the evidence, and understand the arguments, which he considers it necessary to present to them, often at a ruinous expense, to enable them to judge of the merits of the measure on which they are bound to report with the impartiality of judges.

I was anxious to learn whether any similar evil exists under the democratic institutions of the United States, in which the elections are frequent, the suffrage nearly universal, and the responsibility of the representatives to the people complete.

A gentleman who has been a member of the senate of Pennsylvania informed me, that the same mischievous machinery is at work in their legislature. There is extensive jobbing and treating relative to private bills, or bills for the establishment of public companies. The parties who apply for the bill, or their agents, come to Harrisburg while the legislature is in session, and, under pretence of explaining the subject to the members, flatter them, give them suppers, and open their understandings by means of plentiful libations of wine. Many of the representatives are men from country districts, of

little education, and humble fortune, but of unques-
tionable integrity, who would reject with indignation
a money bribe, but who unconsciously fall before
personal flatteries and champagne. The technical
name for these practices is " lobbying."

In the legislature of New York, some years ago,
" lobbying" was reduced to a system. The agents
for the various private bills concerted their measures together, and made up lists of all the members of the legislature, specifying those whom they
could influence absolutely, those whom they could
probably carry, and those (a very small remnant)
who were altogether independent; and, after " the
order of the day," or list of business before the
chambers, was published, they met in a tavern, and
took the " yeas and nays " on every bill in which
they were interested, either *pro* or *con*. The first
bill, for instance, was named; (probably one for a
charter to a bank); the roll of the representatives
was then called, and the different agents answered
" yea" or " nay" for the members respectively whose
votes they could command. When this was finished, the independent members were distributed according to the best estimate which the agents could
form of their probable course of action ; the balance
was then struck, and the announcement regularly
made, the " yeas" or the " nays" have it. So complete was this machinery, and so perfect the sagacity
with which the opinions of the independent members
were guessed at, that the decisions of the chambers
became ludicrous echoes of those of the " lobby !"

At last a check was given to the practice, but much of it still exists ; and it will exist until a higher education of the people shall raise the standard of their moral and intellectual perceptions. As a stream cannot rise higher than its fountain, so, in social life, if the public mind be blind and selfish, the representatives of that mind will never rise into the regions of truth and justice.

It is a common opinion, that if the suffrage for legislators be universal, and elections be frequent, a due regard to their own interests will lead the people to choose wise representatives, and the representatives to adopt just and beneficial measures ; but this is an error. Phrenology shews us that self-interest depends on the animal propensities, and that every one of them is merely a blind impulsive power, which desires its own gratification, but which needs to be illuminated by knowledge, and guided by morality, before it can successfully attain its own objects. The organs of the propensities are generally the largest and most active in the brain ; and most of us, therefore, are by nature abundantly selfish ; but we are not equally clear-sighted in regard to the best means of promoting our own interests. Indeed self-interest more frequently defeats than accomplishes its own objects, through ignorance of the obstacles that lie in its way, and of the means which nature has appointed as indispensable to its own gratification. Every legislature, therefore, which is founded on the maxim that self-interest will discover the best means of attaining its own ends, and that where all

are represented it will necessarily lead to the general
good, rests on a bed of sand.   In the conflict of selfish desires of equal force, justice may be reached as
the only point at which adjustment will be possible, as
objects propelled in opposite directions by equal forces
fall into diagonal lines, and meet in a central point ;
but this is a dangerous, circuitous, and uncertain
method of attaining to truth.   The moral sentiments
alone desire universal happiness, and intellect, extensively informed and highly cultivated, is necessary to discover the means of realizing their desires.
High moral, religious, and intellectual training,
therefore, in the people at large, and nothing else,
will produce pure and wise legislation.   The most
consolatory view of the present condition of the
people of the United States is, that their institutions give such unlimited play to the selfish principles of their nature, that, by their very blunders
and sufferings (which are neither few nor small), they
will be forced into the discovery of the incapacity of
self-interest to find its own way to happiness, and
be led, by the very necessity of their circumstances,
to call in the aid of morality and knowledge—in other
words, to increase and improve the moral, religious,
and intellectual cultivation of their rising generations.

Phrenology —One third at least of my auditors,
now exceeding 500 persons, belong to the Society of
Friends, including both orthodox and Hicksites, and
they tell me that Friend John Joseph Gurney, who
has recently come to the United States on a mission
of charity and religion, is warning his friends, and

the circle which he influences, against Phrenology, as a dangerous doctrine, and one to be shunned by sound believers. As they have now heard a pretty full exposition of it, they take the liberty to judge for themselves, and I do not find that their fears keep pace with those of Mr Gurney. In answer to the question, whether Mr Gurney meant to affirm that it is dangerous to religion to teach the true functions of the brain, or only that Phrenology is false, and therefore dangerous ?—my friends replied, that, so far as they could learn, he knew little about the subject, and appeared to condemn it on vague impressions existing in his own mind, rather than on any specific information concerning its merits.

Jan. 29. Ther 30° *Mr De Ponceau, Baron Hammer, and Captain Basil Hall.*—This day I met Mr De Ponceau in society, and he asked me about the accentuation of the Gaelic, which he reads, but has never heard spoken. Unfortunately, I could give him no information on the subject. He came to the United States from France in 1775, and has realized a fortune in the law, chiefly as a notary. He is highly celebrated as a philologist. He corresponds with Baron Hammer of Vienna, and mentioned that he had translated and published the Baron's Letter in answer to Captain Basil Hall's statements in his work called Schloss Hainfeld. The Baron had written to him that he could not induce any periodical in England to publish it. He was much interested when I told him that I had formed an acquaintance with Baron Hammer, now Baron Hammer Purgstall, when I visited Vienna in 1837, and had received from him a copy of the Letter in question, printed in " the New York American" of 6th Dec. 1836; and that I had subsequently succeeded in getting it inserted in a London newspaper. This led to an interesting conversation concerning Captain Hall and Schloss Hainfeld, when I mentioned to him that Baron Hammer had requested me to peruse several original letters written by the Countess of Purgstall to him, all in English, in which she expressed herself in the most kind and confidential terms towards him. I had read also a letter from the Countess Rzewnska to him, which shewed that Captain Hall received his invitation to Schloss Hainfeld through him, communicated to the Captain by the Countess Rzewnska, and afterwards confirmed by the Countess Purgstall herself. Baron Hammer's interposition is not mentioned in the work. In one of the Countess Purgstall's letters to the Baron, she mentions that Captain Hall had not brought much information that interested her that she found him given up to admiration of the Duke of Wellington, and that his high Toryism annoyed her, all her sympathies being with the Whigs. In another letter, she tells Baron Hammer that, on reflection, she is satisfied that she acted wisely in refusing to subscribe a letter which Captain Hall had drawn up and pressed her to sign, expressive of sentiments which she did not entertain towards her sister Mrs Dugald Stewart. In another letter, she confides her most private wishes, and expresses the greatest gratitude, to Baron Hammer. She likewise tells the Baron that Captain Hall is obviously writing a journal in her house, but that he never informs her what he is inserting in it. The Countess had informed him also that Captain Hall frequently spent only the hour after dinner in her society, and did not even send to ask how she had passed the night. The Baron remarked that Captain Hall took Schloss Hainfeld for " his own man-of-war," and ordered every thing for himself as if he had been owner. After the Countess's death, the Baron succeeded to the property, and he invited the Captain and his family to continue in the castle as his guests until they found it convenient to return to England. He detailed a series of incidents that occurred after this invitation, that are better buried in oblivion, and which I forbear to specify; but they conveyed to me a strong impression of the indiscretion of Captain Hall's publication, and of the injustice done to Baron Hammer in his work. The Baron has placed several of the Countess's letters to him, which throw light on Captain Hall's statements, in the Imperial Library at Vienna, where they are open to the inspection of every one who desires to peruse them. He made these communications to me with a request that I should publish them, as he considered himself injured and ungratefully treated by Captain Hall. I should have had great hesitation in doing so, had not Captain Hall, in the work complained of, converted the incidents of the private life of a lady, into whose house he was received in the confidential characters of a friend and a guest, into the materials of a romance, and by the incorrectness of his statements, done injury both to the living and the dead. Captain Hall is a man of great talents, but his hostility to the Americans, and the inaccuracies of his statements in regard to them, are loudly complained of by the most respectable men in the city of Philadelphia.

Common Schools —I visited a common school in the city, and found the system to be similar to that pursued in Boston and New York. The master of a primary school must be capable of teaching " orthography, reading, grammar, geography, history, writing, arithmetic, and book-keeping;" and, where a majority of the parents of the children attending the school require it, he must also teach German. The teachers are appointed, after examination, by the Board of Directors of common schools, and may, at the end of any month, be dismissed for " incompetency, neglect of duty, cruelty, or immoral conduct." No teacher is allowed to receive " any compensation from parents or guardians in addition to that paid by the district." The *tenth* head of the " Regulations for common school districts," is in these words, and it is here printed in the same types as in the original :—" 1st, THE RELIGIOUS PREDILECTIONS OF PUPILS AND THEIR PARENTS OR GUARDIANS SHALL BE SACREDLY RESPECTED 2d, No *catechism, creed, confession, or manual of faith*, shall be used as a school-book, nor admitted into the school; sectarian instruction not being the province of the schoolmaster, but of the parent or guardian, and the spiritual instructor selected by him."

The teacher is required to " pay most especial

regard to the morals, habits, and general behaviour, as well as to the mental instruction of his pupils. The punishments to be inflicted by the teacher, shall be, 1st, Reading aloud the rule violated. 2d, Insertion of the offender's name under the head of ' bad conduct,' in the monitor's book. 3d, Private and public admonition. 4th, Detention after school hours. 5th, Special reports or complaints to parents or guardians. 6th, *The rod.* The rod shall be applied, whenever, in the teacher's judgment, it shall be necessary; when used, it shall be inflicted with certainty and effect; but passion or cruelty in its application shall be avoided. The hours of instruction shall be from 8 till 12 in the forenoon, and from 2 till 5 in the afternoon, from the 1st of April till the 1st of October; and from 9 till 12, and 1 till 4, during the rest of the year."

" The Old and New Testaments, containing the best extant code of morality, in simple, beautiful, and pure language, shall be used as a school book for reading, without comment by the teacher, but not as a text-book for religious instruction."

The Monitors in Schools —The Regulations provide for the appointment of monitors, who shall be members of the highest classes, and whose duty shall be to enter in a book the offences of which the scholars shall be guilty; but I was informed that the employment of monitors has been abandoned in all the common schools in Philadelphia, and that each school is now under the charge of a male and two female teachers; the females having a salary of $200 each.

This arrangement is new in the boys' schools, and one of the directors mentioned that it has been found to answer well. The young women treat the boys with a kindly interest, obviously influenced by sex, and the feeling is reciprocal. The boys, when studying under the young women, are more gentle and refined in their manners than when taught by male teachers, and they perform their tasks more obviously from a desire to please. This is as it should be. There is nothing necessarily indelicate or improper in the feelings of the sexes towards each other. Indeed, I have heard ladies of the strictest principles and the most refined delicacy, acknowledge that they were conscious of receiving an additional stimulus to exertion from the influence of a teacher of the opposite sex. There is no reason why this excellent ordination of Nature should not be employed to promote the training and instruction of the youthful mind.

The High School of Philadelphia is now forming under the charge of Mr John Frost and Mr Wines. I had read an excellent abridgment of the History of the United States, by " John Frost," reprinted in London, but imagined that this was a mere *nom de guerre*. It gave me pleasure to meet with the real author, and to find him an accomplished teacher instead of a shadow. Mr Wines also has written two valuable works on education.

Phrenology —I was taken, by a medical friend, several miles out of town, to visit a boy of seven or eight years of age, who, in July last, had received a kick from a horse in the region of the organ of Time (above the centre of the eye-brow) on the right side. It had completely driven in a portion of the skull an inch in length, and half an inch in breadth, and the fragment of bone must have rested on the superorbitar plate. The convolution constituting the surface of the organ of Time must have been injured, with parts of the organs of Tune and Eventuality, and probably also the organs of Colouring, Order, and Weight. All the organs on the left side were untouched. The integuments had completely reunited over the wound, but the skull was not restored. When the boy walked smartly, the pulsation of the brain was distinctly seen. The boy had been kept quiet in the house, without bodily or mental labour, ever since the accident; and he appeared to be intelligent and healthy when I saw him. It will not be until he shall have been exposed to intellectual efforts and anxiety, that it will be seen whether his faculties have suffered by the injury; or whether the brain has been restored. The practitioner first called in after the accident, had sewed up the integuments and left the bones sticking in the brain, and the arteries bleeding into it, and the boy was quite insensible when visited by my friend from Philadelphia. Owing to the imperfect education of many of the medical men in the United States, such instances of mistake are not uncommon in the rural districts.

Jan. 30. Ther 40° *The Judges* —Under the former constitution of Pennsylvania, the judges held office for life, but under the recent amendment, which came into operation on the 1st of January current, they are henceforth to receive appointments for ten years only. The reason assigned for the change is, that, under their life tenures, they were indolent in their proper spheres, but became active as political partisans. It is feared that under the new system, they will make the law bend to popular sentiments; so that there appears to many persons to be only a choice between two evils. The salary of the Chief-Justice of the Supreme Court is only $2666.67 cents a year, a sum so small that a trader in moderate business, will regard it as an unproductive year when he does not realize as much. Each associate Justice of the Supreme Court receives $2000 per annum. I record these statements as they were made to me; but I must add, that I have met with several of the judges, and they appeared to me to be strong minded able men, possessed of extensive information.

Practical Phrenology —My class met this day at eleven, and remained till past three o'clock engaged in the examination of skulls and casts. About two hundred ladies and gentlemen attended.

Feb. 1. Ther 40° *The Alms-House* —We visited this Institution, which is situated on rising ground lying on the right bank of the Schuylkill, a little below the city. " The main buildings, which are four in number, are arranged in the form of a parallelogram, and cover and enclose an area of about ten acres." It has a handsome architectural front, which appears to great advantage when viewed from the city. The entire building cost above one million of dollars, and it is altogether so magnificent in reference to its objects, that it is commonly denominated " the Pauper Palace." It includes a pauper lunatic asylum and an hospital for the sick. It was erected and is supported by assessments on the city and liberties. Its fame stands so high, and has extended so widely, as affording comfortable quarters for the destitute, that some of them have been known to walk two hundred and fifty miles to reach it. Although only the poor of the city and suburbs have a legal right to enter it, these distant strangers throw themselves down at the door during the night, and refuse to rise or go away, stating their resolution to make good their quarters after such a toilsome march. It contains at present about 1800 inmates.

I was surprised equally at the magnificence and extent of the building, and at the number of paupers, in a city of only 200,000 inhabitants, situated in a young, fertile, and prosperous country where labour is greatly in demand, and highly remunerated ; but I was assured that three-fourths of the inmates are foreigners who are cast forth from all the countries of Europe, and fall as a burden on the United States.*

* The number of paupers I find is really small when contrasted with that of Edinburgh, a city without manufactures or any other great source of pauperism. On 1st October 1840, Mr Small, Treasurer to the Edinburgh Charity Workhouse, reported the number of persons receiving permanent support from that institution to be 3500, besides 400 supplied with temporary aid. The population is under 100,000, as the poor of the parish of St Cuthbert's, as well as those of the Canongate, are separately provided for. These two parishes nearly surround the ancient city, and St Cuthbert's includes many new streets and populous suburbs.

This is probably too true ; because, in general, only those individuals who find a difficulty in providing for themselves at home emigrate ; and hence many of the foreigners landed in America are feeble in mind, dissipated, or reckless persons, whom their friends in Europe have shipped off to rid themselves from the burden of their maintenance. One of the Directors of the Alms-house, mentioned to me that the Managers for the poor of St Cuthbert's parish in Edinburgh, had actually shipped off a body of paupers and landed them very recently at New York, two of whom are said to be idiots.*

The Alms house has a medical and surgical hospital attached to it, where clinical lectures are delivered by the professors of the University once a week. It is unfortunately two miles from the city, and in consequence the students do not *see* the regular course of clinical treatment ; but only hear it described on Saturdays.

* I expressed my astonishment at this statement and disbelief in its accuracy, and afterwards ascertained that it is essentially incorrect. A Mr Johnston came to Edinburgh, and engaged a number of the younger inmates of St Cuthbert's Charity Workhouse to go with him, as indented servants, to his farm in Canada. He entered into a legal bond to the Managers to carry them to that country, to provide for them, and to remunerate them suitably for their labour. He proceeded with them to New York, but there his means failed him, he was imprisoned for non payment of the " head-money," a tax exigible by law on emigrants, and they were left destitute. The newspapers in New York represented the matter as if the paupers had been deliberately shipped off by the Managers of St Cuthbert's parish, in order to relieve themselves from the expense of maintaining them, and to impose them as a burden on the United States ; but this was not their intention.

The whole establishment is kept clean to the eye, but the nose and lungs detect imperfect ventilation, particularly in the departments for the children; who are afflicted with ophthalmia, languid looks, and other indications of a low condition of the corporeal system. It is extremely difficult to induce paupers voluntarily to admit fresh air into their apartments, except in very warm weather, and in building an alms-house, adequate means for involuntary ventilation as well as warmth should be provided. I was glad to observe that pictures, objects, and apparatus, are supplied for teaching the children; an advantage not enjoyed in many of the city schools.

Sorcery.—The following advertisement appeared in the " Public Ledger" newspaper a few days ago. " A Card. Madame Dusar, thankful for fast favours, respectfully informs the ladies and gentlemen of Philadelphia, that her residence is No. 6 Watson's Alley, *Locust, 1st Alley below Tenth*, where she will be happy to solve all questions relating to dreams, marriages, journeys, losses, gains, and all other lawful business, sickness, death, &c. &c. j. 30. 3 t." The small letters at the end mean " January 30. three times ," and we may presume that Madame Dusar meets with customers who indemnify her for the expenses of advertising, and leave her besides a suitable remuneration for her skill and trouble. There are ignorant and superstitious individuals in all countries; but the circumstance which gives this announcement interest in my estimation is, that the male customers above twenty-one years of age of

this lady have votes for the civic rulers of Pennsylvania, and may exercise an influence on its banks,
public works, credit, and general prosperity.   It
would certainly be desirable to bring this profession
to a close by a higher and more general education of
the people.   I have been informed (but perhaps the
story is an old "Joe Miller") that within four or five
years from the present time, the cashier of a bank
in Philadelphia applied to one of these ladies to learn
who had committed a robbery on the bank, and that
she directed him to a certain house, in the garret of
which he would find an old chest, and in the chest
the lost money.   He found the house, the garret,
and the chest, but no money : The sorceress had
sent him thither to annoy a family whom she dis-
liked !

Feb. 3. Ther 26° *The Free Negroes* —Our apartments at the Marshall House are under the charge
of a coloured man, who, although a complete negro,
has a brain that would do no discredit to an European.   It is of a full size ; the moral and intellectual
regions are well developed; and his manner of thinking, speaking, and acting, indicates respectfulness,
faithfulness, and reflection.   He was originally a
slave, and purchased his own freedom.   His wife
also is of pure African blood, and his children of
course the same.   One of his sons named " Rob
Roy," (what would Helen Macgregor have thought
of her husband's name-sake ?) was extremely desirous to hear some of my lectures, and his father asked
if he might be permitted to go into the room.   No

objection existed on my part to lecture to an audience of any colour, if they were intelligent and attentive ; but Americans feel differently. I consulted some liberal friends as to what could be done without giving offence, and it was arranged that, after the audience was assembled, Rob Roy should enter and stand near the door, at the back of all the seats, and thus pass for a servant in waiting. He followed this plan, and no notice was taken of his presence. I have not introduced the question of abolition into my lectures, because it is foreign to their object. So far, however, as the subject lay incidentally in my way, I have not shrunk from it, but have introduced the skulls and casts of Negroes among those of other varieties of mankind, and freely expressed my opinion of the moral and intellectual capabilities indicated by their forms.

Quaker Preaching.—We attended the Meeting-House of the Hicksite Quakers this day. The women were seated at one end, and the men at the other. One male Friend spoke, and afterwards Mrs Lucretia Mott delivered an excellent address. We had previously formed the acquaintance of this lady, and of her husband Mr James Mott, and observed that in private society she manifests the power of intellect of a philosopher combined with feminine refinement and delicacy. In delivering her address, her manner of speaking was so clear, yet so soft and touching, and the matter of it was so full of wisdom and goodness, that it drew tears from the eyes of C——, and intensely rivetted my attention.

Feb. 4. Ther 33° *William Penn.*—We visited the Pennsylvania Hospital in Pine Street. It is a Medical and Surgical Hospital and a Lunatic Asylum in the heart of the city, surrounded by ample grounds and stately trees. In front there is a well-executed bronze statue of William Penn, standing in full Quaker costume, hat and all, with the charter of Pennsylvania, granted by Charles the II. in 1681, in his hand. From the top of the dome, an extensive view is enjoyed, and an emotion of astonishment presses on the mind, that this large, rich, regular, beautiful, and enlightened city, should all have grown up from an absolute wilderness since 1681, and that Penn should have had the vigour and sagacity of mind to look forward to its increase with the eye and hope of a prophet, and should at that time have laid it out in streets, and squares, and ways, almost exactly as it now appears, with so much to approve of, and so little to amend.

Phrenology in Baltimore.—After repeated advertisements in the Baltimore newspapers, requesting those citizens who desired that I should lecture there, to enter their names at a book-store, twenty-six individuals have appeared, and this success has been reported to me. As the number which I require is 150, I have declined to lecture in that city. I have been solicited to repeat my course in Philadelphia, and offered to do so, if 200 subscribers appear for a second course.

Loss of the Use of Words, &c.—Dr Parrish jun. called and introduced a man of slender stature, bilious and nervous temperament, retreating forehead, and prominent eyes, a policeman, about thirty-eight or forty years of age, who, after sleeping in a very cold bed in December last, at Harrisburg, (whither he had been conveyed as a soldier to suppress the riot,) had felt some uneasy sensation in his head, and then discovered that he had lost the use of words. Although he understood language and could articulate, he could not find words with which to express his own ideas. He saw distance erroneously : a house distant one street, appeared distant a mile or a mile and a half ; he lost the perception of numbers also, and could not reckon. He felt no pain in any particular part of the head. He gradually recovered the use of the lost faculties, but even now he cannot use numbers readily : he calls numbers " times." In endeavouring to name dates, he says it was " last time," or " a time before that." The lower part of the anterior lobe is narrow and projects considerably. If one may hazard a conjecture, I should say that the intense cold had produced congestion of some of the intellectual organs ; those most affected being the organs Language, Size, and Number ; the other intellectual faculties were unimpaired. The cause of these affections is obscure ; but the fact of only three faculties, and these so distinctly marked, being involved in this case, not only confirms the general principle of a division of the brain, but affords grounds for presuming that the phrenological divisions are real.

Fashion.—The British public appear to have a great

difficulty in understanding the condition of the fashionable world in the United States. They generally imagine that little refinement and elegance, but
abundance of vulgar glitter and ridiculous pretension
prevail there. They forget that the United States
embrace a country of vast extent, exhibiting society
in all its stages. The love of distinction being innate in the human mind, fashion is found in the social circle of the savage as well as in that of the mo-
narch of France or England. In the United States,
every condition of society, from that of the newly-
cleared wilderness to that of the opulent eastern cities, has its circle of fashion, and great differences
may naturally be expected to exist. Philadelphia
presents a great amount of female grace, beauty, and
accomplishments, and of handsome young men, rather verging towards dandyism ; while the shops contain the most expensive and elegant wares, and the
public rooms in many of the houses of wealthy citizens, are richly furnished and decorated. The refinement and elegance of manners which distinguish
the highest circles in London may not abound, but
there is more of nature in its genuine forms. In
short, there is no difficulty in finding society in which
any mind, less fastidious than that of a Beau Brum-
mel, may feel itself at home. Indeed, the contest for
superiority in fashion between different circles, is
here as keen and active as in any European city.
Market Street is the northern boundary of fashionable residences. The fashionable inhabitants of Ches-
nut, Walnut, and Spruce Streets, which lie to the

south of that line, will scarcely recognise as compeers
families living to the north of it.   If a stranger were
to come to the city and occupy a house of the first
class, beyond the northern boundary, and give the
most splendid entertainments, he would nevertheless
find it difficult to make his way into fashionable society.   This is neither more nor less absurd than the
rule in London thirty years ago, which limited all
good style to localities south of Oxford Street, and
doomed the north to irretrievable vulgarity.   Many
families of good fortune and the highest respectability live north of Market Street, but few of them aim
at figuring in the fashionable circle.   We were told
that one fashionable family have ceased to invite the
English to their house, on account of the ungrateful
conduct of the visiters of that nation, who have from
time to time published their travels.

Feb. 5.   Ther 32°   *Residences of the Poor* —It
is distressing to learn, that even in this beautiful
city the houses of the poor too much resemble the
residences of the same class in European towns.   Dr
Parrish informed me that great numbers of young
children die here every season in hot weather from
cholera infantum, or, as it is commonly called, the summer complaint.   The poor live in small houses, never
intentionally ventilate their rooms, and seem not to
know the use of cold water.   He would enter one of
these dwellings on a summer morning when the thermometer stood at 90°, and find an infant shrivelled
and bedewed with a clammy perspiration.   It had
been gasping all night for breath, and not drawn one

mouthful of fresh air, and had, perhaps, never been washed from its birth. Death speedily relieves it. Many of the parents who thus treat their children are Irish. He hired an Irish nurse to suckle one of his own children. She gave her own son to an Irish family to board. When the hot weather came, he thought of her infant, and went to see it. It was in the condition before described. In three hours more it would have been dead. Without a day's delay, he sent the whole Irish family with the child to his farm, and saved it. " I should have felt very uneasy," said he, " if it had died, because my child was thriving under the care of the mother whom nature had given to it, but whom I had taken away for the benefit of my own."

We were a good deal in Quaker society in Philadelphia, and enjoyed it highly. The principles of moderation, truthfulness, and simplicity, in which they are trained, render their manners pleasing, and those individuals among them who possess in addition high moral and intellectual qualities, are not only excellent specimens of good breeding, but most interesting companions. We knew female quakers who, if introduced at the court of Victoria, would be regarded as perfectly well-bred.

Feb. 6. Ther 14° *Emigrants.*—This evening a well-dressed respectable-looking Scots woman called and introduced herself to me, and told me that she and her husband had been servants in the family of one of my friends in Edinburgh; that they had come to the United States a few years ago ; that her hus-

band now acted as assistant in keeping a store in
Market Street, Philadelphia, for which he received
$ 350 per annum : that she also had found employ-
ment ; and that both were well, happy, and respected.
She had a child with her, equally well dressed with
herself, and thriving in its appearance.   She added,
that " this is the country for poor, honest, and industrious people to come to."   The visit afforded me
much gratification.

Musical Instruments.—An Italian gentleman mentioned to us, that the climate of Philadelphia destroys
musical instruments imported from Germany or England.   He had an excellent pianoforte sent to him
from Germany ; but the first summer dried up the
wood so thoroughly, that the keys would not act, and
the instrument became useless.   He hoped that the
winter would restore it ; but was disappointed.   The
German instruments are not varnished, but polished.
The air takes off the polish, and in one year the
naked grain of the wood appears.   The American
instruments are made considerably stronger than the
European, and are nearly as delicate in their tones.
The wood is seasoned up to the demands of the climate before being used, and it stands it better.   The
manufacture of pianofortes is a very extensive branch
of trade in the eastern cities of the Union ; still, the
Americans cannot be called a musical people.   Most
of the really accomplished musical amateurs in Philadelphia are Italians or Germans, or descendants of
these nations.   This is very natural ; for the Eng-

lish who settled in these colonies were not the musical part of that nation, and the pursuits of their descendants, since they came hither, have not been favourable for the development of the fine arts. The stimulating climate, however, and active brains of the Americans, may be expected, in due season, to bring forth both taste and talent for painting, sculpture, and music. The coloured population shew considerable capacity for music. Frank Johnston's brass-band, which has been collecting large crowds of listeners in the upper rooms of the Philadelphia Museum (and disturbing my audience) is entirely composed of coloured men, and the music is said to be very creditable to the performers.

Useful Knowledge.—This city produces many works adapted for popular use, written by professional and philosophical authors. Dr John Bell edited an admirable work " the Journal of Health," from 9th September 1829 to 24th August 1831, in which the results of the experience and scientific knowledge of himself and other physicians regarding the preservation of health, were presented to the public in simple and pleasing forms. The Journal had reached a circulation of 4000 copies, when it was stopped in consequence of the bankruptcy of the publisher. The same author has published a valuable treatise on " Baths," and another interesting volume named " Health and Beauty," shewing the relation between the two. These and similar works, such as those of Mr Wines on popular education, are calculated to be of great advantage to the rising generation in the United States. The competition among authors to get their works introduced into schools is exceedingly keen, on account of the great extent of the sales, and consequent high profits. All sorts of influences, independent of the utility of the works, are put in requisition to obtain this object; and it would be highly desirable if the books of real merit were better known.

CHAPTER II.

Preservation of School-books—Dr Franklin and Lord Hillsborough
— Phrenology—Animal Magnetism—The African Church—The
House of Refuge —Mr Clay's Speech against Abolition—Clerks—
Lecture-Room—Railroad to Baltimore—Baltimore—Phrenology—
Washington City—Negro Slavery—Visit to the President—Conser
vatism of the Law—La Signorina America Vespucci—Manners and
Morals of Mississippi—The Capitol—and Congress—American So-
ciety for the Diffusion of Useful Knowledge—The Senate—The
Sub-Treasury Bill—Dr Duncan and the House of Representatives
—Dr Sewall the Anti-Phrenologist—Ex-President Adams—Dr
Duncan—Petitions against Slavery—General Washington's Birth-
day—The Negro Brain—Journey from Washington to Philadelphia
—" How do you like our country ?"—Wilmington Delaware—
State Lotteries.

1839.

Feb. 8. Ther. 39°. *Preservation of School-Books.*
—I visited a private school for Greek, Latin, arithmetic, geography, drawing, &c. taught by Mr James
in Market Street. The arrangements and modes of
teaching seemed remarkably good, but the circumstance which struck me most, as being new, was Mr
James's method of preserving the school-books from
destruction: the use of which is included in the school-
fees. He covers the books with cotton cloth, and
enjoins care of them on the boys. To give efficacy to
this injunction, he withdraws every book immediately
on perceiving the slightest tear or stain on it; sacrificing it altogether, and substituting one clean, new,
and perfect, in its place. This practice stimulates

the boys to preserve their books; those among them who are naturally careless becoming ashamed of the frequent renewals which they render necessary. He mentioned that he had found that when the books continued to be used after being soiled or torn, however little, they all made a rapid progress to decay; but that, by requiring them to be kept constantly in a high condition, the waste is surprisingly small. The principle involved in this practice is capable of being extensively applied. Erect a high, but still an attainable standard, in manners, cleanliness, and moral deportment in schools, and the children will work up to it with greater earnestness and success than many teachers believe.

Dr Franklin and Lord Hillsborough —On visiting Mr Vaughan at the apartments of the American Philosophical Society this day, he shewed us, and read, a manuscript report by Dr Franklin of his interview in London with Lord Hillsborough, Secretary of State, when the philosopher presented his commission as agent for the *people* of Massachusetts. He describes the Secretary as having scolded both him and his constituents, and declined to recognise him as their agent, because his commission had not been sanctioned by the Governor. The report is in the handwriting of Franklin, but it is not subscribed by him.

Phrenology.—I gave the last lecture of my course this evening, and received the thanks of the audience in a series of gratifying resolutions, which, with a table shewing the attendance at this course, are

printed in the Appendix, No. II.   They guaranteed
a class of 200 hearers for a repetition of the lectures,
and a second course was immediately announced.

Feb. 9.   Ther 45°   *Animal Magnetism* —This
subject is exciting considerable interest in Philadelphia; and the proceedings of Dr Elliotson, and the
attacks on him in the London Lancet, are much
spoken of in medical society.   The medical men
here who do not admit the existence of animal magnetism, ascribe the phenomena to hysteria.   As some
cases in the Institution for the Deaf and Dumb in
this city have attracted attention, we visited it, and
saw a deaf and dumb girl of about nine years of age,
of a nervous and bilious temperament, lively, and in
good health, magnetised.   The operator seated her
in a rocking-chair, placed his hands and thumbs in
contact with hers, and thus induced the magnetic
sleep.   Her head fell on her shoulder, and she appeared to lose consciousness.   He raised her up,
pushed her about the room, and raised her arms.
She then seemed to acquire an internal consciousness,
appeared as if in an ecstasy, answered questions in-
telligently, walked, and jumped, and threw her arms
about, as if extremely happy.   Passes were then
made with the hands across and nearly touching her
forehead, when she awoke.   She was again magnetised, and repeated the same evolutions.   The questions were put by means of touch and the finger
alphabet, and were answered in the same manner.
Another girl, of the same age, fair, and of the sanguine and lymphatic temperament, and who was not

deaf and dumb, was next magnetised. In her natural state she was so bashful (she had very large Cautiousness and Love of Approbation), that she would
scarcely speak even in answer to a question. After
being magnetised and put into a state of somnambulism, her bashfulness disappeared, and she became
lively and confident, answering questions readily.
She was asked what certain pictures which were put
into her hands represented, and although her eyes
were not bandaged, but closed as in sleep, she carried
the pictures to the lamp, and placed her head, and
occasionally her fingers, on them ; she also held them
up to the light, as one would do who enjoyed faint
but natural vision. In some instances she told correctly what objects they represented, in others she
did not. She was requested to read, but did so very
imperfectly, and obviously directed a chink of her
eyelids, which she opened, to the book. A mask,
having the eye-holes pasted over with thick paper,
was put on, and she was requested to read. She
could not do so ; but by holding back her head she
brought the opening at the nose into the line of the
axis of the eye, and then offered to read.

There was no reason to believe that these young
children were taught to act a part, although the latter in some of her actions appeared as if doing so.
The gentleman who operated on them was most reasonable in his remarks. He professed only to shew
the effects of an experiment which he had been led
to try in consequence of the general interest which
the subject had excited, and offered no theory to ex-

plain the phenomena. I asked him if he would allow me to try the experiment also. He consented most readily; and I selected the deaf and dumb child as the one whose conduct gave me the greatest confidence in her simplicity of character. To my own surprise, my passes were effectual. They brought the girl out of her state of somnambulism; afterwards induced it again, and once more awoke her out of it. This was my first and only experiment in animal magnetism; and as I came to the house with the intention of being a spectator merely, there was certainly no concert between the girl and me, and her appearance and actions did not lead me to suppose that she had been trained to deception. In this case the deception, if there was any, must have been at least extemporaneous.

It is possible that some of my readers may conclude from this narrative, that I am not only a phrenologist, but an animal magnetiser, a union of faiths and professions which they may think natural and appropriate; but I merely report facts. I profess to have neither studied nor practised animal magnetism, and to be a stranger to its merits; but I do not shrink from witnessing experiments on any subject, or from trying them, if in my power; and still less from reporting what I see. The whole subject of animal magnetism appears to me to be involved in the profoundest obscurity; but this is a good reason why it should be subjected to the most searching scrutiny by observation.

Feb. 10. Ther. 25°. *The African Church.*—We

heard a sermon to-day in the Episcopalian church occupied by the people of colour in Philadelphia. The
slightest tinge of colour in the skin, perhaps discerni-
ble only by a practised eye, excludes its owner from
social intercourse and social worship with the whites.
The church was commodious and comfortable, and
the congregation respectable in their appearance.
The service was performed, and a fair average sermon preached by the Rev. Mr Douglas, also a man
of colour. Many persons may imagine that ludicrous
incidents must have presented themselves in such a
church. They would expect to hear the minister and
congregation mistaking and mispronouncing the English language; reading with strange accentuation, or
curtailing the sentences with baby-like abruptness;
but all such ideas are utterly groundless. The service
was read and the sermon delivered in pure good English, equal to that of any of the other clergymen of
the city, and the whole demeanour of the congregation was becoming and devout. Some of them are
rich and well educated, and not a few are marked by
such faint traces of African blood, that in Europe
they might mingle in any society without their origin being suspected, unless some lynx-eyed American were present to detect it. One large and commodious pew, which I am told belongs to Dr Rush's
family, is generally reserved for white visiters. So
intense is the aversion even of many humane and
educated persons in this city to the coloured race,
that apparently they would shrink back from the gate
of Heaven, if it were opened by a coloured man and

shewed coloured people within. Only the warmly philanthropic view them as men, and treat them with real regard. I have not been able to discover whether there is a sufficient number of rich and well educated coloured persons in this city to form a cultivated society among themselves. I suspect that there is not; and that the most accomplished individuals of the coloured race live here as in a social wilderness, raised by their attainments above the mass of their own people yet excluded from the society of the whites.

Feb. 13. Ther. 32°. *The House of Refuge.*—We visited the House of Refuge for Juvenile offenders of both sexes. This institution is similar to the one in Boston for the same purpose, previously described. Children found, by the magistrates or other judges, guilty of petty larcenies, assaults, and vagrancy, and also children whose parents complain of them as unmanageable, are recommended to the consideration of the managers of this institution, who, if they regard them as proper subjects, and have accommodation, receive them, and detain them during their own discretion. They are taught manufacturing furniture for umbrellas, cane-chair making, casting in brass, turning, and book-binding, and also reading, writing, and arithmetic. They attend school two hours, and labour the rest of the day, with the exception of intervals for meals, and of half an hour for play. We were told that these children learn as much by an attendance for two hours a-day at school as those in the city schools do in four or five hours. The alternation of labour and learning brings the mind and brain fresh to the lessons.

The annual report to the Legislature states that, " during the year 1838, 137 inmates, viz. 92 boys and 45 girls, were received into, and 129 left the refuge, viz. 90 boys and 39 girls, and there remained on the 31st ultimo 158, viz. 105 boys and 53 girls.

" Twenty boys were indentured to farmers, seven to shoemakers, one turner, one bookbinder, one butcher, two chairmakers, one tailor, two blacksmiths, one sashmaker, three manufacturers, one miller, one bricklayer, one printer, one baker, one sugar-maker, one cabinet-maker.

" The girls (16) were indentured to learn house-wifery."

These children are not detained long enough to learn a trade thoroughly. They are apprenticed to farmers in the country, to the sea, and to tradesmen in small villages ; but seldom in large towns. A considerable number of them are ultimately reformed. They are supported by gifts, legacies, and appropriations from the State. The managers let out the labour of the inmates to tradesmen in the city, but the recompense is not nearly equal to the expense of the establishment. Religious worship is performed in a chapel by the ministers of all the sects in the city in rotation, except the Roman Catholic, whose priests decline to officiate, because the chapel is not consecrated. Some of the managers attend every Sunday, and the clergy are requested to confine themselves to the broad and practical principles of Christianity, and to omit peculiar doctrines ; also not to address the children as convicts or criminals.

Mr Clay's Speech against Abolition.—Mr Henry Clay, the Senator for Kentucky, is regarded as one of the first American statesmen of the present day. He is named by many of the whig newspapers as candidate for the Presidency at the next election in 1840. On the 7th of February he delivered, in the Senate, a speech against the abolition of slavery, which has been lauded to the skies by the public press, and commended in the highest terms at the public tables and in private society. It is said to be irresistible in argument, overwhelming in eloquence, and altogether fatal to the cause against which it is directed. It is also said to be intended as a declaration of his opinions on this subject, with a view to the Presidency at the election in the end of 1840. I have read a very full and able report of it in the " United States' Gazette" of the 11th of February, and recognise both dexterity and eloquence in its structure ; but few of the commanding qualities of a great mind. As the subject of abolition continues to attract general attention, both in Britain and the United States, a brief abstract of Mr Clay's arguments may prove interesting to the reader.

The occasion which gave rise to the speech was his presenting a petition signed by several hundred inhabitants of the district of Columbia, and chiefly of the city of Washington, stating that " they do not desire the abolition of slavery within the district, even if Congress possesses the very questionable power of abolishing it, without the consent of the people whose interests would be immediately and directly affected by the measure." The petitioners state that many of them are not slave-holders, and some of them are conscientiously opposed to slavery; but they petition because " they justly respect the rights of those who own that description of property," and who do not desire abolition. Mr Clay enters into the whole merits of the abolition question. He declares himself dissatisfied with the rule adopted by Congress not to receive the petitions of the people relative to slavery; he would have received and referred them to a committee, which would have reported on them in such terms as would have checked the progress of abolition. He proceeds to supply this deficiency, and to " dissuade the public from continuing to agitate a subject fraught with the most direful consequences."

The specific objects aimed at by the abolitionists are described by Mr Clay to be, " the immediate abolition of slavery in the district of Columbia, and in the territory of Florida; the prohibition of the removal of slaves from State to State; and the refusal to admit any new State, comprising within its limits the institution of domestic slavery, into the Union. " These," says he, " are but so many short stages in the long and bloody road to the distant goal at which they would finally arrive—abolition, universally abolition." To the agency of their powers of persuasion, they now propose to add " the powers of the ballot box ;" and on this account Mr Clay was induced to address the Senate.

He traces the history of abolition, and assigns the present American excitement, chiefly to the " undecided British experiment," to which he most fervently wishes complete success, while he confesses that he has " fearful forebodings of a disastrous termination to it." Another cause of the excitement is the desire " to mingle abolition with politics, and to array one part of the Union against the other."

The objections to abolition are stated by Mr Clay as follows : The power of Congress over the district of Columbia is conferred by the following words in the constitution of the United States. " To exercise exclusive legislation in all cases whatsoever over said district (not exceeding ten miles square) as may by cession of particular states, and the acceptance of Congress, become the seat of Government of the United States." This provision preceded in point of time the actual cessions of territory which were made by Maryland and Virginia. Both of these were then, and still are, slave holding States; and the grant should always be interpreted as having reference to the object of the cession. This object was " to establish a seat of Government of the United States ;" and Maryland and Virginia could not have anticipated that the cession would be so applied as to abolish slavery in the district of Columbia, while they maintained it. Abolition is not necessary for the purpose of rendering the district comfortable and convenient as a seat of Government of the whole Union ; and the inhabitants of the district do not desire it to promote their happiness and prosperity.

Therefore Congress has no right to abolish slavery. Slavery exists here in its mildest form. At the last census there were only 6119 slaves in a population of 39,834; and the number has probably not much increased since. The language of the grant may possibly be sufficiently comprehensive to include a power of abolition, but it would not at all thence follow that the power could be rightfully exercised. The object of it must always be kept in view in a correct interpretation.

Florida is bounded on all its land sides by slave states, and almost extends within the tropics. Cuba, the nearest important island to it on the water side, is a slave island. " This simple statement of its geographical position should of itself decide the question." Slavery existed in it in 1819, when it was ceded to the United States, and the property of the inhabitants was secured to them. To abolish slavery there would be to rob them of their property, unless a reasonable time were allowed to them to remove it. By the compromise which took place in Congress in 1820, when Missouri was admitted into the Union, it was agreed that the line of 36° 30″ of north latitude should be the boundary between the free and slave states to be created in the territories ceded by the treaty of Louisiana; Florida is south of that line, and therefore within the space intended for slavery.

The clause of the constitution which invests Congress with authority to regulate commerce with foreign nations, and among the several States, and with the Indian tribes, has hitherto remained dormant in respect to the interior trade by land between the States. It was granted to secure peace and harmony between the States. It is a power of *regulation* and not of *prohibition*. It is conservative, not destructive. Regulation, *ex vi termini*, implies the continued existence or prosecution of the thing regulated. Prohibition implies total discontinuance or annihilation. The moment that Negro slaves are admitted to be property, the law secures the right to the owner of carrying them from one State to another, without any hinderance from Congress.

But the end aimed at by the abolitionists is the liberation of the three millions of slaves held in bondage in the United States. The first impediment to the accomplishment of this object, is the want of all power in the General Government to effect the purpose. This belongs exclusively to the Slave States.

The next obstacle arises out of the presence of three millions of slaves, dispersed throughout the land, part and parcel of our population. The slaves are here ; no practical scheme for their removal or separation from us has yet been devised or proposed ; and the true inquiry is, What is best to be done with them for their happiness and our own ? In the slave states the white man must govern the black, or the black govern the white. In several of those States, the number of the slaves is greater than that of the white population. An immediate abolition of slavery in them would be followed by a desperate struggle for ascendency, which would end in the extermination or subjugation of the one race or the other. Is it not better for both parties that the existing state of things should be preserved?

A third impediment to abolition is to be found in the immense amount of capital which is invested in slave property. The average value of slaves at this time may be moderately stated at $400 each. The number of slaves is three millions; the total value then, by estimate of the slave property in the United States, is $1,200,000,000. This property is owned by widows, orphans, the aged and infirm, as well as the sound and vigorous. It is the subject of mortgages, deeds of trust, and family settlements, and in many instances is the sole reliance of creditors. Does any considerate man believe that it could be annihilated without convulsion, revolution, and bloodshed?

There is a visionary dogma that Negro slaves cannot be the subject of property. " That *is* property which the law declares TO BE property. Two hundred years of legislation have sanctioned and sanctified Negro slaves as property." The British Government recognised them as property, when they paid twenty millions sterling as a compensation to the Colonies for their loss. The FACT that the law has for two hundred years regarded them as property stands opposed to the wild speculations of theorists and innovators that they are not. The abolitionists should, therefore, raise the funds among themselves necessary to indemnify the owners of the slaves before they demand their emancipation.

The proceedings of the abolitionists have thrown back the cause of emancipation, and increased the rigours of legislation against slaves in most, if not all, of the slave states. Forty years ago, Kentucky was preparing for a gradual abolition, like that adopted in Pennsylvania in 1780, at the instance of Dr Franklin, according to which the generation in being were to remain in slavery, but all their offspring, born after a specified day, were to be free at the age of twenty-eight, and in the mean time were to receive preparatory instruction to qualify them for the enjoyment of freedom. The proposition in Kentucky for a gradual emancipation did not prevail, but it was sustained by a large and respectable minority. That minority had increased, and was increasing, until the abolitionists commenced their operations. The effect has been to dissipate all prospects whatever, for the present, of any scheme of gradual or other emancipation.

Prior to the agitation of abolition, there was a progressive melioration in the condition of slaves throughout all the Slave States. This is all now checked.

If it were possible to overcome the insurmountable obstacles now described, extermination of the blacks, or their ascendency over the whites, would be the sole alternative. The emancipated blacks would flow over on the free States in quest of labour, reduce the rate of wages, and spread misery among the white labouring population. I have seen with regret, grief, and astonishment, the resolute opposition (of the abolitionists) to the project of colonization. "The scheme is characterized by unmixed benevolence and utility. The abolitionists, whatever they may declare, must be in favour of amalgamation. It has been the divine pleasure to make the black man black, and the white man white, and to distinguish them by other repulsive constitutional differences." "Those whom God has created different, and has declared, by their physical structure and colour, ought to be kept asunder, should not be brought together by any process whatever of amalgamation."

"It is frequently asked, What is to become of the African race among us? Are they for ever to remain in bondage? The true answer is, that the same Providence, who has hitherto guided and governed us, and averted all serious evils from the existing relation between the two races, will guide and govern our posterity. Sufficient to the day is the evil thereof." "And taking the aggregate of the two races, the European is constantly, though slowly, gaining upon the African portion. This fact is demonstrated by the periodical returns of our population." "In some one hundred and fifty or two hundred years hence, but few vestiges of the black race will remain among our posterity."* "I prefer the liberty of my own country to that of any other people, and the liberty of my own race to that of any other

---

* In his speech, Mr Clay alludes to his published exposition of the manner in which this may be accomplished. I have not seen this exposition, but was told that he proposes to transport the young females to Africa by the aid of the Colonization Society of which he is President.

race ; and the liberty of the descendants of Africa in the United States is incompatible with the safety and liberty of the European descendants."

Such, then, is a brief, but I trust, a correct outline of Mr Clay's defence of the CONTINUED EXISTENCE of slavery (for he declares himself hostile to its first institution), and I must confess, that it did not excite in me the same grand conception of his powers as a statesman and orator, which it seems to have created in the minds of the Americans in general.

The fundamental question is, whether slaves can, by any law, be constituted property ? If they can, Mr Clay is in the right : if they cannot, his whole speech is a structure without a basis. The question necessarily leads us back to inquire into the foundation of all law. If force be the fountain of law, then slaves may be made property ; for the white race, by superior organization and cultivation, have, *de facto*, subdued and reduced to bondage their African brethren. But, according to this principle, the white men and their descendants, who were captured and reduced to slavery by the Barbary Corsairs, became lawful property whenever they were brought within the jurisdiction of the laws of Algiers, Tripoli, and Tunis, which were much more ancient than two hundred years. But all Christian nations recognise, as a first principle, that might does *not* constitute right. The thing declared must in itself be just, before any human enactment can render it legitimately binding on those on whom it is imposed. Were Mr Clay, with his present intelligence and attainments, to change place with his own Negro slaves, and to be

told that the law had made him their property, the
whole of the argument which he has now adduced,
with such apparent self-satisfaction, would appear to
him to be slender and feeble as a gossamer thread.
He would take his stand on the law of Christianity
and the law of Nature, and demonstrate triumphantly
that as he or his ancestors had been reduced to bondage at first by force and fraud, no enactments of the
plunderers, or of those who had trafficked with them
for their plunder, or of the posterity of either, could
ever convert this wrong into right, or deprive him
of his title to freedom. Phrenological observation
satisfies me, that the force with which this argument will come home to the minds of individuals,
will be different according to the size of the organs
of Conscientiousness and Benevolence in relation to
those of Acquisitiveness and Self-Esteem in their
brains ; affected, however, to some extent, by their
circumstances and education. If the Americans do
not recognise its soundness in the abstract, they will
probably understand it better when I add, that their
title to assert their own independence against the
arms of Britain, was founded solely on the indestruc-
tible and inalienable right of man to exact justice at
the hands of his fellows ; that the right of the Greeks
to throw off the Turkish yoke, with their desire to
effect which the Americans manifested so profound
a sympathy, was based on the same foundation ; and
that the right of the conquered Canadian French to
demand their freedom from England, of which the
Americans cordially approved, can be justified on no

other principle of reason or morality. The law which declared the African Negro to be property, did not unmake him a man; and if so, it could not annihilate his human rights. In all the arguments in defence of slavery which I have read, the fundamental error seems to be committed, of assuming that Negroes are not men, but merely goods and chattels. When Mr Clay opposes the *fact*, that for two hundred years they have been considered as property by the law, to what he calls the theoretical and visionary assertion, that they are men, he opposes merely the acknowledgment of a wrong to the statement of the moral principle by which it is condemned.

Mr Clay regards it as certain, that if slavery were abolished, a war of extermination would ensue between the races, which would lead to greater evils than those generated by slavery. This is the argument of the white man, of the master, in whose eyes his own losses or sufferings are ponderous as gold, and those of three millions of Negroes light as a feather. Ask the Negroes their opinion of the miseries of the existing system, and weigh this against the evils anticipated by the Whites from emancipation, and then strike the balance. Before I had an opportunity of studying the Negro character and Negro brain, I entertained the same opinion with Mr Clay, that a war of extermination would be the consequence of immediate freedom. More accurate and extensive information has induced me to change this view. I may here anticipate a statement which belongs, in chronological order, to a more advanced date, namely, that I have studied the crania of the North American Indians and of the Negroes in various parts of the United States, and also observed their living heads, and have arrived at the following conclusions. The North American Indians have given battle to the Whites, and perished before them, but have never been reduced either to national or to personal servitude. The development of their brains shews large organs of Destructiveness, Secretiveness, Cautiousness, Self-Esteem, and Firmness, with deficient organs of Benevolence, Conscientiousness, and Reflection. This indicates a natural character that is proud, cautious, cunning, cruel, obstinate, vindictive, and little capable of reflection or combination. The brain of the Negro, in general (for there are great varieties among the African race, and individual exceptions are pretty numerous), shews proportionately less Destructiveness, Cautiousness, Self-Esteem, and Firmness, and greater Benevolence, Conscientiousness, and Reflection, than the brain of the native American. In short, in the Negro brain the moral and reflecting organs are of larger size, in proportion to the organs of the animal propensities now enumerated, than in that of the Indian. The Negro is, therefore, naturally more submissive, docile, intelligent, patient, trustworthy, and susceptible of kindly emotions, and less cruel, cunning, and vindictive, than the other race.

These differences in their natural dispositions throw some light on the differences of their fates. The American Indian has escaped the degradation of slavery, because he is a wild, vindictive, cunning, untameable savage, too dangerous to be trusted by the white men in social intercourse with themselves, and, moreover, too obtuse and intractable to be worth coercing into servitude. The African has been deprived of freedom and rendered " property," according to Mr Clay's view, because he is by nature a *tame* man, submissive, affectionate, intelligent, and docile. He is so little cruel, cunning, fierce, and vindictive, that the white men can oppress him far beyond the limits of Indian endurance, and still trust their lives and property within his reach ; while he is so intelligent, that his labour is worth acquiring. The native American is free, because he is too dangerous and too worthless a being to be valuable as a slave : the Negro is in bondage, because his native dispositions are essentially amiable. The one is like the wolf or the fox, the other like the dog. In both, the brain is inferior in size, particularly in the moral and intellectual regions, to that of the Anglo-Saxon race, and hence the foundation of the natural superiority of the latter over both; but my conviction is, that the very qualities which render the Negro in slavery a safe companion to the White, will make him harmless when free. If he were by nature proud, irascible, cunning, and vindictive, he would not be a slave ; and as he is not so, freedom will not generate these qualities in his mind ; the fears, therefore, generally entertained of his commencing, if emancipated, a war of extermination, or for supremacy over the Whites, appear to me to be unfounded ;

unless, after his emancipation, the Whites should commence a war of extermination against him. The results of emancipation in the British West India Islands have hitherto borne out these views, and I anticipate that the future will still farther confirm them.

I do not enter into an examination of the detailed impediments to abolition which Mr Clay has mentioned; because, if the slaves be entitled, as human beings, to refuse to acknowledge the authority of all laws which declare them to be " property," and if it be safe to restore them to the rights of men, these obstacles will not be found to be insurmountable. Mr Clay speaks of Providence having separated the Negro race from the White, and "declared by their physical structure and colour, that they ought to be kept asunder." This is unsound. When Providence intends to prevent races from mingling, he renders the product of their union unprolific, as in the case of the mule. The slave-holders have impressed on the slave population striking evidence that no such prohibition exists between the African and European races. The white tint distinguishable in thousands of them shews, that both parents were not of African blood; and it is generally admitted, that the whiter the skin, the closer is the approach of the individual to European qualities of mind. The quadroons are described as a handsome and talented race.

The Anglo-Americans in some degree admire the American Indian character, invest it with a kind of nobleness and dignity, and some families even boast of their inheriting Indian blood; while the Negro

is despised, hated, and by some even abhorred, as
scarcely belonging to the human species.   This
opinion has neither philosophy, religion, nor experience, to sanction it.   Much as Mr Clay's speech
was admired, I often asked in society, whether any
one meant to justify slavery, or to maintain that a
time will not come when it must cease.   The answer
generally given was, that few persons defend slavery
as in itself right, or desire its unlimited endurance ;
but that, since the abolitionists commenced their agi-
tations, few will avow even these sentiments in public.

Feb. 14. Ther. 39°.   *Clerks.*—Young men educated
as clerks, capable of writing letters and keeping books,
superabound in Philadelphia, and receive only $4,
while a porter is allowed $6 a-week.   A young
Scotsman belonging to this class assured me that he
had found it extremely difficult to procure employment, and when he was successful, he received only
$4 a-week.   I asked some persons in trade, who
corroborated the statement, for an explanation of the
fact itself.   They said that the common schools qualify a great number of young men for the counting-
house ; that the sons of labourers are often ambitious,
and although only moderately gifted with talent, become clerks, conceiving this vocation to be more genteel than labour.   To them are added a multitude of
clerks constantly arriving from Europe.   Between
the two, the market is over-stocked, employment is
not to be obtained, and they solicit engagements for
the means of a bare subsistence.

Feb. 15. Ther. 34°.   *Lecture-room.*—So much dissatisfaction was expressed with my late room, that, after visiting every other apartment in Philadelphia fit for the purpose, and attainable, I have been under the necessity of engaging the Music Fund Hall in Locust Street at $800 for sixteen lectures, or L.10 a night ; besides paying for attendance. It is the usual concert room, too large for my class ; but I could find no other room, at a more moderate rent, that was large enough.

Feb. 16. Ther. 34°. *Railroad to Baltimore.*—This morning at eight o'clock we left Philadelphia, and travelled in large and comfortable cars, warmed by stoves, to Baltimore. The railroad consists of a single track ; the distance is ninety-four miles, and although we suffered considerable detention by the bridge over the Schuylkill having been lately carried away by a flood, and not yet restored, we arrived at 3 P. M. There is a " ladies' car" in each train, appropriated for ladies, and the gentlemen who are travelling with them. It is divided into two apartments, and a place of retirement is added. This is a great accommodation, particularly when children are in the party.

Baltimore.—In the United States, Baltimore is often called the monumental city, because it possesses two public monuments ; one a column in honour of General Washington, and the other a structure of a less definite description, to commemorate the citizens who fell in defending Fort M'Henry against the British in 1814. The city stands on irregular ground, some of the streets are steep, and those recently built are wide and handsome. Brick is generally used, but the fine quality of it, and of the masonry, gives an appearance of taste and elegance to the fabrics. We were told that the trade and population are increasing rapidly, and that the present estimate is, that the city contains 80,000 white and 20,000 coloured persons. The latter are mostly slaves.

Phrenology.—I had the pleasure of meeting with several medical gentlemen of this city, previously known to me by correspondence as Phrenologists. Among these was Dr Stewart, who, many years ago, sent to the Phrenological Society of Edinburgh casts of the heads of Pepe, Courro, Felix, and Tardy, pirates of atrocious character executed in Baltimore. He mentioned to me, that, some years ago, he had removed a tumour from the head of a man, a manager of slaves on a plantation, who, when in health, was remarkable for steadiness, firmness, and decision of character. The tumour was situated externally over the organs of Firmness, and after it was formed, he lost these characteristics of mind and became undecided, and finally imbecile. He lingered for some weeks after the operation, and died. A *postmortem* examination of the head shewed that the convolutions of the brain below the tumour, and constituting the two organs of Firmness, were disorganized by suppuration. Dr Stewart received the report of the state of the brain from a country surgeon who knew nothing about Phrenology, and the account of the change of character from the gentleman who had employed his late patient. Neither of these knew the relation of the fact which he communicated to the fact communicated by the other.

Feb. 18. Ther. 33°. *Washington City.*—This morning, at 9 o'clock, we left Baltimore, and travelled to Washington by a railroad. The distance is thirty-eight miles, and the country is undulating, but the railroad finds a practicable track through the valleys. The soil seems to be poor, but clothed with small trees. A chill wind blew, and the ground was covered with snow. On approaching Washington, the first object that presents itself is the Capitol, a large massive building painted white to resemble marble, with a dome not of very successful proportions. The town looks like a large straggling village reared in a drained swamp, with the navigable Potomac about a mile distant.

Negro Slavery.—We are now in the district of Columbia, the seat of government of the United States ; and on taking up the " Daily National Intelligencer" in Gadsby's hotel, my eye was attracted by the following advertisements, among many others of a similar kind :—

" Cash for Negroes.—The subscriber wishes to purchase a number of Negroes for the Louisiana and Mississippi market. He will pay the highest prices the market will justify. Himself or an agent at all times can be found at his jail, on Seventh Street, the first house south of the market bridge on the west side. Letters addressed to him will receive the earliest attention.

" aug 23—d&ctf   Wm. H. Williams."

" Cash for Negroes.—We will give cash and liberal prices for any number of likely negroes, families
included. We can be found at B. & Shekell's tavern, a few doors below Lloyd's tavern, opposite the
centre market, on Seventh Street.

" We wish to purchase for a gentleman's own use,
a good cook twenty-five or thirty years of age, also a
a good seamstress eighteen or twenty years of age,
and a male house-servant between thirty-five and
forty-five years of age.

" may 1—dtf　　　　　BIRCH & SHEKELL."

" A likely Boy for Sale.—For sale, a smart and
likely well grown boy, aged about sixteen years,—to
be sold to any gentleman wanting him for his own
use. He is sold for no fault, but because the owner
has no further use for him. For terms, &c. inquire
of　　　　　EDW. DYER, Auctioneer.

" feb 16—d3t."

Mr Clay assures us that slavery exists in this district in its " *mildest form*," and I believe the statement to be correct; but these advertisements shew
that even the tenderest mercies of slavery are very
terrible. Since we entered Maryland, we have been
attended in the inns by coloured servants of both
sexes, who are slaves. Some of them have children,
who may be seen, in all the innocence and gaiety of
youth, playing about the courts and passages of the
hotels. They are " property" daily increasing in
value, and in due season will probably become fit for
" the Louisiana and Mississippi market," when they
may be sold to Mr " Wm. H. Williams *at his jail* on

Seventh Street." The Americans who have been born and reared in familiarity with these scenes not only do not perceive the malignity of them, but have a variety of commonplace palliations, if not positive eulogiums, to offer in their favour; and these are not selfish and degraded Americans, but persons of education and good standing in society. Familiarity with slavery obviously blunts men's moral perceptions in regard to its qualities. Without pretending to any uncommon degree of sensibility, I confess that my mind could never look on slaves, particularly children and young men and women, without involuntarily first placing myself in their stead, and then following them to the "Louisiana and Mississippi market," to the cotton and sugar plantations, where they are forced to labour to the limits of their strength, till toil and misery send them to the grave. These ideas haunted my imagination, until the whole subject became deeply distressing.

I have already mentioned, vol. i. p. 258, that the Americans are not justly answerable for the institution of slavery, and that it ought to be regarded as a great calamity bequeathed to them by their ancestors, including the British Government of the last century; but after every apology has been framed for slavery which the ingenuity of man can invent, the discord between it and the dictates of man's highest and noblest faculties ever jars upon the soul, and ever will jar, until it be abolished. Those who defend its continuance do not recognise the fact that this discord exists, will exist, and will never allow peace to

the highest minds, while such outrages to humanity
pollute the soil. The supporters of slavery seem
not to perceive that a just God governs the world,
and that the dictates of man's highest sentiments are
His voice denouncing it as wrong. They speak of
it as an institution permitted by His providence, and
say that in His own good time He will bring it to a
close. But slavery, like piracy, murder, and fire-
raising, proceeds from *abuses* of man's animal propensities. It is true that God has *permitted* man to
abuse all his faculties, but he never *approves* of these
abuses. In his government of the world, he takes
care that, sooner or later, those who sow the wind
shall reap the whirlwind; and thus it will probably
be with the patrons of slavery, if they leave it to
God's providence to put an end to the institution,
without making any moral efforts themselves to abolish it. It is certain that He will abolish it; but it
will be in tempest and whirlwind, in blood and devastation, amid cries and misery. He now calls on
them to abolish it in mercy and in peace. In listening to the debates of Congress, in which the most
high-toned appeals were made to justice and right,
and the noblest sentiments were uttered in favour
of universal freedom;—and afterwards, on returning home, casting a glance at Mr " Wm. H. William's jail" for the purchase of Negroes for the
Louisiana and Mississippi market, I could not avoid
the idea that I was looking on the representation of
a drama written by a madman. The spirit and
principles in operation in Congress, and in the " jail,"

were so wildly in discord, that it seemed as if only the delirium of insanity could have placed them so directly in juxtaposition.

Feb 19. Ther. 27°. *Visit to the President.*—Dr Sewall, to whom I brought a letter, called and undertook to introduce us to Mr Van Buren, the President. The " White House," as the presidential residence is named, lies at one end of the chief street of Washington, and the Capitol at the other, the distance being one and one-eighth part of a mile. It is a large square building; not particularly striking in its architecture. We entered as if going into a public office. We opened the door, met nobody, and were asked no questions. At last we reached the anteroom, and here a servant appeared. Dr Sewall sent in his own name and ours, and in less than a minute, we were requested to enter a large room, which resembled the business-room of a chief secretary of state. Mr Van Buren immediately appeared, received us kindly and politely, and entered into conversation. He spoke of steam-navigation, the cornlaws, Mr O'Connell's quarrel with the Dublin Press, and the rising of the Chartists, and appeared to me to possess accurate information, and to state sound views on every topic on which he touched. His manners are very agreeable, combining the ease of a gentleman accustomed to the best society, with the dignity of a public character. The busts and portraits of him, and even the caricatures, which every where abound, are excellent likenesses.

Conservatism of the Law.—Each State has a writ-

ten constitution, which defines not only the powers of
the magistrates but those of the legislature itself;
and the Supreme Court of the State possesses authority to determine whether any particular act of the
legislature be legal or the reverse; that is to say,
whether or not it transgresses the limits prescribed
to the legislature by the constitution. I lately conversed with an eminent lawyer who had just returned
from Annapolis, where he had pleaded the cause of
the professors of the University of Baltimore, who
sought, in the Supreme Court of Maryland, to nul-
lify an act of the legislature of that State, on the
ground of its being *ultra vires*, or beyond the powers
of the legislature, and had succeeded. I see the decision reported in the newspapers to-day:—" It de-
cides," says the report, " the Act (of the legislature)
of 1825, which gave to certain trustees the government of the university, to be unconstitutional and
void, and all the rights and franchises of the university are declared to be vested in the regents. The
opinion of the court is regarded as an able and
powerful defence of chartered rights against legislative encroachments."

The constitution of the United States is in some
respects similar to that of the particular States. It
also has established a Supreme Court, which has extensive jurisdiction, and performs a most important
office in preserving the integrity of the Union. Its
judicial power comprehends all cases, in law and
equity, arising under the constitution itself, or the
laws of the United States; all controversies to which

the United States shall be a party; controversies between two or more States, or between citizens of different States, and many others. It sits in Washington, and on the rolls of the court may be seen *Maryland* versus *Virginia*, or *Ohio* versus *Indiana*, these sovereign States appearing there as private litigants. They argue their claims before the judges, and implicitly acquiesce in their decisions. If civilization were so far advanced in Europe as to induce the whole sovereignties to support the jurisdiction of such a court, it might avert many bloody and expensive wars. The judges of this court in Washington are men of great talent and erudition, and their decisions are highly respected.

Another case has excited great interest all over the Union. Judge M'Kinley, sitting in the District Court in Alabama, had decided that a bank incorporated in Georgia had no right to sue any person in Alabama; that is, that no corporated company could sue beyond the State in which it was incorporated. The effect of this decision would be virtually to repeal the Union in so far as the privileges of incorporated companies are concerned, and to leave each State, in regard to its chartered companies, in the same condition as if surrounded by foreign countries. The Constitution of the United States provides, that " the citizens of each State shall be entitled to all privileges and immunities of citizens in the several States," and that " full faith and credit shall be given in each State to the public acts, records, and judicial proceedings of every other State." The decision of the

Judge of Alabama was regarded as a refusal to acknowledge the " public act" of the Legislature of Georgia which incorporated the bank, as inconsistent with these provisions of the law, and therefore unconstitutional; and the cause was brought into the Supreme Court of the United States by appeal. Mr Webster argued powerfully in favour of the efficacy of the privileges of chartered companies in all the States, in so far as they are consistent with the common law. The judgment of the Court of Alabama was reversed by a majority of the judges, and the following propositions are reported as being established by the decision :—

" 1. That, by the comity of nations, corporations can contract, as well as sue, in other nations, as well as in that in which they exist, or by whose government they are created.

" 2. That this comity exists, in a still stronger degree, between States connected together as are the States of this Union.

" 3. That the Constitution and laws of Alabama establish no such POLICY as is infringed by the purchase and sale of bills of exchange within her limits by the agents of foreign corporations.

" 4. An admission that there are some rights of citizens of other States, secured by the constitution, of which a State cannot divest them. This was not the ground of the decision, but was intended, as we suppose, to be, in legal phrase, the *exclusion of a conclusion.*"

La Signorina America Vespucci.—We met this

lady in society this evening. She is here as a solicitor to Congress for a grant of land in return for
the name which her ancestor Americus Vespuccius
furnished to this great continent. On the 29th of
January last she presented a memorial in the French
language to the Senate, in which she sets forth her
name and descent, and states that " she has been
obliged to quit her country (Italy) on account of her
political opinions. She has separated herself from
her family, in order to avoid drawing upon them the
displeasure of her government. She is now alone,
without country, without family, and without protection." She "has been travelling from country to country, without a stay, and without security." " The
good Queen of the French restored her to courage
by granting her protection, so far as even to permit
her to travel under the auspices of the French flag.
But this generosity does not give her a country ;
this protection does not bestow upon her the title of
citizen." " She is now in this quarter of the globe,
which has been baptized by her ancestor ; by him
who has bequeathed to it his imperishable name."
" America Vespucci will make no demand on the
American Government." " She knows that the
Americans have been magnanimous," " that they
have been generous towards all who have done a
noble act for their country; and that they have,
moreover, granted protection and an asylum even to
emigrants from other nations. There is but one
Vespuccius who has given his name to a continent.
Will the Americans do nothing for the descendant of

Americus ?" Her friends made it known to the Senate that she desired " citizenship, and a grant of land."

This eloquent appeal was remitted by the Senate to a committee of five of their number to consider and report. The chairman of the committee was taken ill, and the committee met in his absence. They divided, two for, and two against, recommending a grant. When the chairman resumed his duties, he found himself in the unenviable position of being called on to decide this delicate question by his single vote. America Vespucci is a tall handsome Italian lady, " young," and " an exile from her own country." She has the sweetest smile and most expressive eyes ; and she bent the whole force of her charms and eloquence on the chairman to induce him to espouse her cause. But he was an American Senator of business habits, and had also the fear of his constituents before his eyes. He therefore constantly asked her for " a reason," for " a principle intelligible to men of business habits," why the United States should make a grant of land to the descendant of Americus, who, if history might be relied on, had received too much honour, when his name, instead of that of Christopher Columbus, was bestowed on the country. But the lady, who understood no English, urged, in the most beautiful French, the romantic incident of a young female descendant of Americus, an exile from home, coming to Congress, after the lapse of so many centuries, and soliciting only a small portion of the territory which already bore her name ! She enforced this view with all the persuasive arts of eloquence, and could not comprehend what more satisfactory " reasons," or " business-like principles," the Senator could require, in order to authorize him to report in her favour. But all her efforts were in vain. The Senator stood fast by his " business principles," and the committee reported against a grant either of citizenship or of land, as being unauthorized by the constitution ; but strongly recommended a subscription by the American people in her favour. The report was subsequently approved of by the Senate, whose individual members subscribed a handsome sum for the lady's benefit, but which she declined to accept.

Manners and Morals of Mississippi.—The ferocious quarrels and dissolute manners of Mississippi have been described by many travellers. They appear to me to indicate a condition of mind in the people somewhat resembling that which prevailed in Scotland three centuries ago, and which is strongly depicted by Sir Walter Scott in his Tales of a Grandfather, and still more strikingly illustrated in the records of the High Court of Justiciary for the same period. Rapine, falsehood, and bloodshed, seem then to have been occurrences so common as to have attracted no particular attention. The Western States of the American Union, with similar mental dispositions, possess more of the physical elements of civilization ; and as Scotland has thoroughly changed her character for the better, there is ample reason to expect a still more rapid improvement in the morals of these portions of the American people.

I have had the pleasure of becoming acquainted with a gentleman from Mississippi who has the best means of information regarding it, and whose own talents and dispositions would render him a welcome visiter in any society. He informs me, that in Mississippi the Legislature has passed severe laws against rioting, in other words, lynching, and using the Bowie knife. This knife has a long blade like a carving-knife, with a thick back to give it strength, an edge as sharp as a razor, and the point rounded off like a scimitar. Its weight and sharpness render it a frightful weapon either for stabbing or cutting. It is carried in a sheath under the waistcoat, on the left side, and can be drawn in an instant. About one in forty of all the western people go thus armed. A law recently enacted, renders it criminal to *draw* a Bowie-knife, although it be not used. The general complaint against these States is, that their laws may be good, and may prohibit ferocious actions ; but that they are not regularly executed. Great efforts are making by the respectable portion of the inhabitants, to wipe off this stain from their country. A lawyer of some respectability lately drew a Bowie-knife in a quarrel and threatened his opponent. He was carried before a criminal judge, convicted under the recent law, and sentenced to three months' imprisonment. He petitioned the governor for a pardon. His petition was refused, and the governor stated publicly, that in no circumstances would he ever pardon any individual convicted under the Bowie-knife act. The law, also, has recently made

the town or district liable in cases of damage or destruction of property by mobs.   There may be difficulty in inducing juries to convict under this statute.

Feb. 20.   Ther. 29°.   *The Capitol and Congress.*—
This morning we proceeded to the Capitol.   In approaching it, I could not help feeling ashamed of the
barbarism of my countrymen, who in the war of 1814
consigned it to the flames.   The external walls have
been painted white, to obliterate the smoky traces of
that unworthy deed.   The grand vestibule is under
the dome, and has no opening upwards to allow of
the escape of air.   The consequence is, that the effluvia of human bodies and of tobacco-juice greet the
nostrils and afflict the lungs the moment it is entered.
We found also, that the Senate chamber and House
of Representatives are, in this weather, hermetically
sealed, except at the doors and chimneys.   Although
these may provide some change of air for the members,
who are all accommodated on the floor, the unhappy
visiters in the galleries receive all the vitiated air from
below, render it worse by their own breathing, and are
nearly doomed to suffocation.   The ladies are accommodated with the front seat, and occasionally faint
from the impurity of the atmosphere.   I sat three
hours in the gallery of the Senate chamber to-day,
and afterwards experienced those debilitating, irri-
table, and unpleasant sensations, which are generated
by imperfectly decarbonized blood.

Mr Calhoun of South Carolina spoke two or three
times.   He seemed to be about sixty, tall and slender, and of a highly bilious and nervous temperament.

The lower ridge of his forehead projects much,* indicating great powers of observation, but the superior ridge, devoted to reflection, is much smaller. Although the latter region looks narrow and retreating, yet there is enough of brain to give average power to his reflecting faculties. He has very large Self-Esteem and Firmness. The head indicates much self-will and determination ; great powers of perseverance ; a capacity for details, but little profound judgment.

I saw also Mr Clay, but he did not speak. He is nearly bald. The anterior lobe of his brain is long and high, the middle perpendicular portion predominating. He seems to have large Acquisitiveness and considerable Ideality. In him also Self-Esteem and Firmness are large. The coronal region rises moderately high above Cautiousness and Causality, and the head altogether is high and long, rather than broad. It is of ample size. His temperament is nervous-sanguine, with a little bilious. He is tall and slender ; and apparently between 60 and 70. This combination indicates great natural vivacity, readiness of apprehension, facility of illustration, with force of character ; but there are two defects in the brain which will prevent such an individual from rising to the first class of minds. Causality and the moral organs do not present the highest degree of development. Men thus constituted do not suffi-

* Busts and portraits of all the public men whose heads I shall here describe, abound in the United States. As they are thus presented to public inspection, I do not consider myself as guilty of any indelicacy in introducing sketches of them into this work.

ciently appreciate the influence of the moral sentiments as a natural *power*, nor do they trace the causes
with which they deal, to their first elements, nor follow them to their remote consequences. Mr Clay's
head, however, bespeaks a man greatly above an average in point of mental power, and also practical in
his tendencies ; and therefore well adapted to the
general American mind of the present day.

Here, also, sits Daniel Webster, looking like an intellectual giant among the senators. His enormous
anterior lobe, and generally large head, reinforced
by large lungs, mark him as a natural leader ; but his
reflective organs are too much developed in proportion to his Individuality to render his eloquence
equally popular with that of Henry Clay. Mr Webster needs a great subject, involving a profound principle and important consequences, before his strength
can be called forth. Give him these, and he will
rise to the highest eminence as a pleader and a
statesman ; but his intellect is too profound and comprehensive to be fully appreciated by the people. On
seeing the man, therefore, I am not surprised at a
circumstance which I have remarked, that, while Mr
Webster is regarded by a few as *the* great political
character of the United States, Mr Clay has at least a
hundred devoted followers for each one of Mr Webster's admirers. Webster, however, like Burke, will be
quoted for the depth of principle and wisdom involved in his speeches, when the more fascinating
but less profound orations of Mr Clay have sunk into
oblivion.

I heard Mr Cuthbert, Senator for Georgia, make a long speech on a bill for preventing the officers of Government from interfering in elections. He is a slow and forcible, but not a refined speaker.

The appearance of the members of the Senate is favourable. With few exceptions, their brains, and especially the organs of the intellectual faculties, are large, while there is a good average development of the organs of the moral sentiments. Collectively, they seemed to me to be a highly respectable and gifted body of men.

The American Society for the Diffusion of Useful Knowledge.—In the evening I attended a meeting of this Society (incorporated by the Legislature of New York) in the Capitol. The Honourable Joseph Story, one of the Judges of the Supreme Court, was called to the chair. After some appropriate and instructive remarks by the chairman, the Reverend John Proudfit of New York stated the objects of the Society. " It aims at the diffusion of pure and wholesome knowledge imbued with the spirit of Christianity." One great object of the Society is the publication and general introduction of a National School Library. " It is estimated that there are at least 50,000 schools in the United States, and it is now generally, if not universally, admitted that every one should be supplied with a library." The Society proposes the publication of a series of popular works upon all those branches of knowledge that are most interesting to the people ; also, the publication of a popular " Journal of Useful Knowledge and of Public Instruction," congenial to the institutions of America. Another object is the preparation of text-books for schools, many of the books now in use being inferior and improper.

Mr Abbott, the secretary of the Society, next addressed the meeting, and exhibited a mass of statistics relative to the publication of newspapers, magazines, and books, in England, in France, in Germany, and in the United States; and shewed that the United States is one of the most reading communities in the world. He exhibited a case, containing 50 volumes of books already published, the price of which is $20; mentioned that the cost of placing one similar library in every one of the 50,000 schools of the Union, would be $1,000,000, and asked " what sum will express the benefits ?"

Towards the close of the proceedings, being requested to address the meeting, I offered a few remarks on the spur of the moment to the following effect : " It appears to me that the elementary principles of all the natural sciences, when contemplated in their primitive forms by superior minds, are simple, and that they constitute the native food of the intellect. I include in these sciences the knowledge of man's physical, moral, and intellectual nature, and the relations subsisting between them and external objects and beings. One advantage of communicating instruction in these truths to youth is, that it furnishes them with a solid basis on which to found their judgments. Under the old system, there was much of conflicting opinion ; authority stood against authority, and in the phases of human life, chiefly intricacy and inscrutable evolutions were presented.   The causes of good and evil did not appear, and the consequences of actions were scarcely traceable.   A people invested with political power, whose education leaves them in such a condition, must, to a great extent, be exposed to the seduction of their passions, to be misled by imperfect views of their own interests, and even to the delusions of an excited imagination, leading them into wild speculations and impracticable adventures.   An education in natural truth has the tendency to steady the whole mind, and to place passion, imagination, and ambition, under the guidance of reason.   America needs an education of this kind, because she has no controlling principle in her institutions except the religion, morality, and intelligence of the majority of her people.

" This Society. in framing books for schools, will do well to ask themselves, as each volume is presented, ' What does this book teach the people to *do ?*'   It is good to *know*, but it is better still to *act*. In the present state of civilized society, the history of the past is not a guide to the future.   We are in a state of *transition*, and it is of greater importance to furnish sound, practical principles for the future, than to load the memory with too minute a knowledge of the past.   The pages of history are useful chiefly as charts, indicating the shoals on which human happiness has been shipwrecked.   We must chalk out new and better lines to direct our future movements.   It is extremely difficult to frame books

embodying scientific principles, and applying them
to practical purposes; but in your country, where
the law excludes works on theology from your schools,
this object must be accomplished before a truly valuable library of secular school-books can be created." The object of the meeting was to commend
the Society and its works to the consideration and
support of the Union, and to induce the Representatives from the different States to make known the
merits of its library in their several districts. The
attendance was large, and the proceedings were interesting. They were subsequently reported in the
" Christian Statesman," from which I have extracted the foregoing remarks, as a short specimen of
the terms in which I generally addressed American
audiences. The library proposed by this Society
will enter the field as a rival to that now preparing
by Messrs Marsh, Capen, Lyon, and Webb of Boston, under the superintendence of the Board of Education of Massachusetts; but there is scope enough
for both in the vast territories of the United States.

The Hall of the Supreme Court, in which the
meeting was held, was destitute of ventilation, and I
suffered severely for several hours after leaving it
from the effects of bad air. On mentioning this next
day, I was told that several lawyers have fallen down
dead on the spot while engaged in the most animated
pleadings in this hall, and that, although apoplexy
was assigned as the cause, some medical men, who
knew the state of the atmosphere, had expressed an
opinion that the catastrophes were probably hastened,

if not caused, by asphyxia. The late arrangements by Dr David B. Reid for ventilating the British Houses of Parliament are well known here; but no person has yet proposed to adopt them, or any other means, for the preservation of life and health in the public chambers and apartments of the Capitol.

Feb. 21. Ther. 43°. The weather to-day is beautiful, and gives indications of the approach of spring. *The Senate.—The Sub-Treasury Bill.*—I heard part of the debate on a bill for regulating the office of treasurer, and more effectually preserving the public money in the hands of the officers and agents of Government; but none of the speeches was particularly interesting. This subject has excited a great deal of discussion in the public prints. There have been great embezzlements of public money by the officers of Government in various departments of the United States; and also losses and embarrassments arising from its having been deposited, until needed, in banks in different States of the Union, many of which have embarked in large speculations with the Government treasure, and when called on for repayment, either declared themselves bankrupt, or suspended cash payments. From the want, also, of an efficient machinery extending over the whole Union for effecting the exchange of bank-notes, the rates of exchange between the different parts of the country are constantly fluctuating, and are often ruinously high. When the General Government deposits its funds in banks, it is subjected also to the loss and annoyance arising from this state of the monetary system. The Democratic party, now in power, have attempted to pass a bill requiring the custom-house duties and the price of the public lands (the chief sources of the revenue of the General Government), to be paid in specie, and this treasure to be locked up by the public officers in strong boxes, and held subject to the orders of the Government at Washington; and farther providing that any public servant who shall abstract any portion of it shall be held to have committed felony, and be punished with confinement as a common criminal at hard labour in the State prison.

Nothing seems to me to be more wanted than some such regulation as this to protect not only the public money, but the public morals; for the mode in which the revenue has of late years been distributed, has acted like a forcing stove applied to public cupidity, and tempted many men from the paths of virtue, who, under a better system, would have maintained their honour without a stain. But it has been, and continues to be, violently opposed by the whig party, who are regarded as the patrons of paper currency, and the " credit system" with which it is generally supposed that the prosperity of the United States is indissolubly bound up. The democrats have offered various modifications, such as introducing the demand for specie gradually, accepting for a time the notes of specie-paying banks, and other accommodations to the merchants; but the opposition is as violent and inflexible as ever in regard to the payment of custom-house duties in gold and silver.

Dr Duncan and the House of Representatives.—
While these discussions were proceeding in the Se-
nate, an extremely stormy discussion arose in the
House of Representatives on a question of privilege.
Mr Prentiss, of Mississippi, offered the following re-
solutions :—

" Resolved, That this house proceed forthwith to
inquire—

" 1. Whether Alexander Duncan, a member of
this house, from the State of Ohio, be the author of
a certain publication or publications under his name,
in relation to the proceedings of this house, and certain members thereof, published in the Globe newspaper of the 19th inst.

" 2. Whether, by said publication or publications,
the said Alexander Duncan has not been guilty of a
violation of the privileges of this house, of an offence
against its peace, dignity, and good order, and of
such grossly indecent, ungentlemanly, disgraceful,
and dishonourable misconduct, as renders him unworthy of his seat in this house, and justly liable to
expulsion from the same."

There was a call of the house, and 125 members
answered to their names.   After a great deal of fu-
rious disputation and vociferation, Mr Thomson of
South Carolina moved to substitute the following
motion for that of Mr Prentiss.

" Resolved, That Alexander Duncan, a member
of this house, having avowed himself the author of
an article published in the Globe of the 19th instant,
grossly libellous of honourable members of this body,

that the said Alexander Duncan be reprimanded by the Speaker in the presence of the house."

After this resolution was presented, the house adjourned, it being then 6 P. M., and the usual hour of adjournment being three.

Dr Sewall, the Anti-Phrenologist.—Dr Sewall, to whom, as already mentioned, I brought a letter, has been exceedingly attentive to us, notwithstanding the different views which we entertain on the subject of Phrenology. We met a large party of senators and members of the House of Representatives at his residence this evening, and had much pleasant and interesting conversation. One of the gentlemen present took me by the button, and placing Dr Sewall and me face to face, said, " Now we have got Phrenology and Anti-Phrenology fairly before us, let us hear you fight it out." I replied that there was really nothing between us to fight about ; that, if the views to which Dr Sewall had given the name in his work were really Phrenology, I should be altogether on his side ; that he had, in truth, created a phantom, called it Phrenology, and then knocked it down, but that no Phrenologist took any interest in such a feat." Dr Sewall asked if I said this seriously. I answered that I did so, and mentioned that Dr George M'Clellan of Philadelphia, from whom I had brought a letter to him, had previously gone along with him in his views, but now acknowledged publicly to his class that it was not Phrenology which he had previously ridiculed, but erroneous conceptions of his own regarding it ; and that he had informed me that

he had stated as much in his letter to him (Dr Sewall). " Then," added Dr Sewall, " I suppose that I
must revise my opinions. They are not unalterable
like the laws of the Medes and the Persians." And
here the conversation terminated, to the disappoint-
ment, perhaps, of some of the members of Congress,
who would have enjoyed a " set to" between us considerably. I shall have occasion, at a subsequent
time, to mention how far Dr Sewall profited by the
revisal of his opinions which he here indicated as
possible.

Ex-President Adams.—I was introduced by Dr
Sewall to the Ex-President, Mr John Quincy Adams,
who was one of his distinguished guests ; and was
just entering into conversation with him, when a
young Scotch lady, overjoyed at hearing, at so great
a distance from home, the accents of the Land of
Cakes, placed herself between him and me, and
poured forth such a volume of questions about Scotland and Scots people, that the patience of Mr
Adams was exhausted. I attempted, by remarks
made to him past her shoulder, to retain him, but in
vain. He turned off and went to another part of the
room, where a circle of admirers was formed around
him, which I was never able subsequently to penetrate.

Mr Adams, after having been President of the
United States, now sits in the House of Representatives as one of the members for Massachusetts, a
position which appears to me to be in every respect
consistent with republican principles, and perfectly

compatible with the dignity of his previous office. A real patriot is ready to serve his country in any station in which his talents may be useful, and there is true magnanimity in descending at his country's call from the station of supreme power to that of an ordinary representative ; and still more so, as at present he is the only president who has not been re-elected for a second term.

Numerous busts of him are published, but I doubted their accuracy, for I was disappointed in the development of his head ; but I now see that they are correct. He is stoutly made, and his temperament is sanguine-nervous bilious, giving him great activity, and power of enduring fatigue. His brain is large : The base of it is large, particularly Combativeness and Destructiveness. Self-Esteem and Firmness are very large ; Acquisitiveness and Benevolence large ; Veneration and Conscientiousness full. The anterior lobe is of considerable size, although not large in proportion to the regions of the propensities and sentiments. This indicates a man of impulse rather than of clear, sound, and consistent judgment. His organs of the observing faculties, however, particularly those of Individuality, are well developed, but they are larger than those of reflection, giving rise to talents for observation, for accumulating knowledge, and for producing it when required ; but without a corresponding power of penetrating to the principles of things, and tracing consistently distant consequences. With much kindness of disposition, and stubborn independence of charac-

ter, the head indicates a liability to heat of temper,
and to occasional obstinacy; also, a deficiency in tact,
and a difficulty in preserving a continued consistency;
the latter imperfection arising not from any tendency
to wavering in his dispositions, but from a limited
intellectual capacity to perceive fine and distant relations, combined with a self-confidence which will
rarely allow him to doubt the soundness of his own
inductions.

Most of the Presidents of the United States are
said to have injured their private fortunes by the
expenses of office, except Mr John Quincy Adams.
He is spoken of as an economist, who spent what the
Government allowed him, but no more. The small
pay allowed to American functionaries is attended
with some evils. Only men of large fortune, of
whom there are not yet a great number in the United
States, or men in whom ambition is more powerful
than prudence, are likely to become candidates for
public offices. The latter are the very men whom
the people should avoid as public servants; for a
democracy, above all other governments, needs men
of prudence and of incorruptible integrity to conduct its affairs. A system of government which has
the natural tendency to elevate imprudent and ambitious men to power, may be designated as a hotbed
to generate jobbers and peculators. I hear it stated,
also, that the foreign ministers of the United States
are often ruined by the extra expense entailed on
them by their office. " The pay of ministers pleni-
potentiary is $9000 per annum as salary, besides

$9000 for outfit. Chargés d'affaires receive $4500 per annum, and secretaries of legation $2000.* I am told that some of the members of the House of Assembly contrive to save four or five hundred dollars out of their own pay during the session in Washington, and would regard any man as an extravagant waster of the public money who should propose an increase of salaries.

Feb. 22. Ther. 42°. *Dr Duncan.*—The debate on the motions to expel or reprimand Dr Duncan was resumed this morning, and finally the resolutions moved by Mr Prentiss were " laid on the table," which means that nothing was done with them. A vote of two-thirds of the members is necessary for expulsion : this could not be carried, and nobody cares for a " reprimand" from the chair. The only alternatives left were " laying on the table" or exculpation, and the former was preferred.

I have introduced this discussion chiefly for the sake of the following remarks :—I heard the whole subject extensively discussed by American gentlemen at the public table in Washington, and subsequently in the railroad cars on the way to Baltimore ; and the result was generally approved of, on the ground, expressly stated, that the *rifle* is the only method of settling such disputes. Some few persons lifted up their voices against this sentiment, but they were the minority. While such a state of feeling prevails, the laws recently enacted by Congress and many of

* American Almanac.

the States against duelling must remain nearly a dead letter. One effect which attends the meeting of Congress in Washington is injurious. It withdraws these fierce legislators from the wholesome influence of a more humane public opinion which would reach them in the larger cities. In Washington they themselves constitute society, and give the tone to opinion.

Petitions against Slavery.—The ingenuity and perseverance of the abolitionists have already discovered an antidote, to some extent, to the resolution of Congress that their petitions should not be received. They continue to present petitions as if no such resolution existed, and take care that the presentment be reported in the newspapers. The " Daily National Intelligencer " contains a list, extending to four columns of close small type, of petitions " handed to the clerk" of the House of Representatives on the 18th of February, the great majority of which relate to the abolition of slavery or the right of petitioning. The list contains the *name* of the *first* person who subscribes each petition, and the *number* of the other subscribers, and specifies briefly what they pray for.

General Washington's Birthday.—This morning the great guns at the Navy yard, a short distance from the city, were fired to celebrate Washington's birthday. In the evening we attended a grand national ball given in honour of the day. The President of the United States, and all the foreign ministers, attended ; the latter in their official costumes.

Much of the youth and beauty of the city were assembled. The President entered about ten o'clock, leaning on the arms of two stewards of the ball. He wore no costume, and was attended by no insignia of office. The dancing, however, was suspended, and he walked up the middle of the floor between a double row of the company of all ages and both sexes, who formed a way for him. They bowed, and he returned the compliment; but not a sound was uttered. The band played " Hail! Columbia." He ascended a platform at the upper end of the room, which was free to all, and on which many ladies and gentlemen were already standing. He then mingled with the company as an ordinary visiter.

The young ladies took the lead at the ball; but I was assured that ladies, however young, gay, beautiful, and accomplished, after being married, are no longer recognised as constituent elements of a ball in the city of Washington. A pretty and engaging lady of nineteen, who has been married for one year, mentioned to me, that while in the single state she remorselessly assisted in deleting the names of her acquaintances from the ball lists as soon as they were wedded, and never dreamt that she was inflicting any hardship on them; but that now she considers it rather hard to be cut off at her age, when her taste for gaiety is yet fresh and unsatisfied, from all active participation in these scenes. There is little *retenue* or shyness in the youthful fair in the ball-room. They act as if the floor belonged to them and their " beaux" (their own expression for young gentlemen); and if the time allowed to them for gaiety before marriage be short, they certainly make the best use of it while it lasts. There is much beauty and amiability, but their forms are fragile, and indicate liability to premature decay.

Opinion seems to be unanimous, that no perceptible evils result from the freedom with which young ladies conduct themselves in the festive parties of the United States. The means of providing for a family are so easily acquired, that most of the men contract marriage at an early age, and seductions are extremely rare. We are told, also, that the young ladies in general display great tact and discrimination in their selection of partners, and very rarely commit themselves to imprudent or unprincipled characters.

The Negro Brain.—In the Negroes whom we have seen in this city, the average size of the brain is less than the average size in the free Negroes of New York and Pennsylvania. Here the Negroes are chiefly slaves, and in some of them the brain is so small, that their mental powers must be feeble indeed. It is a reasonable inference, that the greater exercise of the mental faculties in freedom has caused the brain to increase in size ; for it is a general rule in physiology, that wholesome exercise favours the development of all organs. But I fear that another reason may, to some extent, be assigned for the difference, namely, that the condition of the free Negroes, when they come into competition with the whites, is so unfavourable, that those of them in whom the brain is deficient in size, and the mental faculties weak, are overwhelmed with difficulties, and die out, and only the most vigorously constituted are able to maintain their position ; and hence that in the free States we see the highest specimens of the race.

Feb. 23. Ther. 40°. *Journey from Washington to Philadelphia.*—We left Washington at six in the morning by the railroad, arrived at Baltimore at half-past eight, breakfasted, and started at nine by the railroad for Philadelphia. The axle of the baggage waggon broke, and we were detained for two hours. Nothing could exceed the good humour with which the passengers submitted to the loss of time while the luggage was transferred into the passengers' cars. The rough treatment, however, which the baggage itself sustained in the act of transference was very reprehensible. The trunks and packages were thrown about, and dashed against each other on the ground most recklessly, yet this is one of the best managed railroads in the Union. Mr Newkirk, the manager, told me that in engaging all the men employed by the railway company, it is stipulated that they shall practice habitual temperance, and if their breath even shall at any time be observed to smell of intoxicating liquor, although they may be perfectly sober, this shall be regarded as a voluntary resignation of their places ; and that, by rigidly acting on these stipulations, no serious accident has occurred since the railway was opened in 1838. Urgent solicitations are often made to him to overlook one transgression, and the most positive assurances given of future good conduct, but he meets all such applications by reminding the petitioner of the rule : " When you put the liquor to your head, you knew that by doing so *you resigned* your situation. You were *then sober*, and therefore resigned deliberately ; and it is inconsistent to solicit my consent to your remaining after you have done so. I accept your resignation, and you must go." We arrived in Philadelphia at 6 P. M.

Feb. 24. Ther. 41°. "*How do you like our country ?*"—Mr Charles Matthews has announced a book on the United States, bearing the title, " How do you like our country?" This is a very common question, varied sometimes in this fashion, " How does Boston impress you ?" It is generally the first question put, and it is embarrassing to a stranger, because it will often force him to give an answer that will do violence to the feelings either of the querist or of himself, unless he deliver a long discourse expressive of modified likes and dislikes. By this question, however, the Americans in general mean nothing more than an invitation to conversation, as we do in England by the observation, " This is pleasant weather," or the question, " How far have you travelled to-day ?"

Feb. 25. Ther. 41°. *Wilmington.—Delaware.*—In the interval between my first and second courses of lectures in Philadelphia, I was solicited to deliver three lectures on education in Wilmington, a town of 8000 inhabitants, at the distance of twenty-eight miles from Philadelphia, on the line of the Baltimore railway, and proceeded thither this day at 3 P.M.

We were forced to wait a full hour before leaving the station on the right bank of the Schuylkill, because the train from Baltimore had not arrived, and there being only one track of rails, we could not pass it. The most perfect good humour prevailed among the passengers during the detention. In the cars I have repeatedly met people of colour travelling as passengers, and saw no indignity offered to them. Wilmington enjoys a supply of water raised from the Brandywine river by force-pumps, and distributed in pipes through the town. It has one street paved; but the others present beds of unredeemed mud ankle deep. Mr Gilpin, from whom I received great kindness, carries on an extensive manufacture of writing-paper in the neighbourhood of the town, from fine linen rags exclusively, and he was the first to introduce machinery into this branch. Much of the American paper is made from cotton, and is not durable. Bank-notes are made from *new* Russia duck, and it is the newness of the linen that renders them so tough.

State-Lotteries.—Massachusetts, New York, and Pennsylvania, have established State-lotteries, and prohibited the sale of tickets for the lotteries of other States. Delaware, Maryland, and the district of Columbia, continue to patronize them as well as slavery.

CHAPTER III.

1839.

March. 2. *Phrenology.*—I commenced my second course of lectures in Philadelphia this evening in the Music Fund Hall. The attendance was 342, of whom a large proportion were " Friends," both orthodox and Hicksites. Many of those who attended the first course have subscribed also for this one.

The Maine Boundary.—War with England.—On the 9th of February Mr Van Buren presented to the House of Representatives at Washington a report from the Secretary of State, with the relative documents, regarding the dispute with England about the Maine Boundary ; and on the 1st of March both Houses of Congress were engaged from noon till midnight in discussing the subject, and finally passed a bill to authorize the President to engage 50,000 vo-

lunteers, and take other measures of a warlike character, to support the Governor of Maine. Mr Webster, on whose cool judgment great reliance is placed,
is reported to have said in his speech in the senate,
that " if England did not settle this matter by the
4th of July next, the disputed territory should be
seized by the United States."

The effect of these discussions on the public mind
has been very striking. In every circle into which
we enter, almost every voice is raised for war. The
battles, both by land and sea, in which the Americans have been victorious over the British, are fought
over again in the newspapers; and if one were to
judge from the tone of the public mind, war would
appear inevitable. Amidst this excitement, however,
a few individuals of advanced age and experience may
be met with, who, in private conversation, strongly
deprecate hostilities; but they regard the popular
current of opinion as too strong to be at present stem-
med with success.

The opinion is generally entertained in Britain, that
the Americans are so intensely devoted to gain, and so
averse to taxation, that they are not a warlike nation;
but my conviction is different. The history of their
country, which, in one form or another, constitutes
the staple of their instruction at school, records heart-
stirring adventures of their ancestors in their contests with the Indians, and afterwards many successful battles in the cause of freedom when they fought
for their own independence. Next comes the war
with Britain in 1813, in which the existing generation

boasts of many victories. All these achievements
are described in the most fervid language, and every
battle in which the Americans were victorious is illustrated by engravings or cuts, and celebrated in
songs. In the hotels, and in innumerable private
houses, pictures representing their triumphs by sea
and land adorn the walls ; the panels of some of their
stage-coaches are ornamented with representations of
their frigates capturing their British antagonists ; in
short, in the United States, the mind of each generation is rendered familiar with tales of war, and excited
by their stirring influence from the first dawn of reason till manhood.

Nor are these seeds sown on a barren soil. The
Americans inherit the cerebral organization of the
three British nations, in whom the organs of Combativeness, Destructiveness, Self-Esteem, and Firmness,
the elements of pugnacity and warlike adventure, are
largely developed. In them this endowment is accompanied by a restless activity of mind, which finds
natural and agreeable vent in war, and by a degree of
intelligence which renders them capable equally of
individual enterprsie and of combination in action.
Add to all these the influence of extreme youth, and
the belligerent spirit of this people is easily accounted
for. In mentioning their extreme youth, I do not
refer to their short national existence of only sixty-
three years, since the 4th of July 1776, but to the
extraordinary proportion of young persons in their
population. It is well known that the population of
the United States doubles every twenty-five years by

natural increase alone, and every twenty-three years when assisted by immigration; but I have not observed that any just appreciation has been made by travellers of the influence of this fact on the character of the people. Nearly three generations are on the field at the same time, and as nearly every male, on arriving at twenty-one years of age, has a vote, the preponderating influence of the young on the national resolves is very striking. From attending their public political meetings, my conviction is, that the majority of their voters are under thirty-five or thirty-six years of age. Here, then, we have a people of naturally pugnacious dispositions, reared in the admiration of warlike deeds, imperfectly instructed in the principles on which the real greatness of nations is founded, possessed of much mental activity, impelled by all the fervour of youth, and unrestrained by experience. It would be matter of surprise if they were not predisposed to rush into a contest, especially with Britain, whom they still regard as their hereditary foe.

Fortunately, however, for the people, and for the interests of civilization throughout the world, there are numerous and strong impediments to the gratification of their warlike propensities. Their actual pursuits are all pacific; they live in plenty, and suffer no grievances except those which flow from their own errors, and which they have the power to remove; they have no warlike neighbours to threaten their frontiers; and the constitutions of the General Government, and of the several States, leave the executive power so feeble, that it can only add to its own embarrassments by engaging in hostilities. The American standing army consists of only 12,539 men of all arms and all ranks, while its corps of militia are altogether unadapted to aggressive warfare. The nation, therefore, has no force, except seven line-of-battle ships, twelve frigates, and twenty sloops of war (exclusive of those on the stocks), with which to maintain a war of aggression. So thoroughly ineffi-cient was the militia found to be in the last war, ex-cept as a defensive force, that the General Govern-ment resorted to the expedient of engaging volun-teers; and on the present occasion, Congress has authorized the raising of 50,000 men on the same terms. Fifty thousand volunteers may not appear to be a very formidable host to those who do not know the American people; but it would probably be found to consist of tough materials. A proclama-tion for the enlistment of such a force, would call forth that number of young, ardent, enthusiastic men, with heads full of fancies about glory, and tempera-ments burning for the gratifications arising from en-terprise and danger. A few months would suffice to confer on them the advantages of discipline, and they would then closely resemble the hosts of excited Frenchmen whom Napoleon led to the easy conquest of Italy and Germany. It is a blessing to the civilized world that so many impediments exist to this class of men attaining the ascendency in the national coun-cils.

March 3. Ther. 31°. *The Universalists.*—This

day I heard the Rev. Mr Thomas, a Universalist
minister, preach on the text " Charity suffereth
long," &c. The inscription in front of the pulpit is
" God is Love." He described one great difference
between the character of God, as revealed in the New
Testament, and that of the gods of the Greeks and
Romans, to consist in the " Love" of the God of the
Christians. The heathen deities were personifica-
tions of " power," much resembling the devil of some
Christian sects (" in whose existence," said he, " we
do not believe. regarding him as a mere phantom of
the imagination"). The discourse was very able,
well composed, and delivered from short notes. The
congregation presented that respectable appearance
in point of dress and deportment which characterizes
the American churches in general; but it was not so
numerous as some others.

The Universalists are stated, in the American Al-
manack, to have 653 congregations or churches, 317
ministers, and 600,000 people, in the Union. They
believe in universal salvation; but in applying this
doctrine they differ among themselves. Dr Chauncy
of Boston, who is regarded as a high authority among
them, in his work on " *The salvation of all men*," lays
it down as a rule that those individuals who, in
this life, have been enabled, by the Son of God,
to make great attainments in virtue, shall, in the
next, enter on the enjoyment of happiness immediately after death; while the incorrigibly wicked in
this world will be " awfully miserable" hereafter,
not to continue so for ever, but that they may be con-

vinced of their folly, and recovered to a virtuous frame
of mind.   Another class of Universalists follow Mr
Relly of England, and Mr Murray of the United
States, in admitting " no punishment for sin but
what Christ suffered; but speak of a punishment
which is consequent upon sin, as darkness, distress,
and misery, which they assert are ever attendant
upon transgression.   But, as to know the true God
and Jesus Christ is life eternal, and as all shall know
him, from the least to the greatest, that knowledge
or belief will consequently dispel or save from all the
darkness, distress, and fear, which are attendant upon
guilt and unbelief, and, being perfectly holy, we shall
consequently be perfectly and eternally happy."*

I was informed by several individuals in different
parts of the Union, that the Universalists are making
more progress among the common people than the
Unitarians; and that Unitarianism, where it exists,
attracts a larger proportion of the higher and better
educated circles.

March 4.   Ther. 21°.   *Morus multicaulis, American Silk.*—The Americans are at present labouring
under an excitement about the cultivation of the
mulberry tree, the rearing of silk-worms, and the manufacture of silk.   The newspapers teem with advertisements, announcing the sale of Morus multicaulis trees in innumerable quantities; and many persons are reported to have realized handsome fortunes
by rearing and selling them.   To-day, I saw at Wilmington a waistcoat and pair of pantaloons made of
American silk; and although the cultivators may be

* Dictionary of all Religions, by Hannah Adams, fourth edition.

much further from success than they at present believe, it appears not improbable that, with their ingenuity and perseverance, they may ultimately succeed in adding silk to their other products.

Wilmington.—Lectures on Education.—I delivered
my third lecture on education in the Lyceum at Wilmington this evening, which was attended by 170
persons of both sexes. Handsome resolutions ap-
proving of the lectures were passed and afterwards
published.

At the close of the lecture, an old gentleman rose,
and asked me whether there were not brains so deficient, that their owners had it not in their power to
act according to the moral law ? I had been told that,
since my first lecture, there had been a grand debate
in the Lyceum on the question whether Phrenology
leads to fatalism, and that this gentleman had opposed
it, on the ground that it does lead to this result. This
question was obviously calculated to furnish matter
for more argument. In answer, I stated that, before
one can judge of what any doctrine leads to, it is necessary to know the doctrine itself; that I had not
lectured on Phrenology, but only on education, before
the present audience, and, therefore, presumed that
they were strangers to what Phrenology teaches ; that
in Philadelphia, after devoting twenty hours to the
exposition of Phrenology, I had dedicated a large portion of one lecture to its connection with " moral responsibility ;" and that, as I could not now recapitulate expositions given in these twenty hours, I
hoped that the audience would excuse me for not entering on the results deducible from them. This

was accepted as a sufficient reason for declining to answer the question.*

March 5. Ther. 18°. In going to Wilmington yesterday, and returning from it to-day, I observed a considerable number of lambs newly dropped in the fields, with their mothers, also numbers of cattle out of doors. There is scarcely a tinge of green to be discovered in the grass. These animals are fed on hay and the leaves of Indian corn, which are saved in harvest, and are said to make good fodder. Autumn-sown wheat is now visible, but it looks dark, small, and sickly. No field-labour is going on, as the ground is deeply frozen.

March 8. Ther. 37°. *The Bad Health of the American Women.*—In the February number of the Southern Literary Messenger, Dr Harvey Lindsley, of Washington City, makes the following remarks on this subject. I copy his own words, because I believe them to represent the facts correctly, and also because a similar description, if given by a European visiter, would be more likely to give offence than when it proceeds from an American physician.

" The remark," says Dr Lindsley, " has often been made by Europeans who have visited this country —and the melancholy truth has been confirmed by Americans who have travelled on the eastern continent—that American women suffer much more from ill health than those of other countries. My attention has for some time past been particularly directed

* In my work on Moral Philosophy, under the head of " Treatment of Criminals,' I have discussed the question referred to in the text.

to this subject ; and I am convinced that the remark is undoubtedly true to an alarming extent, and that it is the duty of the medical profession to examine into its cause, and, if possible, to suggest and urge upon the public the appropriate remedies.

" Not only is the average health of our country-women much less robust than that enjoyed by cor-responding classes in Europe, and particularly in Great Britain, but it is much more infirm than that of the other sex in our country ;—I mean, after making due allowances for those diseases and afflic-tions peculiar to their situation and duties in society.

" With respect to their inferiority in point of vi-gour, strength, and robustness, to the women of Eng-land, as well as of the Continent, I believe there is not one dissenting voice among those who have en-joyed the most ample opportunities for comparison, and whose attention has been attracted to the subject. The European has a much more florid and healthful com-plexion—a much more vigorous person—and is cap-able of enduring much more fatigue and exposure, and of performing much harder labour. The slender, and delicate, and fragile form—the pale, sallow, and waxen complexion—which are so common among us, are comparatively seldom seen abroad. The feats of pe-destrianism which are almost daily performed in Eng-land, even by ladies of rank and fortune, would appear almost incredible to our feeble and sedentary country-women. As an illustration of this remark, it is men-tioned by a recent traveller, in his letters from Eng-land, that, while staying for a few days at the house of a friend in the interior of the country, it was pro-

posed one morning that the family, including the ladies, should make a call on another friend, who lived
about five miles distant.　They accordingly started
on foot, without any remark being made as to the
mode of locomotion, as if it were an ordinary occurrence, and on their way home, were so little fatigued
as to be desirous of making a digression of some two
or three miles, in order to exhibit some picturesque
view, which they thought might be interesting to
their guest, as a stranger.　Such a pedestrian excursion by an American woman would be an event to
be talked of for life !

" That the females of our country are likewise
much greater sufferers from ill health than our sex,
is a fact which the daily observation of medical men
has abundant opportunity of confirming, and a class
of diseases, from which they suffer most, are pre-
cisely those which we would suppose would be produced by the peculiar causes operating upon them.
They are derangements of the digestive and nervous
apparatus.　Every physician of much experience
must have been struck with the fearful extent and
obstinate nature of these affections—always difficult
to remedy, and frequently even to alleviate ; and they
seem confined almost exclusively to females and men
of sedentary habits.　They are always productive of
great and protracted suffering."

The American ladies generally ascribe their ma-
ladies to the very variable climate of their country.
This may have some influence; but their own habits
appear to me to contribute much more to their sufferings.　They rarely walk abroad for the sake of

fresh air and exercise. In general, they live and sleep in ill-aired apartments. Their duties press constantly on their minds, and they do not give sufficient effect to the maxim, that cheerful amusement and variety of occupation are greatly conducive to health. They do not properly regulate their diet; pies, pastry, and animal food, are consumed in quantities too abundant for a sedentary life; and baths and ablutions are too rarely used. Almost every family house in Philadelphia, built within these fifteen years, has a bath; but many of the ladies either do not use them, or, from some misapprehension of their influence, do not remain long enough in them to enjoy their full benefit. We met with a married lady in one of the American cities, whose florid and healthy colour attracted my attention; and on my remarking it, she mentioned, that in all seasons she slept with the bed-room window partially open. We have followed the same practice since our arrival in the United States, and also walked abroad every day, however cold, and with great advantage to health.

It is not for want of knowledge that the American ladies suffer so much inconvenience from bad health. The works of Dr John Bell, before mentioned, are highly practical, and in extensive circulation, as are also Dr A. Combe's Physiology applied to Health and Education, and many similar books. Nay, these works are taught in female academies. But there is a wide interval between knowledge and practice. In one female seminary in which Dr Combe's " Physiology" (with questions appended to the chapters) is used as a class-

book, its rules appeared to me to be violated in the
very act of teaching them ; that is to say, the brains
of the young ladies were strained by excessive tasks,
and by undue excitement of the spirit of emulation.
The distinction between *instructing* and *training* is
still imperfectly understood, both in the United States
and in Great Britain. These young ladies were
taught to repeat the laws of health, but they were not
trained to carry them into practice in their daily habits. Apparently, their leading objects in learning
them were, to be able to shew off their knowledge at
the public examinations, to gain prizes, and to establish their reputation for superior talents. The pupils of a distinguished teacher in Edinburgh used
to astonish the public by the great extent, accuracy,
and readiness of their knowledge of history, exhibited
at their annual examinations ; but the admiration of
their exploits diminished when the secret of his
teaching was known. Questions were printed at the
end of each chapter, and in reading the work he desired them to mark certain words in the text with a
pencil ; he added that these constituted the answers
to the questions, which they must learn to repeat
promptly whenever the questions were asked. They
did so ; but their knowledge was not an intellectual
conception of the historical events, but resulted from
a mere parrot-like exercise of verbal memory, and
faded as rapidly as it was acquired. I fear that, in
the United States, the laws of health are still taught
in a somewhat similar manner.

One general defect in the mental condition of all
of us is, that in ten instances we act from impulse

and habit for once that we do so from reflection.
This arises from imperfect training in youth. Our
impulsive faculties, being early developed, and possessing great natural energy, are constantly liable to
err, and to lead us into evil, when not controlled and
directed by enlightened intellect. One object, therefore, in teaching the young, should be *to communicate knowledge*, and another to *train* the propensities
and sentiments to submit to the control of the intellect. This last department of education is greatly
neglected, except in the infant schools conducted on
Mr Wilderspin's principles. In the United States,
training is needed above all things; for the public
institutions of the country, in fostering a spirit of independence, encourage the young to rely on themselves; in other words, to act from the impulsive elements of their nature, much more than from reflection. Reflection, when founded on knowledge, produces habits of self-denial, self-restraint, and obedience. The want of this practical training and discipline is seen in the males, in the recklessness with
which they dash into speculation and adventure, pursuing their leading impulses at all hazards; and in the
females, in the pertinacity with which they adhere to
practices which they know to be injurious to health,
and in their deficiency of mental resolution to submit to the temporary sufferings which always accompany a change of evil habits.

If the conductors of the female seminaries would
require their pupils to recapitulate, once a-week, what
they *do* in obedience to the laws of health, and *train*
them for two or three years to the practice of these

laws, they would form habits that would last during life, and thus render the knowledge which they communicate effectual.

March 9. Ther. 35°. *Supremacy of the Law: The Grand Jury.*—Judge Bouvier has just delivered an excellent charge to the Grand Jury. The following extracts represent faithfully the spirit in which the judges in the United States generally enforce the claims of the law on the people.

" Besides finding the bills which are prepared by the Attorney-General and sent to you, you have the right, and it is your duty, to present such offences and offenders as you may know of your own knowledge, or of which proof has been given to you. Sometimes grand juries present nuisances in classes, as gambling-houses, tippling-houses, and the like. This may be well enough, gentlemen, and doubtless such presentments have a good effect in some degree. But if such things are known to exist, it is much better to present the offender and the offence individually. In the generality of the charge, the heinousness of the crime is indistinctly felt or not perceived. One presentment of one such offence and the name of the offender, followed by a conviction, would have more terror in it to such evil doers than a thousand such fruitless presentments.

" Our exertions to enforce obedience to the laws cannot be too great. The law must reign supreme, or anarchy have the sway. Justice, order, and right, must be sustained, or rapine and murder take their place : we have no middle ground, and it is for us to say, whether our noble institutions, justly our pride, and the admiration of the world, are to be sacrificed to the spirit which has manifested itself in so many places, of disregarding the law, and of having recourse to brute force, to redress real or imaginary wrongs. We censure, very justly, those foreign travellers, who, after sharing our hospitality, return to their own country, and publish their views of American manners in such a way as to caricature rather than to paint them. Gentlemen, let us not give them any occasion or apparent justification for such slanders, by a disregard of the laws which we have ourselves made. Upon you depends whether the laws shall be properly enforced ; use every exertion, then, to punish its violators ; bring all who have been guilty to punishment, and particularly those who make it their business to ensnare others into crime.

" I regret to say, that, with all the exertions which our very vigilant mayors and the police magistrates in the districts make, still the laws are, in many respects, as a dead letter. The fault is not in the officers, for they do all in their power, but in the system, which is not sufficiently energetic to prevent the habitual commission of crime. The laws should not be placed on the statute-book as a dead letter, to be brought into action only when accident may lead to detection, perhaps one of a thousand cases, but be constantly active, ready to apply a remedy to every evil felt by society. Who, that looks around, but must admit the laws relating to the sale of spirituous liquors are daily, hourly violated, not in one or two places only, but throughout the city and county of Philadelphia ? And yet the mayor of the

city and mayor of the northern liberties, and the police magistrates of the districts, have but little power,
and less means, to break up these dens of iniquity.
The same observations may be made in regard to
gaming-houses and lottery-offices, which, though not
so numerous, no doubt exist to a great extent, as is
evident by the casual discovery occasionally made
of some of them."

I have often heard the judges complain of the
want of power in the law, and of the deficiency of
the means for executing it, as evils which characterize their institutions. The remark of Aristotle
in his Politics, that the great danger to democracies
lies in the reluctance of the people to part with as
much power as is necessary to restrain their own ex-
cesses, seems to be recognised by them as too applicable to this country.* Yet a democracy, with
such institutions as those of the United States, can
have no good grounds for withholding power from
their judges and magistrates ; because these officers
are completely under the control of the people. The
laws may be altered, and the judges and magistrates
removed, at the will of the people ; and it is the interest of all that order should be preserved and property protected. The judges, however, have a na-

---

* Aristotle's words are these : Speaking of the establishment of
that form of democracy in which the public business is performed by
paid functionaries, he says, " Above all, demagogues must never cease
to convince the people that, under their favourite democracy, they will
be at liberty to live as they list ; this will procure for them the assistance of the majority : for the greater part of mankind will always
be better pleased to live licentiously, than to submit to the restraints
of salutary discipline."—*Politics,* B. viii. *Gillies's Transl.* p. 469.

tural desire to increase the power of the law and of the magistrates, just as the clergy have to augment the influence of the church; and perhaps it is also a safe rule for them to depict, in strong colours, its defects and the weakness of its executive department, in order to induce the public to lend a vigorous support to both ; but, on the whole, it appears to me that life, property, and social order, are fully more secure than a stranger, judging from the charges and conversations of some of the judges, would infer.

The Firemen.—I was amused to-day to see a troop of boys training themselves, in their play, to be future firemen. They had a miniature carriage of a fire-engine, named " Hero," with ropes attached to it, and one of their own number sat on it and represented the engine. They ran round Franklin Square, braying through a tin trumpet, and uttering many unearthly sounds, in excellent imitation of their seniors. The real firemen are all volunteers, and serve without pay; and it is thus that their numbers are recruited.

Governor Porter and the Banks.—On 7th March, the lately elected democratic Governor of Pennsylvania sent a message to the Senate and House of Representatives, informing them that no offer had been made for a loan of $1,200,000 wanted for the commonwealth, at 5 per cent. interest, payable half yearly, and redeemable at any time within twenty years from 1st July 1839. He ascribes the nonappearance of bidders to a combination among the banks. I am told that other reasons than this exist why nobody will lend the money : first, the annual

expenses of the State, and the interest of its debt,
exceed its revenue, and no proposal is made to raise
taxes to cover the deficiency; and, secondly, the
people are clamouring for war with England, where
alone money can be obtained on the terms offered,
and it is not expected that the English will be disposed to make loans which may possibly be employed
in fighting against themselves.

The Maine War.—The engrossing topic of conversation continues to be the prospect of a war with
England: It is unpopular to doubt that it will take
place.   Nevertheless some of the wiser men have at
length begun to operate on opinion in favour of
peace.   The first step has been to bring Mr Webster into a right position.   Mr David B. Ogden, of
New York, has addressed a letter to him, asking him
for an explanation of his speech, recommending that
the United States should seize the disputed territory on the 4th July next; and he has written an
answer, mentioning that what he meant to say was
only this—" that it was high time for the two Governments to adjust this controversy;" that they should
do every thing possible to accomplish this end ami-
cably; but that, if they should unfortunately not succeed, " a time must come, of necessity, when the
United States must perform that duty for themselves."   He did not intend to say " that our Government ought to take possession of the disputed territory on the 4th of *next* July," but some time or other
when it could no longer be avoided.   These letters
have been published, and Mr Webster's explanation,
although regarded as a lame one in itself, is giving

satisfaction, as the first step towards a sounder view of the interests of the country. Two reasons are assigned for the precipitate advocacy of a war which the printed report of Mr Webster's speech contains : It is said by some persons that, by opposing the last war with England, Mr Webster injured his popularity so deeply that it has never fully recovered, and that, by now leading the van in advocating another war, he hopes effectually to wipe off this stain from his reputation : By others it is affirmed that the warlike speech was made altogether without premeditation or design, and that it was inspired solely by champagne and the excitement which glowed on all sides around him. The bill authorizing the enlistment of 50,000 men was passed by the Senate in a session held after dinner ; and I have been assured by one of the few senators who voted against it, that, but for that circumstance, it never would have passed at all. Some of the members had indulged in large potations before coming to the evening meeting, and they were all on fire for maintaining the national honour !

Mr Espy's Theory of Storms.—This subject has excited much attention in Philadelphia, and the scientific men concur in expressing an opinion in favour of its essential truth. The following is a condensed abstract of Mr Espy's principles :—

By ascertaining the dew-point, we discover the quantity of vapour which the air contains. Mr Dalton of Manchester made this discovery. The following table exhibits the relation of the temperature to the quantity of vapour :—

Dew-Point.			Quantity of Vapour.
32°,	.	.	$\frac{1}{240}$
52°,	.	.	$\frac{1}{270}$
73°,	.	.	$\frac{1}{60}$
80°,	.	.	$\frac{1}{48}$

The equilibrium of the air may become disturbed by heat or moisture below. Ascending columns or currents will then be formed. As they ascend, they will come under less pressure, and consequently expand. This expansion will produce one degree and a quarter of cold for every hundred yards of ascent. The dew point will fall only one quarter of a degree for every hundred yards. Cloud will begin to form when the air rises as many hundred yards as the dew-point is below the air in degree. When the vapour condenses, it will give out the latent caloric into the air. This will prevent the air from cooling more than half as much as it would do in its farther ascent. Thus, the higher the air rises, the warmer will it be when compared to the air outside of the cloud at the same height. For every degree that it is warmer, it will be $\frac{1}{844}$ lighter than air at zero. Thus the barometer will fall under the cloud; the air will run in on all sides under the cloud, and upwards, with a velocity of 240 feet per second for a fall of one inch, and so on in proportion to the square foot of the fall.

An application has been made to the Legislature of Pennsylvania for a grant to defray the expense of an experiment, causing rain to fall by producing an ascending current of air by means of a great artificial fire. The petition was referred to a committee, and on

6th March, Mr Smith of Philadelphia, on their behalf, reported in favour of granting Mr Espy " a sum equal to the expenses of making the experiment, if he shall cause it to rain over a territory of 1000 square miles; the sum of $25,000 if he shall cause it to rain copiously over a territory of 5000 square miles; and the sum of $50,000 if he shall cause it to rain copiously over a territory of 10,000 square miles, or in such quantities as shall keep the Ohio river navigable during the whole summer, from the city of Pittsburg to the Mississippi river; the larger sum in each case to exclude the smaller;" and the committee farther proposed, that the Governor should be " authorized and required to appoint three impartial and competent persons to witness and judge of the said experiments, who shall, at the times and places appointed by the said James P. Espy, attend for that purpose; and upon such experiments being fully made and completed, the said persons shall certify to the Governor the result thereof, and if the same shall be successful, the Governor shall draw his warrant on the Treasurer of the Commonwealth in favour of the said James P. Espy, for such of the said sums as he shall be entitled to under this resolution."

The New York Evening Star objects to this report, because " the proposition savours of blasphemy!" Surely steam-boats, which not only sail without the wind, but even against it, must be moving masses of " blasphemy" in the eyes of the editor of the Star! As the " Report" wears a ludicrous aspect, and as the subject is scientifically interesting, I pre sent in the Appendix, No. IV., a letter from Mr Espy himself in explanation of his views.

Working-Men's Grievances.—On the 7th January last, the working men held a convention, and appointed a committee of twelve of their number to deliberate on their condition and affairs, and to report. The address of the committee " to the working men of the city and county of Philadelphia" has been published. In a country which enjoys an unlimited field for the profitable employment of its people ; in which, consequently, labour is highly paid, and in which nearly universal suffrage prevails, an exposition of the working men's grievances may be regarded as a kind of psychological curiosity. The imagination is tasked to divine in what their sufferings can consist. Yet here is a manifesto which might almost literally be adopted by the Chartists of England, or the workmen of Lyons. " It is necessary," say the committee, " to restore the equilibrium to society which your indifference has permitted others to monopolise."—" We cannot, must not, disguise the fact, that other portions of the community have arrayed themselves against your interests, and, while you stand single and alone, and oppose with naked truth their unhallowed schemes, you are only exhausting your strength in an unequal and profitless contest."—" The committee cheerfully assent that the interests of the whole people are identical under our republican form of institutions ; but this equality or reciprocity of rights is no longer regarded,—the great principles which aroused the latent energies of freemen" " are now lost in corporate interest, which controls nearly all the avenues to wealth, absorbs the whole attention of the Legislature, while it leaves you, who are the majority, in a state of abject servitude, and the fruits of your toil to be enjoyed by those who have obtained special grants of the Legislature to retain the product which you have produced We also admit, that no system can be introduced which will free, perhaps, a majority of the people from manual labour; but we do insist that a better system than the present, which inflicts upon the many perpetual toil and eternal poverty, can be devised. What argument can be adduced why a *more equal distribution of wealth should not be made ?* Be not alarmed at the annunciation of an equal distribution of wealth, or rather the equal means of obtaining wealth. No surer index can be desired where overgrown wealth and luxury are enjoyed on one side, that squalid wretchedness and misery is the inevitable doom of the other; this is an unerring test, adapted to all ages and countries."

The reader probably expects the next sentence to contain a recommendation to spoil the rich, and divide their wealth among the poor; but the committee entertain other views. They proceed—" There is a natural *innate* repugnance to be found in us all of associating with those whom we consider not our equals in point of general intelligence—this should be the only distinction known in society. This feeling of superiority may be found in the higher walks of life as regards their own members." " Remember, intelligence is a passport everywhere—com-

manding respect where aught else has failed." " *You
are accused of wishing to level down society and appropriate to yourselves the proceeds of others' industry. Throw back the imputation with a vengeance,
for you know that the mass are levelled almost below
the common feelings of humanity, and your toil appropriated to fill other coffers.*"

" Do not retaliate." " You are for a system which
will level up instead of down." " Fellow working
men ! The levelling system we speak of is a system
of education which shall teach every child in the commonwealth his duty and interest as a citizen and free-
man ; working men are now allowed to take but half
a drink at the rippling rill as it flows beneath their
feet—and this, too, as a public charity.

" We speak not of the hackneyed system of education which is now the order of the day--of schools
where the same prejudices are taught, and the same
partial influences exist, as are found out of doors—of
high schools which are said to be founded to carry
out more perfectly the system of common schools,
where the children of affluent parents are taken from
private schools and placed in the common schools,
barely sufficient time to have them become members,
that they may be taken into the high schools in preference to those who have prepared themselves in
the primary institutions, simply because they are
more proficient and advanced in their studies ; but
we speak of a democratic republican education, which
regards all the children as equals, and provides food
and clothing during the period they are receiving
an education to fit them as members of society and

component parts of a free government ; so when they shall arrive at maturity, and are thrown upon the world and their own resources, they may start equal in the race for the accumulation of wealth, or in pursuit of the honours of the Government. *This is the levelling system we desire—the only equal distribution of wealth we ask.*

" No system, fellow working men, will tend so directly to a more equal distribution of wealth as an equal and perfect system of education.

" Knowledge is power ; the committee, therefore, exhort all to bind up their resources, and let their exertions tend to one mighty and simultaneous effort for the accomplishment of this desired object."

They recommend, *first,* The formation of trade societies and associations ; *secondly,* The formation of united trade societies and associations ; *thirdly,* The formation of a literary and scientific institute ; *fourthly,* A joint-stock company for the erecting of a hall for the use of the united trade societies, associations, and institute.   They add—" Let not the genius of our institutions, which is based upon the intelligence of the people, reproach you, or the award which posterity will accord to you, grate upon your consciences, as you turn a deaf ear to those imperative demands.

" Remember, fellow working men, you have a responsible duty to perform, and unless you shew a disposition to help yourselves, it will be difficult to make others believe your complaints are well grounded ; and it may be a question, but one of immense magnitude, whether men, who have the power to re-

dress their grievances, but will not apply it, deserve
the sympathy or aid of a discerning public.

(Signed)

E. A. Penniman, of the coach-makers' society.

Samuel C. Thompson, cordwainers' society (men's
branch).

Wm. Gilmore, ditto (Ladies' Branch).

E. Dallas, of the brush-makers' society.

Townsend Yeadrsley, of the house-carpenters' society.

Thos. O'Neil, of the jewellers' society,

George G. Clark, of the house-painters' society.

John Botsford, of the bricklayers' society.

Samuel Sayer, of the tailors' society.

Thomas Steel of the curriers' society.

James J. Pierce, of the oak-coopers' society.

John Wright, of the cabinet-makers' society.

Committee."

This document exhibits a striking combination of
native talent, with deficiency in literary and philosophical education; and apparently both the composition and the scheme have emanated from a single
mind. It is instructive, however, to observe the
tendency of the human mind when left free, to appreciate knowledge and mental refinement. In the
circumstances in which the working men are placed
in Pennsylvania, any other remedy for their grievances than the one recommended would have carried
inherent absurdity in the face of it.

American Roads.—At this season, the roads are
in their worst condition. A friend who has just come
from Easton, fifty miles distant, in the stage, describes the road as composed of soft mud, nearly 18

inches deep, with alternate masses of unthawed clay and large stones. A gentleman who heard this description said, that he saw an Italian music-master, whom he named, who had the top of his head bruised. He asked him if he had met with an accident. " I have only had it bruised," said he, " by its being constantly knocked against the top of the stage coming from Pittsburg." At the time when this was told, I thought it a facetious exaggeration; but within less than three months, I had the best reason for believing it to be literally true; for I had the crown of my own head severely beaten against the top of a stage coach in the western regions of the State of New York!

March 12. Ther. 33°. *The Friends' Lunatic Asylum at Frankford.*—We visited this institution, which contains sixty-six patients. The situation is favourable; and the house well adapted to the purpose, except that the apartments have no proper provision for ventilation. There are a garden and walks, and a circular railroad on which the patients move themselves in a car by turning a crank. But they decline to labour, and there is no moral force sufficient to induce them to give up their prejudices against it. They are not all Friends; but all belong to the middle classes of the community, and come chiefly from towns. These classes regard labour as mean, and the free institutions of America render compulsion inadmissible, even for a patient's good. I was told, that the average of insanity is higher among the Friends than among the general community. Two reasons were assigned for this fact : first, their doctrine of the workings of the Holy Spirit, and the inward light, their narrow circle of interests, and limited education, act unfavourably on minds predisposed to disease ; secondly, they intermarry extensively within close degrees of consanguinity. This institution belongs to the Orthodox Friends.

Education among the Society of Friends.—Many individuals among both classes of Friends in Philadelphia are highly educated and intelligent, and are ardent promoters of moral and intellectual improvement ; but the mass is represented as considerably deficient in educational attainments ; and some of them, of no mean weight in their society, oppose every advance in education as a dangerous innovation. The young Friends, however, of both sexes, are in the course of discovering their deficiencies, and encourage and support those few among their seniors who advocate a more liberal course of study. I am informed that my lectures constitute a subject of anxiety to some of the Orthodox Friends, whose prejudices prevent them from hearing them. Those who do attend feel no alarm ; but the absent regard these as misled, and are of opinion that they themselves, who know nothing whatever of the subject, are the best judges of its tendency. They have remonstrated with and prayed for some of my audience to induce them to withdraw, but without success. About one-half of the present class is said to consist of Friends of both denominations.

Animal Magnetism.—The following case was mentioned to me, separately, by at least half a dozen persons, some of them highly respectable physicians, and others ladies, who were present and saw the facts which they narrated. A young woman, a domestic servant, was severely afflicted by the toothache, but was of such a nervous and sensitive constitution, that she never could summon courage to have her tooth extracted in the usual way. Dr Mitchell, with her own consent, had her magnetised, and she fell into a profound magnetic sleep. A dentist who was in attendance extracted the tooth, and one of my informants said that she gave no symptoms of sensation, but another told me that she contracted her brows. She had no consciousness of blood trickling from the wound, but the magnetiser desired her to spit it out, and she did so. He restored her to consciousness, and she had no knowledge of having lost the tooth, till her attention was drawn to the fact. She was again magnetized, and the dentist punched out other three stumps of old teeth without her once moving a muscle. About thirty ladies and gentlemen were present, many of them unbelievers in animal magnetism, and most of whom were satisfied that in this instance deception was impossible.

The Organ of Colouring.—This evening I met with a gentleman in whom the organ of colouring is very deficient, and whose powers of perceiving colours are equally feeble. He appreciates blue and green best, but often confounds even them. He has had the names inscribed on a number of colours, and when he wishes to find out the colour of any object, he places them beside it, and when it makes the same impression on his mind with one of them, he judges that it is of the colour inscribed on that piece. This is the way in which I understood his statement; but from his extreme deficiency in all conceptions about colours, his explanations were to me nearly unintelligible. He has no other defect in his sight.

March 14. Ther. 38°. *War with England.*—This subject continues to occupy almost exclusively the public attention. In my last lecture, on Combativeness and Destructiveness, I discussed the sources of war, and alluded to the present extraordinary excitement of these organs in the American people, adding that it was a consolation to think that the excitement would not be responded to on the other side of the Atlantic. I proceeded to mention, that since the Reform Bill had become law, political power in Great Britain and Ireland was placed essentially in the hands of the middle classes of society; that they were moral, industrious, and reasonably intelligent; that, from experience of its horrors, as well as from motives of interest, philanthropy, and religion, they were averse to war; and that the disputed territory in Maine would appear to them such a worthless object compared with the evils of hostilities, that they would not echo the warlike defiance sent to them from the United States. After the lecture, a crowd of persons collected round me, and asked if this was really possible! They regarded John Bull as proud, grasping, pugnacious, and still so flushed with his Continental victories, that he would receive menaces from no people on earth, and they expected that the British nation would be roused into a flame equal to their own. The assurances that John Bull had now become older, wiser, and more virtuous than he once was, were received with delight, but not very generally credited. Events, however, verified my prediction in his favour.

It is edifying to observe how this people is acted on. Their leaders are far from participating in their excitement, but they dare not, in the first ebullition of public passion, decidedly oppose them. Mr Van Buren's message was a rational and statesmanlike document; and I hear the most eminent men in public life daily deploring the headlong impetuosity of their youthful people, and say that they are watching the first moment when the masses may be successfully addressed by reason. There is a want of moral courage, however, in the leaders, which, although easily accounted for, is not the less to be lamented. The impression is nearly universal, that any man who should oppose the public sentiment when under strong excitement, would ruin his popularity, and terminate for ever his public life. The torrent of opinion appears to be so overwhelming, that no efforts of reason will suffice to stem it; and the leading men have no sufficient faith either in their own power, or in the rational elements of the public mind, to induce them to venture opposition. Their reliance even on the ultimate ascendency of reason and virtue is too feeble to allow them fairly to risk their fortunes on the venture. This fact, of

which I am convinced by numerous observations,
indicates an humble estimate by the public characters of the influence of the moral and intellectual
faculties over the mass of the voters. At the same
time, neither the leading men nor the people do
themselves justice. Party spirit runs so high, that
if, at this moment, the wisest and the best men in
the Union, of one party in politics, should present the
most forcible yet respectful appeal to the good sense
of the people against war, their political opponents
would instantly seize the opportunity to manufacture
" political capital" out of it. They would pervert
every sentence of the address, hurl denunciations of
cowardice and want of patriotism against its authors,
and offer the grossest adulation to the vanity of the
nation. The people, having committed themselves
against the appeal, would be withheld by pride from
subsequently doing justice to its authors, who might
struggle for years before they could recover that position in public estimation which they had forfeited
solely by an act of genuine patriotism. The only mode
of avoiding this evil would be for the leaders of both
parties in equal numbers to join in the address; but
they have too little confidence in each other to admit
of such an act of magnanimity.

Among other stimulants to the national appetite
for war, I hear in conversation, and see in the newspapers, the most exaggerated and absurd estimates
of the evils which England must suffer from hostilities. The ruin of her manufactures, the loss of
Canada and her West India Islands, the triumph of

the Radicals and Chartists, and the bankruptcy of her Treasury, are descanted on, with much complacency, as inevitable consequences of her provoking a contest with the United States. This is the counterpart of the equally absurd lucubrations in which English writers indulge about the consequences to the Americans of a war with Britain : The emancipation of their slaves, the devastation of their southwest territory, the ruin of their commerce and of their Atlantic cities, the dissolution of the Union, universal bankruptcy and anarchy, and, finally, a military despotism, are the certain results with which they are threatened if they shall dare to provoke British wrath. This species of threatening and boasting reminds one of two ill-conditioned boys, who, assuming a combative attitude, indulge in reciprocal taunts and maledictions, but shew no particular anxiety to begin the fight. War between Britain and the United States would be an act of insanity in both, and a disgrace to the civilization of the nineteenth century ; but even this boasting and daring each other to war shews a lingering barbarism in their minds, which it is their duty, as well as their interest, to eradicate as speedily as possible.

Political Economy.—Mr Henry C. Carey of Philadelphia has published a valuable work on political economy ; but I am informed that the subject is very little studied in the United States. As a branch of general education, it is nearly unknown, and ample evidence is afforded by the public press that most of the measures which should be regulated by sound economical principles are proposed, discussed, and adopted or rejected, on local, temporary, or private grounds, with the least possible reference to scientific views. In the United States the same outcries are raised from time to time against monopolies, and banks, and other institutions, which one might expect to hear in Austria or Naples if the people of these countries were allowed to publish their sentiments ; but one rarely meets with a public writer who treats of such subjects with a statesmanlike reference to the great principles which regulate the creation and distribution of wealth, and with a comprehensive regard to the interests of the whole Union ; and yet such views are much required by this nation. The Americans appear to me to be trying all manner of social experiments, guided only by their instinctive impulses. The Union may be regarded as a vast field for the cultivation of the science of political economy *by experiment.* The Americans will probably solve some of the most momentous problems in economic science—that of paper currency, for example—by the mere exhaustion of errors. But this is a most expensive and painful method of studying a science. It resembles that of rushing into numerous litigations in order to gain a knowledge of law. It is certain that the prosperity of nations, as well as the motions of the planets, is regulated by positive laws, and that happiness is attained only in proportion as these are obeyed. This truth should be instilled as a first principle into every American child, and the development of it in its specific forms and applications should constitute an important branch of general instruction. The American people need above all things to be trained in the perception and belief that they have a Master; a Master who not only will call them to account hereafter, but who actually rules over them in this world, and regulates the ebbing and flowing of their wealth by fixed laws, without the possibility of their escaping from his sway. If the principles of political economy were presented in this form, they would be understood and appreciated.

The neglect of economic science, although to be regretted, is not surprising in this people. They are the genuine descendants of the English, who are characterized by a larger development of the organs of Individuality, Eventuality, and Comparison than of Causality, giving a practical rather than a speculative tendency to the mind; their institutions render them bold and confident; and their natural position is surrounded by so many avenues to prosperity, that they have a better chance than most people to go right by intuitive sagacity: nevertheless their want of knowledge of scientific social principles exposes them to great evils.

The American constitution is not favourable to legislation on scientific principles. The power of Congress, although extensive as to foreign relations, embraces comparatively few domestic interests. Each State, enjoying an independent sovereignty, is prone to pursue its own welfare with little reference to that of the other States. At this time, a vivid discussion

is proceeding in the press, between New York and
Philadelphia, whether an outlet shall be made from
the Pennsylvania Canal at Black's Eddy, into the
River Delaware, to enable the Lehigh coal, which
now seeks the New York market, to get into the New
York canal (the Delaware and Raritan) directly; or
whether the coal shall be forced to proceed, as
hitherto, to Bristol, thirty-four miles below Black's
Eddy, there enter the Delaware, and re-ascend to the
Eddy! The interest of New York is said to dictate
the former plan, and that of Pennsylvania the latter.
The Legislature of Pennsylvania must decide the
question; but there is reason to fear that its own
apparent direct interest will have a greater influence
over its decision, than a regard to the general welfare of both States. I have no knowledge of the
merits of this controversy, and cite the case merely
in illustration of the impediments which the American institutions offer to the application of comprehensive principles of economical science.

The reader may possibly regard the statement
made in vol. i. p. 296, about the opinions entertained
by well-educated American gentlemen concerning
British legislation on the church, tithes, entails, free
trade, and similar topics, as inconsistent with the remarks now offered; but in the chapter referred to,
I spoke of men of superior attainments, and with reference to questions irrevocably settled and confirmed
by experience. At present I allude to the application of principles still undecided by experiment, and
to the average mind of the country.

March 16. Ther. 41°. *Ship-Launch.*—We were taken to-day by some kind friends to see the launch of the packet-ship " Thomas P. Cope," 800 tons burden. The ship went off in the most graceful style, amidst beautiful sunshine and a vast concourse of spectators. She glided so softly into the water that she did not perceptibly reel, and no perceptible surge was heaved up by her descent.

March 19. Ther. 57°. *Advantages of Training.*—In the lecture on education, forming part of my first course in Philadelphia, I explained the difference between *instructing* and *training,* and remarked that for the latter the field of social life is necessary. In illustration, I mentioned the great difference in command of temper between a body of lawyers and a body of divines when assembled to discuss their own affairs. In their profession lawyers are trained to oppose and to meet with opposition, without losing temper ; while divines are treated with such general deference and courtesy, that they are very little accustomed to contradiction. The consequence is, that lawyers in general discuss their affairs without falling into heats of temper or making personal allusions ; whereas the clergy, when assembled in their public courts, do not treat each other with that deference which they are accustomed to receive from the world ; they meet as equals, espouse opposite opinions, and contradict each other like ordinary men. Their minds, however, being untrained to bear opposition, they lose their equanimity, become heated, fall into personalities, and exhibit extraordinary aberrations from that meekness of spirit which should characterize the Christian, whether clerical or lay. This description was drawn from observations made in my own country, but the latter part of it considerably amused my audience, the precise cause of which I never found out till to-day. I had, altogether unconsciously, described scenes which had recently occurred in the General Assembly of the Presbyterians in Philadelphia, when the ministers quarrelled and split, an event which had attracted great public attention. The utter unconsciousness, on my part, of the blows I was dealing, contrasted with their actual, although accidental, force, excited the risible faculties of not a few of my auditors. The subject has been mentioned to me to-day in the course of a conversation about a cause now depending in the Supreme Court between these two sections of the Presbyterian Assembly, and which is exciting great and general interest.

Unitarianism in Philadelphia.—Dr Friedlander, Superintendent of the Asylum for the Blind, has died at the age of thirty-seven, deeply lamented, and the appointment of his successor is already engaging attention. A Unitarian left this institution nearly $200,000, and Unitarians have been among its most assiduous promoters. They do not object to Trinitarians being elected as directors, if they be good men; but the Trinitarians use their influence to oppose the election of a Unitarian. I have derived this information from a member of the latter sect; and, if it be correct, it shews that the Calvinists of this city are chargeable, to some extent, with the spirit of Popery in one of its worst forms, an unmitigated confidence in the infallible soundness of their own opinions. If they could conceive the possibility of their interpretations of Scripture being as liable to error as those of other sects, and give effect to this conception, they would respect the rights of conscience in other men, and approach so much the nearer to the real spirit of Christianity.

March 20. Ther. 45°. *Female Delicacy.*—The following statement was made to me by a clergyman, who had the best means of knowing the facts, and whom I did not at all suspect of palming on me an " old Joe Miller." In allusion to the fastidiousness of American women about the human figure, he mentioned that the farther south the more ridiculous are the prejudices. The word " leg" must not be mentioned in the presence of a lady, and in whatever part of the abdomen a lady may have a pain, it is always announced as in her " breast." A physician in the south told him that, if he had even proposed to open the body of a young lady, a patient, who had died of a disease imperfectly understood, he should have expected to receive a challenge for the insult from her brother. The physician led him to understand that this had actually happened in his own experience. At the same time these ladies will allow coloured men to come into their bed-rooms in the morning to light their fires, even when they are in their morning undress, without the least feeling of outraged delicacy.

Lynch Law.—I present the following extracts from two American newspapers without commentary :

" HORRID RESULTS OF LYNCHING.—In Schuyler county, Illinois, a man by the name of Sampson stole a trunk, while labouring under derangement of mind, and, being pursued, was caught and whipped to death for the offence. His brother, a highly respectable citizen, was in pursuit of him, when he learnt the melancholy story of his death. His delirium was caused by sickness, and he had escaped from his brother's house but a short time before he was seized, and lynched till he died."—*Boston Times.*

" Thus it always turns out, when any other course than such as is sanctioned by law is pursued 'to remedy an evil, or to bring an offender to justice. Under the plea of dealing *justice* to an offender, crimes are perpetrated far more atrocious than those which are urged as affording a pretext for their commission. Yet we regret that there are to be found, in every community, individuals so ignorant of their own rights as freemen, and of the rights of others, as to publicly advocate this system of ' summary justice,' or Lynch law. Though we are aware that most of these advocates may be found only among the valiant pothouse politicians of the day, yet their influence, small as it may be, and convincing as their arguments generally are of their own ignorance, can be traced, in its effects, in various parts of our country during the last few years. Who is there *now*, among the mob by which this morally innocent man was sacrificed, but would hide his head at his participation in the crime ?"—*Editor of the Philadelphia Public Ledger of the* 20*th March.*

Spring.—Radishes appeared at table to-day for the first time ; they are the welcome harbingers of spring.

Dr Morton's " Crania Americana."—I have had the pleasure of holding many consultations with Dr Morton and Mr Phillips about the best means of measuring the skulls to be described in this work, and have been greatly interested by the ingenuity and perseverance of Mr Phillips in overcoming the difficulties that presented themselves. He has now succeeded to an extent that will enable him to proceed with the measurements. Dr Morton has requested me to furnish an Appendix for his work. He is imperfectly acquainted with Phrenology himself, and has composed his text without reference to it. He perceives, however, that when he presents a correct drawing of an average specimen of a national skull, and describes historically the mental character of the nation, he places in juxtaposition the two elements on which Phrenology is founded; and he is anxious to obtain the means of enabling his readers to combine them, so that they may draw their own conclusions on the accordance or discordance of the forms of the skulls with the Indian characters. I have engaged to supply this desideratum, without having seen one word of his descriptions of the characters of the Indian tribes. My Appendix will consist of a brief outline of the phrenological faculties, of a drawing of a skull shewing the regions of the animal, the moral, and the intellectual organs, with directions how to estimate their relative proportions ; and some remarks on the influence of size in the brain on mental power. The reader of Dr Morton's work, by applying the rules and examples thus furnished to the several skulls delineated in it, will be able to draw his own conclusions. This will expose Phrenology to as severe a test as could well be devised ; but I have confidence in the harmony and stability of truth, and do not hesitate to hazard the experiment.*

March 21. Ther. 43°. *Fires.*—There has been an alarm of fire on five of my lecture nights in succession ; and last night the alarm was so near that I was under the necessity of suspending the lecture till the result should be seen. It was only a chimney on fire, but this is always attended with anxiety in American cities. The roofs of the houses are covered with shingles (thin wood cut into the shape

---

* Since the text was written, Dr Morton's work has appeared and been very favourably noticed in the Medical Reviews of the United States and of Britain. I may be permitted to remark, however, that the Edinburgh New Philosophical Journal, edited by Professor Jameson, and the Edinburgh Medical and Surgical Journal, edited by Dr Craigie, in their ample notices of the work, have omitted to mention not only this experiment, but Dr Morton's own testimony, penned six months after I left Philadelphia, of the result of it. He says, " I am free to acknowledge that there is a singular harmony between the mental character of the Indian, and his cranial development as explained by Phrenology." In the notices of Dr Morton's work in Professor Silliman's American Journal of Science and the Arts (which Professor Jameson professes to copy nearly entire), in the London Medico-Chirurgical Review, and in the British and Foreign Medical Review, this result is stated in Dr Morton's own words, and the interests of truth and justice require that it should be so.

of slates), which are exceedingly dry, and a spark falling on them might raise a vast conflagration. This is one cause, also, of fires spreading so rapidly in this country. To avoid this danger, zinc is now used to cover the roofs of some houses. Notwithstanding this condition of the roofs, it is not an uncommon practice here to set the chimneys on fire and burn them out, to save the trouble and expense of sweeping them! One of the newspapers lately recommended the burning out of chimneys only during heavy rains, when the wet condition of the shingles might abate the risk of the conflagration extending! In a city like Philadelphia, the police should be armed with power to suppress the practice altogether, under severe penalties.

Phrenology.—At eleven o'clock this day, I had a practical exercise with my class on the temperaments, in the manner described in vol. i. p. 126. Two hundred and twenty-three persons attended, who entered into the business of the meeting with great interest and judgment. Many of the members of the Society of Friends stood up to have their temperaments described; but when a call was made for ladies to stand up, there was a pause. I explained the advantages to parents and teachers of understanding the influence of the temperaments of children, as their treatment should vary with their natural constitutions. On hearing this, a Quaker gentleman took his daughter by the hand, and led her up to the platform. Her temperament was described, and then another Friend led up another young lady; af-

ter which there was no farther difficulty with the
ladies. Among the men, the predominating temperaments were the bilious-nervous and nervous-bilious; the next common was the sanguine and its
combinations; and there were very few cases of the
lymphatic. Among the young women, also, there was
surprisingly little of the lymphatic temperament;
nervous-bilious was common, and nervous-bilious-
sanguine.

In the evening we visited one of the Society of
Friends, who with his lady had attended the lectures; and the morning's exercises were talked of.
A lady of the party, who had not attended the lectures, held forth in severe condemnation of the
young ladies who had stood up to have their temperaments described. She accused them of want of
delicacy, compared them to Fanny Wright, and uttered many other disrespectful expressions against
them. This is the only example which has fallen
under my own observation, of the influences by
which the amiable and feminine sentiments of the
young women of this country are perverted. This
female censor of morals was unmarried, and of a certain age. She possessed much volubility, a very slender stock of useful information, great native energy,
and no lack of self-confidence. Her censures fell
like two-edged swords on young, timid, and unform-
ed minds; and she gloried in her power. I told her
plainly that it was by such speeches as hers that the
young women of this country are made slaves, through
the instrumentality of their best feelings, to injuri-

ous customs, to the great detriment of their health and usefulness ; but she only launched out the more vehemently against human improvement, and in commendation of the nations of antiquity.

Difficulty of Describing Events.—This same lady assured me that there was not one word of truth in Miss Martineau's description of a Quaker marriage, at which she had been present. Another lady of the party, who mentioned that she had herself witnessed the ceremony, stated that Miss Martineau's description was substantially correct. Those who describe manners experience strikingly the fate of the painter who pleased nobody and every body. Phrenology shews us that men differ in their original faculties, and hence the same event will make different impressions on different minds : They differ in their education and training, and yet each assumes his own perceptions and emotions to constitute the true standard for judging of all things : They differ in their opportunities for correct observation, yet each believes his own impressions to constitute absolute truth. The traveller is only one mind, with a particular combination of faculties, some powerful and others deficient ; he is trained in his own peculiar way ; he has only his own opportunities of observation, and his own stock of knowledge ; and all that he should pretend to accomplish is to record faithfully his individual impressions, and leave his readers themselves to judge of their value.

Rate of Wages.—The journeymen house-carpenters have published a manifesto, addressed " to the

public in general, and builders in particular," in
which they state that " our present wages is $1.25
cents (5s. 2d. Sterling) per day, out of which sum
we find it impossible to live, and render unto every
man that which is just, although we practise the
most rigid economy.   Men under these circumstances are frequently driven by poverty and care
to intemperance, to dispel for a season the horrid
gloom which envelopes their homes."   They ask
$1.50 cents per day.   They add that all other trades
connected with building receive from $1.50 to $1.75
cents per day.

Working men also complain of another grievance.
There is no arrangement by distant banks for re-
deeming their notes in Philadelphia, and in consequence they are not received by the banks of this
city.   The only way of disposing of them is to carry
them to the exchange-brokers, who buy them at a discount corresponding to the distance and difficulties of
sending them to their own head-quarters, and obtaining Philadelphia money in return.   The workmen complain that their masters buy up these notes
at a discount and pay them over to them at par;
throwing the loss of the exchange on them!   The
Public Ledger, in noticing this abuse, says : " We
consider this extortion most unconscionable, and regard every one who will practise it as a thief of the
very worst description, for he steals from poverty."

The Presbyterian Church Case.—This case excites
great interest, and its present form may be briefly
stated.   It has come into the Supreme Court for the

Eastern District of Pennsylvania *nisi prius*, on a writ of *quo warranto*, which is the form of a summons commanding the parties named in it to appear and shew by what authority they exercise the liberty and franchise described in the writ.

On the 28th of March 1799, the Legislature of Pennsylvania passed an act incorporating certain persons therein mentioned, under the name of " The Trustees of the General Assembly of the Presbyterian Church in the United States of America." It is declared by section 6th, " That the said corporation shall not at any time consist of more than eighteen members ; whereof the said General Assembly may, at their discretion, as often as they shall hold their sessions in the State of Pennsylvania, change one-third, in such manner as to the said General Assembly shall seem proper : And the corporation aforesaid shall have power and authority to manage and dispose of 'all moneys, goods, chattels, lands, tenements, and hereditaments, and other estate whatsoever committed to their care and trust, by the said General Assembly; but in cases where special instructions for the management and disposal thereof shall be given by the said General Assembly in writing, under the hand of their clerk, it shall be the duty of the said corporation to act according to such instructions," provided said instructions shall not be inconsistent with the laws of the United States, of the commonwealth of Pennsylvania, or the provisions of the act of Incorporation.

Differences of opinion crept into the Church, and increased ; two conflicting parties divided each General Assembly, and the terms Old and New School began to be applied to them respectively. For several years the two parties continued nearly equal in numbers. In 1831–2–3 and 1834, the Old School (or orthodox) were a minority in the General Assembly. In 1835 they had a majority ; but again, in 1836, the New School were able to carry their measures. The Old-School party projected to separate from the New, with whom they could not agree ; and in May 1837, a meeting of that party was held in Philadelphia, for deliberating on this project. But the Old School unexpectedly found themselves to constitute a majority of the Assembly of that year. They made a proposal of separation to the New School, and to give force to the proposal, they intimated the design of cutting off from the Presbyterian Church a sufficient number of their opponents to place themselves strongly and permanently in the majority. Resolutions were presented to cite to the bar of the next Assembly " such inferior judicatories as shall appear to be charged by common fame with the toleration of gross errors in doctrine and disorders in practice ;" and also to exclude the " members of said judicatories from a seat in the next Assembly, until their case shall be decided." These resolutions were adopted, and a committee, consisting of five from the majority and five from the minority, was appointed to carry them into effect. " The Assembly engaged in prayer on behalf of this committee, and of the subject referred to them." The committee met, disagreed,—and asked to be discharged.

During these proceedings, the New School intimated that they were willing to separate, and offered terms ; but these the Old School rejected, and proceeded to the work of excision.   They cut off from the Church the four synods which returned the greatest number of the New-School members to the General Assembly, viz. those of Geneva, created in 1812, of Genessee in 1821, of the Western Reserve in 1825, and of Utica in 1829.   There were in those synods 28 presbyteries, 509 ministers, 599 churches, and 50,489 communicants.   They did this without an accuser or accusation ; and the first information on the subject which reached the ears of the great mass of Presbyterians who inhabited the proscribed districts was, that they had been cut off, and excluded from the communion of their church.

At the same time, the Old School *dissolved* the third Presbytery of Philadelphia, containing 33 ministers, 32 churches, and 4850 communicants, without the usual provision of attaching the ministers and churches to other presbyteries.   This also was done without accusation, proof, or trial.   They stated, however, that " great, long-continued, and increasing common fame charges errors and irregularities in doctrine and order" on this Presbytery, and also on that of Wilmington ; but they did not proceed against the latter.   They reserved the privilege to all churches and ministers in the four exscinded Synods, " which are strictly Presbyterian in doctrine and order," to apply for admission into other presbyteries in connection with the Assembly.   They also reserved the same liberty to the ministers, churches, and licentiates of the third or *dissolved* Presbytery of Philadelphia.

The Old School justified these measures on the ground that a certain plan of union entered into in the year 1801, between the General Assembly of the Presbyterian Church, and the General Association of the State of Connecticut, was unconstitutional; that congregationalists had been received under that union; and that the four exscinded synods had been formed under this unconstitutional association. The Assembly first abrogated the union, and then declared that this plan having been unconstitutional and void from the beginning, no rights had ever been acquired by it, and, therefore, that the four synods, which were alleged to have been formed under its operation, had never been parts of the Presbyterian Church.

The Old School required and obtained a pledge from the clerks of the Assembly, that they would not recognise the commissions of delegates from within the bounds of the exscinded synods, if presented to the next Assembly, to be held in May 1838, and then adjourned till that time. No minute, however, was made of this pledge in the records of the Assembly.

On the third Thursday of May 1838, commissioners from the various Presbyteries of the United States, including those coming from the four exscinded synods, met as usual in Philadelphia. The clerks refused to receive the commissions of the exscinded delegates.

All the delegates met in the seventh Presbyterian

church, the place appointed for the meeting of the
Assembly of 1838. After the customary religious
services, Dr Elliott, the moderator of the previous
year, took the chair, until a new moderator should be
chosen.   The clerks read their report, and the moderator announced, that, if there were any commissioners present whose names had not been enrolled,
now was the time to present their commissions.
Upon this call, Dr Mason, a delegate from the third
Presbytery of New York, presented the commissions
from the exscinded synods, mentioned that the clerks
had refused to receive them, and moved that the
names contained in them should be added to the roll.
The moderator declared this motion out of order ; Dr
Mason appealed from the decision ; his appeal was
seconded, but the moderator declared it also out of
order, and declined putting the question to the House.

At this juncture of affairs, the Rev. John P. Cleave-
land, a commissioner from the Presbytery of Detroit,
moved the deposition from office of Dr M'Dowell and
Mr Krebs, the clerks who had refused to receive the
commissions, and of Dr Elliott, the moderator, who
had refused to put the question to the House ; and
that Dr Beman, of the Presbytery of Troy, should be
named temporary moderator, and put the question.
The motion was carried by a large majority : in other
words, the New School had the majority in this Assembly.   Under Dr Beman, it constituted itself the
Assembly ; proceeded to the election of new clerks and
a new moderator, and then adjourned to the first Presbyterian church of Philadelphia, where it sat during
nearly two weeks.

On the 24th of May 1838, this General Assembly of the New School elected six persons to act as trustees according to the provisions of the charter of incorporation, in place of the trustees who at that time held office, and who were attached to the Old School.

The commissioners belonging to the Old School, however, continued their sittings in the seventh Presbyterian church, chose their own moderator, and acted on the principle, that *they* were the real General Assembly of Presbyterians.

The incorporated trustees held property to a considerable amount, which the Church had acquired by legacies and other means, and which had been invested partly in colleges ; and the real object of the action was, to ascertain to which of the parties the moneys, goods, and chattels belonged.

The case went to a jury on the question, whether the trustees of the Old School were lawfully removed from their places, and the trustees of the New School lawfully elected in their stead ? in other words, which of the two bodies was the true and only Assembly.

While the trial was proceeding, I heard several commentaries made on the evidence given by the reverend gentlemen on both sides. It became necessary to prove before the jury the proceedings which took place at one of the great meetings that preceded the separation ; and it was remarked, that by some unexplained action of the laws of acoustics, the witnesses on each side were able to bear testimony only to the speeches which were delivered in favour of their own party ; they did not *hear* distinctly, so as to be able to report on oath, the speeches delivered, and motions made on the opposite side. The clearness of the recollection on the one side, and the obscurity of it on the other, attracted considerable attention in court ; but this was not extraordinary. An indifferent auditor, who is interested in the proceedings, may recollect the arguments on both sides equally well, for his attention is equally directed to both ; but when a *party* is in court, he naturally listens with profound attention to the proceedings on his own side, and relaxes his attention when his opponents speak. As an act of close attention is necessary to distinct recollection, and as none of the members knew that they were subsequently to be examined on oath about the proceedings, I conceive this obliviousness of the hostile proceedings to have been a natural result of the circumstances in which the witnesses were placed.

Judge Rogers charged the jury strongly in favour of the New School ; and after a consultation of about an hour, they returned a verdict in favour of that party, the plaintiffs under the writ.*

I have presented this report at considerable length, in order to shew the true nature of the disputes which led to the separation of the two parties of Presbyterians. It owed its origin to differences in doctrine and practice. Rigid Calvinism was giving way among the Presbyterians, both in the city of Philadelphia and in the distant synods of New York ; and the

---

* The Old School appealed to the Judges in Bank (that is, judges sitting in a body), before whom a very long argument was subsequently maintained. They set aside the verdict of the jury, and the property now remains with the trustees of the Old School.

measures now detailed arose out of an attempt by the orthodox members to check the declension, or, as the other party say, the advance towards sounder doctrine.

Dickenson College, Carlisle.—The State of Pennsylvania granted an annual sum to Dickenson College, on the condition that it should be open to all sects as a seminary of education. The Presbyterians got hold of it, by insensible steps, until, at last, a complaint against them was presented to the Legislature, that they had possessed themselves of all the offices, and had, in fact, converted it into a Presbyterian seminary. A committee of the Senate was appointed to examine evidence and to report. A member of this committee mentioned to me, that about twenty Presbyterian clerygmen were examined, and that never in his life had he encountered such difficulties in extracting evidence from witnesses, as from these gentlemen; and he said, that the same remark was made by all who heard the examinations. The grant to the college was ultimately withdrawn.

Infidelity in the United States.—I have in vain endeavoured to discover to what extent infidelity prevails in those parts of the United States which I have visited. I have seen no outward traces of it; but when in New York, I was told that a society of Deists meets on Sundays in Tammany Hall, that they are persons of respectable station and morals, who act on conscientious conviction, and moreover, that a large proportion of them are Scotsmen. I was asked to explain how the latter circumstance came to pass;

but as I did not see the society, and did not investigate the facts, I declined to offer any opinion on the subject.*

In " The Presbyterian" of the 23d of March 1839, an evangelical newspaper published in Philadelphia and New York, I find the following statement, which, from the high character of the paper, is entitled to far more weight than any opinion which I could possibly have formed. " There is no doubt that many more men than we are willing or accustomed to believe, are secretly cherishing infidelity. It has been widely disseminated through our country, and even in those portions of it where the Gospel has been long enjoyed, and the great mass of the families are moral and religious. Many of our young men in all ranks and classes of society are tinctured with it, and help to extend and perpetuate it." This announce-

* I was told that most of these Scotsmen had been educated in the old country, and had come as emigrants to the United States. While this sheet is in the press, I have perused a work just published, entitled " Religion and Education in America, by John Dunmore Lang, D.D.," Senior Minister of the Presbyterian Church in New South Wales, &c., and himself for many years a minister of the Church of Scotland. He there says : " Accustomed as I had been from my youth up to the lean, gaunt form of Scottish orthodoxy, with neither a heart nor a soul beneath its ribs of death, and with an apron of fig-leaves tucked round it to cover the nakedness of the land, I confess it was not less novel to me, than it was extremely gratifying, to witness the vigour and the life, the piety and the zeal, the self-denial and the self-devotedness, that evidently characterized both sections of the American Presbyterian Church." If this representation of the Scottish Church be correct, it may account in some degree for the facts alleged to exist in New York. Dr Lang has renounced his connection with the Church of Scotland, and prefers the Voluntary system ; but he still professes orthodoxy in faith.

ment took me by surprise ; and it is proper to add, that it does not appear in an editorial form, but in a communicated article, bearing the initials D. N. The editor, however, must have believed it to be correct when he allowed its insertion.   The writer ascribes the prevalence of infidelity to " the disuse of the Bible as a class-book in our common schools ; the importation of European infidelity and agrarianism by Owen, Fanny Wright, and others ; the boastful and arrogant claims to reason, free inquiry, and independence of thought, so universally made by infidel writers and speakers, and so captivating to uninformed and uncultivated minds ; and the natural preference of the human mind of error rather than truth.   It is painful," says he, " to contemplate the wide-spread operation of these causes.   No one can travel on our great highways, in steamboats, on canals, and railways, and mingle with the moving masses he there finds, without being sensible of their dreadful effects."   He proceeds to recommend a work by Dr Nelson, now of Illinois, as the best antidote to this evil.

(173)

CHAPTER IV.

1839.

March 24. Ther. 43°. *Sunday.*—We heard a highly evangelical discourse in a church in Broad Street, a little above Chestnut Street, and found a handsome edifice, a large congregation, and an able preacher ; not the pastor of the church, however, but a stranger. His text was, " Take up the cross and follow me ;" and he drew a lively picture of the difference between what he called the maxims and wisdom of the world, and the obligations of Christianity.

March 25. Ther. 43°. *The Friends of the People.*— I have had the pleasure of meeting in society here an old gentleman who was the friend and associate of Muir, Skirving, and other Scottish Reformers, at the beginning of the French Revolution, and who at that time left his native country on account of political persecution. He settled here, and has been successful in business, having realized a competence. He is much respected.

The Fire Department.—I have already mentioned that the fire-engines are all served voluntarily by the young men of the city; and that they even keep up the engines and hose at their own expense, assisted occasionally by the profits of a ball, or a donation from the civic corporation. I have endeavoured to discover the motives which have maintained this system in full energy for a century. In the first place, in observing the men in one of their processions, I perceived that they were almost all under thirty years of age, and of the sanguine, or sanguine-nervous, or sanguine bilious, temperaments, which give great love of excitement and action. The midnight alarm, the rushing to the fires, and the labour and peril in extinguishing them, are agreeable to such minds. Farther, their emulation is strongly excited. The point of honour is to be first at a fire. The director of the first engine that arrives becomes director-general of all the engines for the evening. He is, as it were, the commander-in-chief of an allied army during a battle. If the director be not out, the engine-man who first attaches his hose to the water-pipe assumes that high honour. There are no recognised differences in rank in this country, but it struck me that there are, in fact, plebeian and patrician fire-companies, drawn from different classes of citizens, and that this adds to the ardour of the competition. The company attached to each engine amounts to from 20 to 100 men, and it starts from its station-house as soon as two or three have arrived to direct its movements. The people in the street assist in dragging it. The competition to be first is so ardent, that ambitious young men sleep as if a part of the brain was left awake to watch for the word " fire," or the sound of the State-House alarm-bell. They will hear either, when no other inmate of the house is conscious of the slightest sound. They will sometimes put on their boots and great-coats, and carry their clothes, which lie readily bundled up, in their hands, and dress at the fire. In rushing along the streets, they often run down and severely injure passengers who are in their way ; or, if one of themselves falls, the rest drag on the engine, regardless of his fate, and often break his legs or arms with the wheels. When two engines arrive at a fire at the same time, the companies occasionally fight for the first place, and then a desperate and bloody battle will rage for a considerable time while the flames are making an unchecked progress. Add to these evils, the circumstances that fires occur so frequently that the firemen are kept in a state of almost constant excitement, and that Sunday furnishes no respite from their labours. They are often called out on very trivial alarms, and being once abroad at midnight hours, they adjourn to taverns, and pass the night in nocturnal recreations. Troops of boys, also, attach themselves as volunteers to the engines, and acquire idle and dissolute habits.   In short, the fire department, which at first sight appears to present a noble specimen of civic devotion and disinterested benevolence, turns out, on a closer scrutiny, to be a convenient apology for exciteable young men indulging in irregular habits, which, if not clothed with an official and popular character, would expose them to censure by a strictly moral community.   In Boston, the evils of the voluntary fire system have been so severely felt, that it has been abandoned, and a regularly organized and paid corps of firemen now serves in that city.   Many respectable persons in New York and Philadelphia desire that their cities also should adopt the same plan.

March 26. Ther. 43°. *The Pennsylvania Judges.* —I have already mentioned that, by the recent amendment of the constitution of this State, the judges were declared no longer to hold their offices for life, but to be subject to election for a term of ten years ; that their salaries are small, and that they are not allowed any retiring pensions.   An incident illustrative of their condition has just become public. At the time of this change in the law, some of them had attained to sixty or sixty-five years of age, had families, and saw old age, without provision, approaching.   Governor Ritner, a whig, continued to hold office for a few days under the amended constitution, until the legal inauguration of Governor Porter, a democrat, who at the last election had succeeded in obtaining the majority of votes.   " Judge Darlington was the first judge whose commission would have expired under the amended constitution. To evade this provision of the new constitution, he, before Governor Porter's inauguration, resigned his seat, and was re-commissioned under the new constitution by Governor Ritner, thus renewing his term for ten years." The Attorney-General, Mr Johnson, has served a writ of *quo warranto* on Judge Darlington, to inquire upon what authority he holds his seat upon the bench ; and the 2d of April is fixed by the Supreme Court for hearing the argument. The case is exciting much interest, because, it is said, that other judges stand in the same situation.

Rotation in Office.—This is the phrase used to gloss over the palpable injustice and the public disadvantages attending the dismissal from office by each political party, on its accession to power, of all their political opponents, however meritoriously they may have discharged their public duties. It is said to have been begun by General Jackson ; and the extent to which it is now carried, may be judged of from the following extract from " The Pennsylvanian," a democratic paper of the 28th March 1839 :—

" The Washington Globe asks for information as to the extent of proscription, for opinion's sake, exercised by the whig party in Pennsylvania. In reply it is perhaps unnecessary to go into particulars, for the aforesaid proscription was exercised upon a principle of the most sweeping generality. For instance, in 1832, when the whig party gained the upper hand in the city of Philadelphia, and found the offices held by democrats, they did not spare a single

man. In the course of that year and the one en-
suing, every democrat was swept out, whether his
office was high or low, the very watchmen being subjected to the operation as inexorably as those who
held places of value. In fact, the treatment of the
watchmen was more severe, if possible, than that
which fell to the share of the other ejected parties;
for they were all discharged in mid-winter, when it
was impossible for them to procure employment. So
much for city matters.

" In the State, upon the accession of Joseph Ritner, the same course of action was followed to the
very letter. Throughout the whole of this commonwealth, in the county offices and upon the public
works, every democrat was superseded by some one
whose politics were congenial to those of the minority leaders, who had been successful by an accidental
breach in the democratic ranks. Still more: in 1838,
when the political struggle became violent, a species
of inquisition as to party faith was established in regard to the very labourers on the public works, and if a
doubt was entertained as to the firmness of their Rit-
nerism, they were at once turned adrift. A devotion
to Thaddeus Stevens was one of the chief requisites
for obtaining a contract; and he who split wood for a
locomotive was suffered to split no more if he would
not bow to Geisler's cap. Proscription was carried to
the utmost extent. No one was so humble as to
escape it. How many democrats did whiggery dismiss in Pennsylvania? The answer is brief and
comprehensive. All!"

This statement proceeds from a party source ; but I have read " The Pennsylvanian" pretty regularly since my arrival in Philadelphia, and so far as a stranger has the means of judging, it appears to me to be ably and *honestly* conducted. Its own party is at present in power ; and, nevertheless, it speaks of the " boring system" in the following terms :—

" *Pennsylvania Legislature—The Boring System.*" —After stating that the Legislature has closed its labours for the present, and " that the amount of business left unfinished by the adjournment is greater than on any former occasion," the editor proceeds to say— " We fully believe that great impediments are thrown in the way of the fulfilment of imperative duties by the monstrous increase of boring and lobbying on behalf of the interests of corporate associations, and it is clear to our minds that the time has come to crush this iniquitous system, which is a disgrace to the state, and is a fruitful source not only of political corruption, but of personal debauchery. It is a common case, when any particular institution feels anxious for certain additional privileges which are at the disposal of the Legislature, for it to proceed upon a regular and well understood *tactique*. Its agents or officers appear upon the ground with purses well furnished from the ' contingent fund,' and commence the work of ingratiation. The railroad cars bring up the boxes of champagne, brandy, cigars, and delicacies of all kinds, and it is said that then a convenient room is obtained as a head-quarters, where the members of the Legislature are at liberty to par-

take gratuitously of the eating, the drinking, and the
roaring frolics carried on in these places of resort,
which are open not only all day, but likewise all
night, (like the entrance to a certain nameless place
described by Virgil,) and where it is also asserted
that gambling is frequently introduced to give additional zest to the delights of the boring system, and
to initiate those who are as yet untainted by the vicious desires which render men an easy prey to the
tempter.   To follow up the work thus begun, the
collateral operations of making presents of liquor and
various articles, with the loaning of money to the
needy and extravagant who are entrusted with power,
are brought into play ; and the fact is notorious that,
of late years, among the members of the Legislature,
many young men, and not a few of more advanced
years, who were deficient in the necessary resolution,
have been utterly and often irretrievably ruined by
the evil influences to which they were thus subjected
at Harrisburg, acquiring habits which led to certain
destruction."

I have already remarked, vol. ii. p. 32, that the
conduct of the legislators on private bills on both
sides of the Atlantic leaves little occasion to either
to boast of a virtuous discharge of public duty.   In
the English House of Commons, the " influences"
used to purchase or to strangle justice before committees are not so humble as those employed to attain the same ends in the Legislature of Pennsylvania;
but in principle they are the same.   They are a disgrace to both countries ; but no opposition print in

London could have condemned the committees of their political opponents with greater force and a more just indignation than is here exhibited by the democratic " Pennsylvanian," in commenting on its own party.

Fortune-telling.—I have already, p. 47, adverted to the exercise of fortune-telling as a profession in Philadelphia, and observe that in New York it stands in an equally dignified position. " Fortune-telling," says the Journal of Commerce, " has become such a regular branch of business in New York, that cards with the names and residences of professed fortune-tellers are almost daily handed to ladies and gentlemen while walking through the streets. The matter having, however, reached Justice Merritt in the shape of a complaint, he sent officers to the residence of a Mrs Louisa Kraft in Christye Street, and a Mrs Theresa George Medier in Orchard Street, each of whose cards had been left at the police-office by gentlemen who complained that their wives or daughters had been considerably annoyed by boys thrusting those cards into their hands in the street. The officers easily obtained access to the fortune-tellers, and had their fortunes told them for the low sum of fifty cents each, and then marched off the two ladies to the police-office as common vagrants. Mrs Louisa Kraft, on being examined, very candidly admitted " that she did not pretend to tell the fortune of any individual ; but that if persons were foolish enough to go to her for that purpose, she would receive their money." The two ladies were both ordered to find bail in $500, to be of good conduct for one year, and in default of such bail were committed to prison.

Such occurrences would excite only ridicule in a European monarchy, where the people exercise no political power ; but they are more momentous in a country in which universal suffrage prevails. The " persons who are foolish enough to go to" Mrs Louisa Kraft to have their fortunes told, are regarded by the law as " wise enough" to choose state officers and legislators.

March 28. Ther. 57°. *Marriage Vows.*—A friend from a neighbouring State, newly married, came to our hotel to-day with his bride. In conversing with the party, they mentioned that some of the clergymen omit the promise of *obedience* on the part of the wife from the marriage service, as unconstitutional ! This probably is a joke ; but so far as my means of observation extend, I should say that American wives in general display the most exemplary devotedness to their husbands. whether they vow obedience before the altar or not.

Conversion of the Jews.—I am assured that in this city Jews are treated in much the same manner as individuals are who belong to the Christian sects. They are received in society according to their attainments and condition. Jewish physicians attend Christian patients, and *vice versa.* Jews fall in love with, and marry pretty Christian women, and within three generations the Jew is sunk, and the family merges into the mass of the general po-

pulation. There is a Jewish synagogue, in which
the brethren hold meetings on Saturdays; but the
spirit of free discussion which has loosened the bonds
of orthodoxy in other sects, has not been without
some influence on the Jews. They use considerable
freedoms with Moses and the prophets; preach and
discuss general ethics and natural religion, and altogether wear the chains of Judaism so loosely, that
probably their brethren in Europe would disown
them.

This description of their condition was not derived
from one of their own number, but from a friend,
who said that he obtained it from an educated and
highly respectable Jew. I inquired of several gentlemen whom I regarded as likely to be well informed
on the subject, whether it might be relied on, and
they said that it was highly coloured, but that it
contains essential truth. I conclude from this example, that the best method of converting the Jews
is to treat them with justice and generosity.

How to Manage the People.—The American people
may be led by promptness, good nature, and tact;
but they will not be driven. In 1812, previously to
the declaration of war against England, the mob of
Philadelphia seized the rudder of a British brig,
lying at the wharf, to prevent her from sailing,
there being at that time no legal authority for de-
taining her. Mr ———, a highly respectable and
well known citizen, met them dragging the rudder
through the streets in triumph; he joined them, and

hauled the rope and cheered with the rest. They proposed to go and break the windows of the British Consul. He went with them; and when they came opposite to the house, he addressed them, as if he had never heard of the proposal to break the windows, and said, " Now, my brave lads, let us give him three cheers to shew that we are not afraid of the British, and be off." He cheered instantly, and they all joined. At the close of the last cheer, he gave the word " off to the State-House ;" and suited the action to the word so rapidly that nobody had time to suggest or do any thing else. Arrived at the State-House, he said, " Let us give three cheers for America, and lock up the helm in the State-House."— " America for ever ! Hurrah ! Hurrah !" The key of the cellar was obtained, and the helm locked up, three cheers were given " for ourselves ;" " Dismiss" was then uttered, and acted on by his walking away ; and all followed his example. As the whole proceeding had been illegal, Mr ——— went quietly to the ship, and desired the captain to send up to the State-House for his helm in the night. He did so; put it on ; and when the sun rose, he was down the Delaware on his voyage to England.

Another anecdote of the same gentleman is equally characteristic of the " way to manage the people." Between Walnut and Spruce Streets, and Sixth and Washington Streets, lay a piece of ground named the Potter's field, or burial place for strangers. Interments in it had long been prohibited, but it contained some graves and monuments inclosed by railings. There was a strong desire in the minds of many enlightened citizens to clear these away and to turn the ground into an ornamental square, as it now lay in the heart of the city ; but every proposal to obliterate them was resisted by the public sentiment, although no living person could be found who was interested in any of them. Mr ——— suggested to a marble-cutter to carry off the monuments quietly, and by slow degrees, at dead of night. In the course of two years, they all disappeared mysteriously, nobody knew how. The rails followed. Nobody interfered ; nobody noticed the change until it was complete. He employed men quietly at night to level the surface over the graves. Thus was completed, in less than three years, without any authority whatever, a change which the enlightened residents had in vain solicited permission to accomplish. The ground being reduced to a waste, the civic corporation, without any hesitation, voted money to inclose it with a handsome rail, to plant it, and to furnish it with gravel walks. It is now Washington Square, one of the greatest ornaments, and a great benefit to the city.

March 29. Ther. 63°. The weather is so warm that we have left off fires. The following table has appeared in the newspapers, and is interesting.

" *The Baths of Philadelphia.*—Owing to the copious supply of water from Fairmount, the city and suburbs of Philadelphia enjoy the luxury of bathing, in a way superior to most cities of Europe or

America, as the following table will shew. It is
taken from last year's report of the Watering Committee.

" The City proper has 1673 private baths,

paying . . .			$5,061 00
" Ditto 10 public, one of which pays			300 00
" The other 9 pay . .			360 00
" Northern Liberties, 195 private baths,			877 50
" Spring Garden,	217 ...	...	976 50
" Southwark,	45 ...	...	202 50
" Moyamensing,	23 ...	...	103 50
" Kensington,	1 ...	...	6 00
	2164		$7,887 00

" Two thousand one hundred and sixty-four baths
supplied with an *unlimited* quantity of water for
Seven thousand eight hundred and eighty-seven
dollars !"

United States Bank.—There it a great sensation
this evening about the resignation by Nicholas Biddle, Esq. of his office of President of the United
States Bank.

Acuteness of Children.—In the course of my lectures, I urged the necessity of women being thoroughly educated for the sake of guiding the opening minds
of children; and this evening one of the Society of
Friends whom we visited, read to me in illustration
of the lecture, a part of a letter which she had just
received from her married sister, living in a neighbouring State. The letter described the questions
put to her by her child on hearing parts of the

Scripture read. The child insisted on being informed whither Ananias and Sapphira went when they were struck dead. " To hell ?" asked the child. The mother gave an evasive answer. " To heaven?" " No." " Where then did they go ?" On hearing the description read of Abraham preparing to sacrifice Isaac, and of his being at last told to spare his son, and sacrifice the ram, the child exclaimed, " Well, I do say that that was cheating !" The mother could go no farther. It would be very interesting and instructive to parents and teachers, if a record were published of the observations of children who have large moral and intellectual organs, on the Scripture narratives. Such a record would shew the relation in which these stand to the human mind in its natural condition, before it has been influenced by commentaries, and explanations, or glosses, and indicate what portions of Scripture are calculated most directly to benefit the juvenile faculties. The advantage of *selecting* passages suited to their capacities would then become evident, and the objection of " mutilating the Scriptures," which is raised in Britain against the proposal to prepare extracts from the Bible for the use of children, would be refuted by evidence that the young are far from being benefited by an indiscriminate perusal of the whole.

March 30. Ther. 53°. *The United States Bank.*— Mr Biddle's letter of resignation is published in the newspapers to-day. He assigns " approaching age and precarious health" as the causes of his retirement. I am informed by the medical friends of Mr Biddle.

that a pressure of labour and anxiety such as he encountered at the last expiry of the charter of the bank, and at the suspension of cash-payments in 1837, would in all probability induce either apoplexy or inflammation, and that he has been strongly urged by them to retire.   One medical gentleman who knew him well, said to me, that if he had continued in office, and any new difficulty had arisen, he should not have been surprised to hear that he was found dead in his business-room.   The stock of the bank has fallen in consequence of his retirement.

March 31.   Ther. 40°.   *Omnibuses and Railroads.*—In this city the omnibuses run on Sundays. Rails are laid on the streets for the Baltimore, the Harrisburg, and the New York railroads.   The passengers are taken up at convenient stations in the city, and the cars are drawn by horses till they have fairly cleared the houses, when locomotive engines are attached to them.   This is found to be a very great convenience ; but children are occasionally injured by heedlessly running on the rails.

Pulmonary Consumption.—The late Dr Benjamin Rush regarded consumption as an inflammatory disease, and applied to it very active treatment.   Dr Parrish told me that he was early struck by the speedy and never-failing death of Rush's patients. Two young students became ill of the disease in the beginning of winter : one of them followed Dr Rush's advice, and was dead in a few months; the other refused all treatment whatever, and lived double the time of the other, although he also died.   Dr Parrish in his own practice abandoned Dr Rush's treatment, and recommended air and exercise as abundantly as the strength of the patients permitted; he also advised them to brave, as far as possible, the weather, and to use little medicine. He resorted to bleeding and blistering only when unequivocal symptoms of local inflammation were present, superadded to the tuberculous disease. By this method he was more successful than Dr Rush. He saved a few, and prolonged, to some extent, the lives of almost all his patients. I have read, with much interest, his exposition of the subject in vols. 8, 9, and 10, of the North American Medical and Surgical Journal.

The Education of the People.—A friend has called my attention to an article in Blackwood's Magazine for February 1839, No. 280, reprinted here. The object of it is to shew that the mass of the people never can become enlightened and refined; that, therefore, education can render them only uneasy and restless; that ignorance is to them the parent of contentment; but that, if they must be educated, a religious education is the only one fitted to do them good. It renders them patient, humble, and moral, and relieves the hardships of their present lot by the prospect of a bright eternity. " How strangely," said my friend, " do such sentiments sound in this country, where we must enlighten and refine the mass of the people or perish, for they rule our destinies. The author obviously considers England as the world, and the present condition of her people as the only one in which the human race can ever exist ! If the article be written in good faith, the author needs much to be educated himself. If he is an aristocrat or a priest, endeavouring to prop up a system which devotes eight out of every ten of the English people to toil and ignorance, without prospect of relief on this side of the grave—for the benefit of the remaining two—he deserves to be doomed to undergo this fate himself, that he may know by experience the efficacy of his own prescriptions for human misery."

Chimney-Sweeps.—The chimney-sweeps here are young negro boys. As they glide through the streets in quest of employment, they have a peculiar and melodious cry, slightly resembling a Tyrolese "yoddle."

April 1. Ther. 40°. "*The Coloured American.*" —This is the title of a weekly newspaper for the use of the coloured people of the United States. It has reached No. 2 of vol. iii. It consists of four pages, each containing four columns; the price is $2 per annum. The paper of 30th March has been sent to me because it contains an attack on Phrenology, a denial of its utility, and a commendation of the philosophy of Dr Thomas Brown, and that of Mr Young of Belfast. It is edited by Samuele Cornish and James M'Cune Smith. I am told that one of the editors is a coloured gentleman, who studied medicine in Edinburgh, and imbibed the prejudices of his teachers against the science, and that he is now labouring to transfer them to his coloured brethren.

Female Delicacy —In my first course of lectures in Philadelphia, I endeavoured to point out the con-

nection between beauty in the proportions and forms
of the human figure,—and health. The handsomest
figure is one in which the abdomen, the chest, and
the head, are all well developed; and this proportion
is also most favourable to health; because on the
first depends digestion, on the second respiration,
and on the third mental energy. The limbs will
rarely be found deficient where the proportions of
these regions are favourable. I recommended to my
audience the study of the human figure in statuary
and painting, not only as an interesting object of
taste, but as capable of conveying knowledge of great
practical utility. A mother, with an eye familiar
with those proportions, and instructed in their relations to health, would watch, with increased attention, the habits, postures, and nutrition of her children. If she saw the abdomen tending to become tu-
mescent, the chest flat, and the head enlarged, she
would early become aware that there was some de-
viation from the laws of health; and thus by timely
remedies might prevent serious disease. There is
no inherent indelicacy in the human figure. It is
the workmanship of the Creator, the temple of the
mind, and there is impressed on it a beauty of form
and an elegance of proportion that render it capable
of exciting the most pure and refined impressions in
a cultivated and virtuous mind. Where indelicacy
is felt, its source must be looked for, not in the object, but in licentious feelings, or in a perverted or
neglected education in the spectator. That individual who is able to associate only impure ideas with

the most exquisite specimens of the fine arts, resembles a man in whom the aspect of a rich and
beautiful domain should excite only feelings of envy,
cupidity, and discontent.

These views appeared to me to be well received;
and some friends even commended them as useful in
tending to correct that false delicacy which injures
the health and usefulness of many American women.

In the United States Gazette, however (a Philadelphia paper), of the 28th of March, a letter, subscribed " Candidus," appeared, which, in allusion to
my lecture on this subject in the last course, characterized it as having been " equally revolting to
the feelings of delicacy of many of the audience, as
it was offensive *to the national sense of propriety;*"
and the writer hoped " either that, notice being given
of its being obnoxious, it will not again be introduced; or, if it be, that it will meet with a prompt
and stern rebuke, which will prevent a repetition."

On the present occasion I intentionally reserved
this topic for the last portion of my lecture on Physical Education. I then read the letter to my audience, and announced that I intended to repeat the
remarks, and that they would form the conclusion of
the lecture; but that before proceeding, I should
pause to allow any lady or gentleman to retire, whose
delicacy might be offended by them. Ladies composed more than one-third of the audience, and many
of them belonged to the Society of Friends. Not a
single individual rose. I then stated, in answer to
the remarks of *Candidus,* that " I did not respect any

feeling merely because it was ' national.' It had been a ' national' feeling in Scotland to hate the English; in Britain to hate the French; and in the year 1776, it was the quintessence of patriotism in England to hate you, the Americans; yet every one acknowledges that these were improper feelings in themselves, and that the fact of their being ' national' did not alter their character. *Candidus*, however, very properly asserts, that, in the present instance, the national feeling ' is founded alike on virtue and reason;' and, if so, it merits respect; but this is the point on which I differ from him in opinion. It has been announced by the highest authority, that ' To the pure *all* things are pure;' but, according to *Candidus*, there is one exception, and the verse should have contained the qualifying words, ' except the human figure.' Has the Creator framed any object that is essentially and necessarily indelicate? Impossible! But my leading design in this exposition is not to initiate you into a love of the fine arts, but to call your attention to the necessity of becoming acquainted with the structure of the human body, and the functions of its organs, as the very basis of a rational view of physical education; and in your country this is an important desideratum. You cannot know that structure without studying it; and you cannot study it without looking on it. If you neglect the study, you suffer: Do you believe, then, that the Creator has rendered it necessary for you to study his works, and at the same time made it sinful in you to do so?" Pointing to an anatomical drawing shewing the intestines, the stomach, the liver, and the lungs, I said that " I had been assured that in whichever of these organs a lady felt indisposed, she told her physician that she had a pain in her *breast*, misleading him, so far as she had the power to do so, by an erroneous statement of symptoms, and offering increased obstacles to the successful exertions of his skill for her own welfare. In some instances (as I have been told) this feeling of delicacy renders it extremely difficult for the physician to extract, even by the most pointed questions, real and necessary information from oversensitive patients. This is false delicacy, and it should be corrected by knowledge. Fortified by these considerations, and also encouraged by the right spirit in which the ladies of Boston, New York, and this city, have received my remarks on the subject in my previous courses, it is my intention again to introduce it to your notice, and I hope to convince you, by your own experience, that it is quite possible to convey valuable information concerning it, without one indelicate emotion or idea being suggested to the mind." The audience repeatedly applauded these remarks as they were delivered, and testified their satisfaction by a loud and general burst of approbation at the close.

April 2. Ther. 53°. *New Lunatic Asylum.*—Dr B. H. Coates kindly drove me about a mile and a half west from the city, over the Schuylkill River, to visit a new lunatic asylum, now erecting by the Trustees of the Pennsylvanian Hospital, for pauper and other lunatics. The edifice is 420 feet long, is two stories high, in addition to the sunk floor, and contains a long corridor with cells on each side. It is built of sandstone-rubble, except the centre, which is cased with *droved* sandstone, veined very like marble. There are two small wings, and the centre is ornamented with a dome. It stands on a gentle eminence fronting the south, in a wooded and cultivated country, and has 108 acres of land attached to it. It is said to be fire-proof, and to possess all the modern improvements for warming and ventilation ; but it is not yet finished. The roof is complete, but the floors are not laid. It appears to be highly creditable to the trustees and architect under whose auspices it has been reared.

Railroads in the United States.—In conversing with an accomplished civil engineer, who had visited Europe, on the temporary character and unfinished appearance presented by the American railroads, he said that here a railroad is made in order to call forth population, commerce, and manufactures ; whereas in England, they are constructed, because they are wanted by a dense, rich, and industrious population. He considered the American plan best suited to their own circumstances. Their works are sufficient to accomplish the main object,—cheap and expeditious transportation. They will be improved as trade increases. Wherever the lines have been judiciously selected, commanding thoroughfares from one important point of the Union to another, as from New York to Philadelphia, and from Philadelphia to Baltimore, railroads have been eminently successful.

The Academy of Natural Sciences.—I attended

a meeting of the Academy this evening. It was instituted on 25th January 1812, and incorporated in 1817 by the Legislature of Pennsylvania. It has a hall at the corner of Twelfth and George Streets, and a valuable and extensive collection of objects of natural history. These are displayed in upright and horizontal cases: they are ranged in accordance with the most approved systems ; and their generic and specific names (wherever these can be ascertained) together with the localities and the names of the donors, are attached to each article. The "Journal of the Academy" was commenced in 1817, and continues to be published, not at stated intervals, but when valuable communications have accumulated to suffice for a number. It has reached to seven 8vo volumes, and is widely circulated among scientific persons in America and Europe. It is replete with important details in every branch of science, and is reputed to contain a greater body of facts in reference to the technical natural history of the United States than any other work. The Academy possesses also the richest library on natural history in the United States. It is indebted for a great part of its property and prosperity to its President, Wm. Maclure, Esq. who has bestowed on it several splendid donations.*

The Pursuit of Wealth.—The Americans are taunted by the British for their exclusive devotion to the pursuit of wealth ; but in this respect, as well as in many others, they are the genuine heirs of English dispo-

* "Notice of the Academy of Natural Sciences," 1837. In November last, it did me the honour to elect me a Corresponding Member.

sitions, with a better apology for their conduct. One
of the earliest injunctions of the Creator to man was,
" to multiply and replenish the earth." The Americans have a fertile country of vast extent placed before them inviting them to fulfil this commandment ;
and it would argue mental lethargy or imbecility were
they to disobey the call. But how can a wilderness be peopled and replenished without the creation of wealth? Houses must be built and furnished ; clothes and implements of husbandry must be
manufactured ; animals must be reared; yet these
are the constituent elements of wealth. The fertile soil of the west, therefore, invites the active and
enterprising spirits of each generation to advance
and take possession of it. Within two years after
it is cleared, it places in the hands of the occupier a
surplus produce after supplying his own wants. He
sends this surplus to the eastern cities to be sold, and
receives in exchange the various manufactured articles which constitute the conveniences and ornaments
of civilized life. The demand of the west on the capital and industry of the east, is incessant and increasing. The rich lands of the west, aided by the rapid increase of population, present investments which
can scarcely fail, after a few years, to yield an immense profit to the adventurer ; and this legitimate
drain for capital affects profits and interest, and the
value of property all over the Union. There are re-
vulsions, no doubt, but the wave never recedes so far
as it had advanced, and those who fail are generally
men who have engaged in enterprises far beyond the

measure of their capital and legitimate credit. Were the people of the east therefore to despise riches, and to become merely the cultivators of literature, philosophy, the fine arts, and all the social graces, they would be fit subjects for their own lunatic asylums. The *physique* must precede the *morale* in the order of nature. We must be well lodged, clothed, nourished, and altogether physically comfortable, before we can bend our minds successfully to refinement, philosophy, and the investigations of abstract science. The people of the United States, therefore, are only fulfilling a law of nature. They are peopling and replenishing the desert, and devoting themselves to this duty with a degree of energy, assiduity, and success that is truly astonishing. It is in vain to blame their institutions or their manners for these results. They owe their origin to nature.

But while I thus hold the Americans as not meriting disapprobation for pursuing wealth as their national vocation, I regard the impulse which prompts them to do so, as one which needs to be watched, and within certain limits resisted, lest it should swallow up all other virtues. Their real prosperity depends on the co-ordinate activity of their acquisitive with their moral and intellectual faculties. If their external circumstances stimulate Acquisitiveness with a power equal to 10, they should put on a power of moral, religious, and intellectual cultivation equal to 15, to guide and restrain it. They are endeavouring to do so by their public schools; and if they succeed, they will in due season become a magnificently great nation; great equally in the possession of physical and moral civilization.

The Americans, although highly acquisitive, are not sordid as a nation. They expend their wealth freely, and where the object meets with their approbation, they are even munificent in their donations. The sums contributed by them to religious and benevolent societies, to the building of churches and colleges, and to the support of hospitals and similar institutions, are very large. I frequently heard of strangers coming from distant parts of the country to the cities, soliciting subscriptions to build churches, and was told that they were successful. Unitarians have repeatedly told me, that they had subscribed to build evangelical churches; but no instance was mentioned to me (though such may be not uncommon) in which an evangelical believer had contributed to the erection of a Unitarian edifice. I heard a scientific gentleman defend his countrymen and himself against the charge of excessive acquisitiveness, in the following pithy sentences : " I have always," said he, " pursued wealth, because I saw that I could accomplish nothing without it. A sordid mind is indicated by the uses which it makes of property, and not by the pursuit of it. I employ two men to assist me in my scientific analyses and experiments, and pay them $1000 per annum. If I had not bought lots of ground which have doubled in value, I could not have done this ; so that in point of fact the money acquired by my lots is devoted to the extension of science."

April 3. Ther. 50°. *Cause of the Decline of Qua-*

kerism.—I have already mentioned that a number of individuals left the Society of Friends at the time of the separation between the Orthodox and the followers of Elias Hicks. A sagacious old Scotsman, who has been many years a citizen of Philadelphia, gave me a novel theory of the decline of Quakerism. " The real cause of it," said he, " is the excessive multiplication of banks. The paper currency is so abundant, and so recklessly issued, that a spirit of gambling speculation has seized the whole community, against which Quakerism cannot maintain itself. Farming is the only occupation, consistent with the simplicity of Quaker principles, which is left to them." The same individual summed up his character of the Americans, the result of forty years' observation, in these words : " They are most awful braggers ; there is no end or limit to their boasting ; yet they are the most active people I ever saw. If they only knew how to go right, there is nothing which they might not achieve."

Sunday Travelling.—The running of the railroad cars on Sundays from Philadelphia to Columbia, is announced and apologized for, as indispensable to overtaking the greatly extended spring trade of this season, and a promise is given, that the arrangement is only temporary, with a view to forwarding an accumulating mass of goods. In the eastern States, the steam-boats and stage-coaches, except the mails, do not run on Sundays ; but there are morning and evening trains on the railroads for passengers.

Franklin's Grave.—After at least ten unsuccessful

attempts to find open the gate of the burial-ground in Mulberry Street, corner of Fifth Street, in which Benjamin Franklin is interred, I succeeded in gaining admission to it to-day.   The number of funerals which one sees is strikingly small for so large a city, and this indicates a young population.   Franklin's grave is covered by a large marble slab, lying on the ground, on which is inscribed :

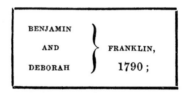

BENJAMIN
AND   } FRANKLIN,
DEBORAH   } 1790 ;

and nothing more.   On a similar slab, to the left, and exactly in the same form, are inscribed the words, " Richard and Sarah Bache, 1811."   These were his daughter and her husband.   The situation is favourable for the erection of a monument, and Franklin certainly merits, although his memory does not stand in need of, this mark of respect.

Imprisonment for Debt.—In conversing on this subject with an Englishman who has been settled for some years, and has prospered, in this country, but in whom not one English notion has been changed, he said to me—" When you go home, recommend this country as a paradise for rogues.   Most of the States have abolished imprisonment for debt, and every one who chooses may issue bank-notes.   A well-varnished story will enable any one to obtain credit ; and having obtained it, there is no law to force him to pay. But for honest men this is not the country at all. Republican institutions will never succeed." He should have added, that imprisonment for debt is not abolished where fraud can be established. There are two sides to every question. I have had opportunities of observing the operation of the law of imprisonment for debt in the old country, and do not think that the United States have committed a great error in abolishing it.

A man who sells goods is pursuing his own interest fully as much as he who buys. In the keen competition to effect sales, sellers use every art of persuasion to induce their customers to buy, and also strive to obtain prices as high as possible. Many well-meaning, but weak men, and also many speculative men, are by these means drawn into purchases far beyond the limits of their regular means of selling. When the day of payment comes, the creditor trusts to the law to enforce his claim; and, through terror of a jail, the buyer, to raise the needful funds, sells his goods at a loss. By a few repetitions of this error, he becomes insolvent; but for some time after this takes place, he continues in possession of as much means and credit as to be able to proceed with his trade. He must now, however, buy and sell largely in order to raise means to meet his obligations as they become due. Acute sellers soon discover that he is in this situation; they calculate how long he will be able to proceed before his losses accumulate to such an amount as to force him to stop payment altogether; and they add per centage to per centage on the price as they reckon the day of failure to approach. If the buyer be a man of resources, he may go on for two or three years in insolvency, and during all this time the persons who sell to him are " spunging him," as they term it, by ever-increasing additions to their demands. He is in such a condition, that he must sell, or fail and go to prison. He sells cheap that he may raise money to avert this catastrophe as long as possible ; and in order to sell, he must buy. Thus, between buying at high, and selling at low prices, he at last arrives at the goal, and openly declares himself bankrupt.

To allow the seller, who has partly induced, and partly profited by this course of transactions, to wind up his proceedings by putting the debtor in jail, is neither just nor beneficial. If the seller be deprived of this power, he will trust to his own sagacity in selecting honest men for his customers, and he will also be more attentive to their interests. In short, instead of trusting to the law to enable him to reap the fruits of his own rapacity, he must conduct trade on higher moral and intellectual principles.

This is no imaginary representation. I have seen the whole machinery in operation, and traced its effects. One example may be mentioned in illustration. A mercantile friend told me that a Mr B——, whom we both knew, had come to him and looked at some goods. " He had rarely dealt with me before," said my friend, " but I had judged from his forced sales that he was below par (insolvent) ; and from the prices at which he was purchasing from Mr C.

and Mr D., that he must be pretty far gone. I wished, therefore, to get rid of him ; and I asked ten per cent. above the market price. To my astonishment, he at once accepted my offer. He selected another parcel of goods, and asked the price. Being already farther in with him than I had intended, I added fifteen per cent. to the price of these. He did not hesitate a moment, but purchased them also. He proceeded to a third parcel, and asked the price. Being resolved now to pull him up at all hazards, I demanded twenty-five per cent. above the market price : he grumbled a little, but gave in, and desired me to send the whole purchases to his warehouse. The prices amounted to L.500. I was convinced that he was now in desperation, and that an immediate bankruptcy might be expected, and I closed the conference by asking him for ' security' for the payment. He turned on his heel and walked off without speaking a word ; I retained the goods, and within a fortnight he was in the Gazette as a bankrupt." I subsequently had the means of tracing the transactions of Mr B—— for several years, and observed that he had run the course before described, and that this was the last and desperate effort to maintain a regularly sinking trade.

I have already described the very strong excitement which the natural circumstances of the Union present to the acquisitive propensity in the Americans. Nevertheless they are incessant in their calls for additional stimulants. They create oceans of paper currency, and proclaim the " credit system" as indispensably necessary to their very existence as a commercial people. With all deference to their judgment, it appears to me that they stand in need of checks and regulators on their acquisitiveness, instead of stimulants. The natural rate of profit is so high, and they are so active and economical, that, if they had only some adequate machinery to regulate their movements, they would advance with extraordinary rapidity to wealth. If the majority of them were sufficiently enlightened to discern (as many of the judicious and better informed among them do) their true position, and the means of promoting their real welfare, they would check their banks, their credit system, and their vast speculations, and advance more leisurely in pursuit of gain. The Scripture proclaims that he that *hasteneth* to be rich falleth into a snare; and the Americans afford striking examples of the truth of this proposition. The philosophy of the text is, that capital, time, and labour, are necessary to the production of wealth; that before we can legitimately obtain it, we must give an equivalent, and every equivalent also requires time, labour, and capital, for its production. He who hastens to be rich, therefore, tries to create wealth, or to acquire it, without complying with these natural conditions. But Nature is too strong for him; he is blind to the obstacles which she presents to his success, and he falls into a snare. It is true that, in a rich and extensive country, a few individuals may, by gambling and speculation, acquire sudden wealth; but some others must lose as much. Time and labour must have been employed to pro-

duce the wealth before it could be lost and won ; and
these men produce nothing.   They shuffle property
from one hand to another, but the nation is in no
degree made richer by their speculations.   All young
Americans, therefore, should be trained to understand the real laws by which wealth is produced and
distributed, and to submit to them as they would do
to the commandments of the Bible.   The natural
effect of the abolition of imprisonment for debt is to
render merchants more cautious whom they trust.
It should check, rather than encourage, " the credit
system."

While, however, the Americans appear to me to
have pursued the right road in abolishing imprisonment for debt, they are, from all that I can learn,
much in fault with respect to their bankrupt laws.
Their laws leave debtors in possession of the power
of distributing their effects among their creditors,
and of conferring preferences on favourites, to an extent that is unknown in other civilized countries.
Besides, there is no general bankrupt law extending
over the whole Union ; and as each State is to the
others a foreign jurisdiction, a man may be discharged
of his debts in one State, and an undischarged bankrupt in another, without the possibility of remedying
his condition.   When imprisonment for debt is abolished, there should be a cheap, efficacious, and ge--
neral law for transferring the whole property of a
debtor directly to his creditors for equal distribution,
and he should have no power whatever either to
obstruct or regulate the operation of the law.   Pro-

vision should be made, also, for his obtaining a complete discharge with consent of his creditors, or a large proportion of them, but not otherwise. At present no public notice is given of bankruptcy; so that an individual may be utterly bankrupt in New York, and the fact be unknown in Philadelphia, unless by private communication. This opens a wide door to fraud, and to unprincipled speculation. If the Americans knew their real interests, they would publish the name of every bankrupt in every town of the Union, as is done in Britain, where the official intimations of bankruptcy are transferred from the London and Edinburgh Gazettes into every newspaper in the kingdom. Honest men gain by this information, for it enables them to know the speculators. Honourable merchants may once or twice become insolvent by misfortune; but there are individuals who pass their lives in swindling and bankruptcy, and the American method of concealment is admirably adapted to their purposes.

It is only a few years since a bankrupt law was passed even in Massachusetts, one of the most enlightened States in the Union. On the 19th of March 1835, a report on the subject of " insolvent debtors," by the Hon. Horace Mann, as chairman of a committee, was presented to the senate of that State. It is replete with admirable views eloquently expressed. The following sentences should be adopted as maxims by the legislatures of every civilized country :—
" The committee entertain a firm conviction that the legal relation between debtor and creditor exerts a

commanding influence, not only over individual and
national wealth, but also over private and public morals. To establish this relation upon the foundations
of natural justice, is one of the primary duties of
government." * * * " Your committee will not
enlarge upon the obligation and utility of making the
legal coincident with the *moral* code. In many
minds ideas of right and wrong are but a transcript
of positive enactment or judicial decision ; and legal
rules are their ultimate conscience. Hence, unjust
laws never stop with extinguishing an individual
right, or inflicting an individual wrong. They
fashion and adapt the general mind to injustice.
They bind the foreign substance of error to the heart,
until the fibres close around it, and it becomes in-
eradicable for ever. Erroneous principles in legislation commend the injustice they ordain ; they impress the form of right upon the substance of wrong;
and they withhold from truth its highest advantage—
the privilege of being seen. But true legislation,
which is the art of applying the rules of right to the
affairs of men, should develope those rules, give them
a bold and conspicuous prominence, and, illuminating
them with a light of its own, make them universally
legible." Effect was given, to a considerable extent,
to these principles in the act for " the relief of poor
prisoners," and in the " Insolvent Act" passed by
the legislature of Massachusetts in 1838, chap. 163.

I find a number of vague ideas afloat among the
mercantile classes here, which have become maxims,
but which appear extremely questionable to a stran-

ger.   It is said that " this is a new country, and we
must encourage enterprise : although we have many
speculators and numerous bankruptcies, yet these are
always helping forward the general advance of the
country; the individuals may fail, but the results of
their speculations remain, and add to the general
wealth." The answer to these views is, that wealth
can be created only by capital, labour, and time; and
that these may be applied prudently or imprudently.
The men who apply them with judgment and discretion succeed, and benefit equally themselves and
their country ; those who, in the employment of
them, infringe every law of nature by which the
creation and distribution of wealth are regulated, are
speculators, and so far from their enterprises bene-
fiting the community, the fact is directly the reverse.
They waste the resources which in more prudent
and skilful hands would have produced double the
advantages which they bring out of them.   It is
true that the houses which they build, or the manufactories which they erect, remain, and that in the
course of years the wealth and population of the
country advance and render them useful ; but they
were not wanted at the time they were built, the
capital expended on them has been unprofitably locked
up, and the enterprise and industry of wiser and
better men, from whose hands it has been withdrawn
by the speculators, have been paralyzed for years.
The American people appear to me to be so extremely
active and enterprising, that no encouragement needs
to be held out to speculators to engage in bold

schemes in order to promote public prosperity. On the contrary, they will prosper more rapidly, and enjoy far greater felicity, if by their laws and institutions they will put a check on such spirits, and encourage the honest, the wise, and the prudent, to lead them forward in their commercial career.

April 4. Ther. 53°. *How to choose a Sect.*—The following ancedote is *not* an old Joe Miller. I relate it because, while it illustrates the kindly feeling which reigns among the members of a sect towards each other, it shews how this amiable trait of character may be taken advantage of by rogues. A bookseller, a native of Germany, came from England, settled in one of the large American cities, and began business in a moderate way. He had a stock of neatly printed bibles which he was anxious to dispose of. After he had been established for some time, he called on an old-established citizen, and told him that he thought of joining one of the religious bodies of the town, and wished to know which of them was the most influential. His friend imagined that he was in joke, and said that there was a simple way of solving that question. He took up the *directory* and shewed the inquiring bookseller the lists of the directors of all the public institutions. He desired him to write down their names, and he would tell him what sects they belonged to. The bookseller accordingly folded his paper for columns, and wrote on the heads of them, "Presbyterian," "Methodist," " Catholic," " Quaker," " Baptist," " Unitarian," " Universalist," " Jew," &c., and under these heads entered the names of the directors of the institutions, according to the information of his friend. The result was a clear demonstration that the " Presbyterians" were by far the most numerous and powerful sect in the public institutions, whence the inference was drawn that in all probability they would be the most influential in the general affairs of the city. He thanked the gentleman (who still believed that it was a jest) and departed. But it was neither a joke nor a mistake. The bookseller found out which was the wealthiest Presbyterian congregation, offered to join them, and presented a handsome gift to the church, and neatly bound copies of his bible to the minister and elders. He was admitted a member, was widely praised among the congregation, sold all his bibles, obtained extensive credit, had a large store and an ample trade, and might have done well. But, like too many others, he speculated and ruined himself. At his bankruptcy, the rich men of the congregation were his creditors, one to the extent of $20,000, another of $15,000, another of $10,000, and so forth, every man according to his means !

This is no uncommon occurrence in other countries, and it is a proof of the real Christian spirit of the individuals who are thus cheated. Having entire confidence in the efficacy of their own faith to regenerate the human mind, and being perfectly sincere themselves, they do not suspect the roguery of others. In reference to an individual of a character very similar to this, who had come from Scotland, I was asked, " How do you reconcile the strange and

striking discrepancy between the religious professions and the commercial reputation of your country-
man Mr A. B?"   The explanation which I offered,
and which I knew to be supported by facts, was,
that in the class of persons to which Mr A. B. belongs, the organs of Acquisitiveness, Secretiveness,
and Veneration, are *plus*, and those of Conscientiousness *minus*.   The large Veneration gives them a
strong interest in religious worship, and to this extent their professions are sincere. It reveals to them
also the power of this sentiment in other minds.
Their large Secretiveness and deficient Conscientiousness, when combined with acute intellect, render
them apt at swindling and deceit; and thus accomplished, they are tempted to employ the religious
feeling as a means of gratifying their Acquisitiveness.

Many religious persons refuse to believe in the
possibility of any individual being sincere in his religious feelings, and at the same time dishonest.
They conceive that his religious professions must in
such a case be entirely hypocritical. The great
cause of their erroneous judgment on this subject, is
that, in their conception of religion, they always include morality, and hence conclude that wherever
devoutness is really present, morality must necessarily be so also. They are right in holding that the
Christian religion embraces both faith and practice,
and that no man is a true Christian who does not
" do justly, love mercy, and walk humbly with his
God." But they err in not knowing that the natu-

ral aptitude of individual minds to discharge these three duties, depends mainly on the size of three separate cerebral organs ; and that one or two of them may be small, and the third large, or *vice versa ;* that, for example, the organs of Benevolence and Conscientiousness may be large, and that of Veneration small, and then the individual will be greatly disposed to justice and mercy, but very little to the externals of devotion ; while in another the proportions may be reversed, and he may be greatly interested in acts of devotion, but very little addicted to honesty and goodness. When religious men shall rise above their prejudices, and use Phrenology as a means of discovering natural dispositions, they will find less difficulty than at present in discriminating between the sheep and the goats within their fold.

The Deaf and Dumb Institution.—Every Thursday at half-past 3 o'clock there is a public exhibition of the manner in which the deaf and dumb are taught. This exhibition, which is well attended by the citizens, serves to support the interest of the public in the institution, and enables strangers to obtain information concerning it without interrupting the ordinary studies of the pupils. Three boys and three girls appeared. They wrote words and sentences with readiness and intelligence, illustrative of any idea or subject that was proposed to them. One of the girls told a little story, in which she employed not only words spelled by the fingers, but also signs and natural language. She was exceedingly animated. Phrenology reveals the natural attitudes, and the ex-

pressions of the features and voice, which accompany
the predominating activity of many of the faculties.
This is called the natural language of the faculties ; it
is universal wherever man exists, and could be used
to great advantage in the instruction of the deaf and
dumb. We visited the workshops, and saw the boys
making shoes and the girls sewing. The children
are numerous, and they seemed healthy and happy.
Mr Hutton, their head teacher, was gentle, quiet,
kind, and intellectual in his intercourse with them.

Exclusion of Sectarianism from the Common Schools.
—On page 40 of this volume, I have quoted the
tenth head of the public " regulations for common
schools districts," which provides that " the religious predilections of pupils and their parents or
guardians shall be sacredly respected." It is only
four or five years since this resolution was practically adopted by the board of directors of the common schools. Before that time, every teacher in-
doctrinated the children under his charge with his
own notions. One was zealous in training up the
children to be Calvinists and Presbyterians ; on the
floor above, a Baptist teacher was busy propagating
his peculiar views ; in another school a Roman Catholic teacher was infusing Catholicism, and next to
him a Universalist was with equal zeal engaged in
imbuing the youthful minds with his faith. The
complaints of the parents were incessant, that their
children were taught dangerous and heretical errors
under the guise of religion ; each applying these
epithets to all opinions that differed from his own.

At last it was proposed to prohibit all doctrinal instruction in the common schools, and to leave to parents, pastors, and Sunday school teachers, the duty of inculcating the peculiar tenets of the different sects.   At first this proposal was vigorously opposed, and described as "infidel;" each sect hoping to obtain the exclusive possession, if not of the whole, at least of a limited number, of the schools, which they should manage in their own way.   All, however, stood firm in objecting to their neighbours obtaining the exclusive direction of any, as they were all supported out of a common fund; and, in the end, the exclusion of all was unanimously adopted, as the only practicable means of solving the difficulty.   This rule is now in force, and it is found to answer well.   In the evenings of week-days, as well as on Sundays, I see troops of children going to the "lecture-rooms" under the churches, where they are taught the peculiarities of their faith by their several pastors.

Defective Teaching in Common Schools.—The infant school system has not flourished in Philadelphia. So far as I could discover, it has never been in operation in an efficient form, and it is now generally laid aside in the common schools.   Pictures, and a few natural objects, may still be seen in some of the schools, but they are rarely if ever used.   The great object aimed at, is to teach the children to read fluently.   They read long passages with ease, without understanding the meaning of them.   One of the female teachers, to whom I remarked this circumstance, acknowledged the fact, and said, in explanation of it, that the parents insisted on the children being rendered great readers ; that they complained to the directors of the time spent in explaining words and teaching objects as being " lost ;" and that the directors, to satisfy them, desired her to make them " read," and not to waste time in giving explanations. She obeyed, and certainly the children read with great fluency ; but the meaning of the words is to a great extent unknown to them. In my lectures on education, I adverted to the errors of this mode of teaching, and told my audience that it reminded me of the mode of teaching English in a certain Highland school in Scotland. The children, whose vernacular tongue was Gaelic, were taught to spell, pronounce, and read English correctly and fluently, and, at a public examination, they displayed such proficiency, that the clergymen present were about to compliment the teacher publicly on his meritorious exertions, when a friend of mine, one of the proprietors of the parish, struck by the mechanical tone of the reading, put several questions to the children regarding the signification of the passages which they had read. He found them ignorant of the meaning of the words. The teacher had omitted to translate the English into Gaelic, and, although they could read, and pronounce the words, they did not understand the former language.

The children in the Philadelphia schools are to some extent in a similar condition : they read works on the history of America and other subjects, the language of which is so far superior to the expressions contained in their domestic vocabulary, that, while unexplained, it is to them a foreign tongue. I urged on my audience the indispensable necessity to the welfare of the country that the education of American children should embrace solid instruction in things, and not consist of words merely; and that *training* also, or *daily discipline of the dispositions*, should be regarded as of great importance to them. I earnestly advised them to invite Mr Wilderspin to visit their country, and to shew them a few good infant and training schools in operation; after seeing which, they would not long tolerate their present inefficient system. I respectfully recommend to the trustees of the Girard College, if they wish to benefit Pennsylvania, to engage Mr Wilderspin to spend six months in organizing an infant and training school in their seminary. In England, Scotland, and Ireland, the most efficient schools are those which embrace most of his principles and practice.

The Yellow Fever in Philadelphia.—Upwards of thirty years ago, Philadelphia was visited with yellow fever, and the disease raged like a pestilence. Dr Parrish, then a young man, volunteered to act as assistant resident physician in the Yellow Fever Hospital. He told me that he never experienced the least fear, and never was sick for a day. All the inhabitants who could leave the city had fled, and at noon it was still as at the midnight hour. The Hospital was situated on the bank of the Schuylkill, a short distance from town, and though for seven months he resided in it amidst the sick and the dying, yet he was happy. He was constantly engaged in discharging his duty, and no seven months of his life seemed to him so pure and bright in the retrospect as these. This is easily understood. He has a beautiful development of the organs of the moral sentiments, combined with fair intellect, and all these faculties glowed with beneficent and pleasing excitement. His first convalescent patient was an old woman. When he saw symptoms of recovery, he removed her into a private apartment to relieve her from the shocking spectacles of the dead and the dying which filled the public ward. She petitioned to be carried back, it was so lonely to be left by herself in a room. He complied with her request, and she recovered. The attendants became so careless, that he often saw a man, when relieved from duty, instead of going into an adjoining house prepared for him to sleep in, enter a bed from which he had just removed a dead patient, wrap himself up in the bed-clothes, sleep soundly, and take no harm. The Catholic priests were constant in their attendance ; while the clergymen of other denominations rarely ventured within the walls. In such scenes the celibacy of the Roman Catholic priesthood has a value.* He saw an aged priest proceed to administer extreme unction to a woman who was fast dying. She refused to repeat certain words. He told her she could not be saved

---

* I hope that I may be excused for mentioning, to the honour of the Scottish clergy, that they ventured boldly into the Cholera Hospitals at Edinburgh, and administered consolation to the sick and dying, at a time when that disease was regarded as even more formidable than the yellow fever.

unless she complied.   He explained, argued, and
entreated.   She continued obstinate, sunk back, and
died.   As she expired, the old priest shed a flood
of tears.   Dr Parrish was deeply affected, and said
that the scene carried home to him a strong conviction of the priest's sincerity and benevolence.   At
a subsequent period of my residence in the United
States, I had the pleasure of meeting with Dr Caldwell of Louisville, who mentioned that he also had
resided in the Yellow Fever Hospital as an assistant
physician, and that, in his opinion, the exciting causes
of the disease were confined to the town of Philadelphia.   Of the hospital attendants, not one who had
never entered the town was taken ill.   Some who
visited the town during the day were seized with the
disease : and of those who slept all night in it scarcely
one escaped.   He never entered the town, and enjoyed perfect health.

Dr Parrish on Liberty of Conscience.—A few years
ago, a young lady wrote a letter to Dr Parrish, who
is a Hicksite Friend, in which she says—" I had no
personal acquaintance with you.   I never listened to
your conversation on general topics, and probably
never may, at any future period.   But I have seen
you at the couch of sickness; I have seen you, by
the benignant smile of sympathy, soothing the suffering invalid, and, with accents of sweetness, cheering the room of sorrow.   And, oh ! I have said, Shall
such a mind be inveigled into those absurdities and
awful delusions, as ridiculous to every truly sober
understanding, as they are dreadful to the view of
any Christian ! Shall such a mind be led captive in

the most fearful species of enthralment, that of blasphemy and infidelity, under the imposing garb of the most refined spirituality—of the most professedly sublime and elevated religion," &c.   She prays that he may become an evangelical Presbyterian.

He wrote a reply characterized by Christian benignity in its most beautiful form. " In the extensive practice of my profession," says he, " for many years I have been accustomed to view poor, frail human nature in its most unveiled forms. The longer I live, the greater is my compassion for erring humanity. I have observed, that, in the hour of deep affliction, the Episcopalian, the Presbyterian, the Methodist, Baptist, Roman Catholic, Friend, &c. &c. notwithstanding their various modes of faith, all call upon one common God and Father. Among these, none manifest more composure than the Catholic, after confession and absolution by his priest. Thou wouldst perhaps call him an idolater, when thou sawest him with the crucifix, on which his dying eye was reposing with confidence and consolation, as he was passing through the dark valley of the shadow of death. Were I in the same situation, and the priest were to offer me similar consolations, I should reject them at once, as ' absurd and ridiculous,' so far as they related to me. Yet never have I dared, at such a moment, to attempt to unsettle the mind of a Catholic by an exposition of my own religious views. I have also seen the poor despised Jew, calm and resigned on the bed of death, unshaken in the religion of his fathers. Surely these things should teach us a lesson of charity, remembering we are dust.

" I have often admired, and been humbled in beholding, the simplicity of the Gospel, as taught by our Divine Master. In the first place, he commissioned poor fishermen to be its promulgators. Does he refer us to nice theological distinctions—or are we called upon to test each other by opinions and speculations? Look at his plain directions delivered in his sermon on the Mount. Hear his positive declarations—' A good tree cannot bring forth evil fruit, neither can a corrupt tree bring forth good fruit; wherefore, by their fruits ye shall know them.' And in the hour of final judgment, on what is that judgment predicated? Is it on orthodox opinions, or on practice? ' Come ye blessed of my Father, inherit the kingdom prepared for you from the foundation of the world : for I was an hungred and ye gave me meat, I was thirsty and ye gave me drink, I was a stranger and ye took me in, naked and ye clothed me ; I was sick and ye visited me, in prison and ye came unto me,' &c.

" From the views now unfolded, it will be perceived, although thou art a Presbyterian and I am a Friend or Quaker, yet, with my present feelings, between us there must be no controversy. Claiming sincerity for myself, I award it fully to thee," &c.

" When I perceive the bitter fruits which are so often produced by the conflicting opinions of professing Christians, my mind is affected with sorrow ; yet it is at seasons consoled by the reflection, that, happily for the human family, they are not to be finally judged by any earthly tribunal, but by a heavenly

and compassionate Father, who pities his erring
children; who sleeps not by day, nor slumbers by
night; but who watches over us for good, and numbers the very hairs of our heads : And although justice and judgment are the habitations of his throne,
yet thanksgiving and praise be ascribed unto our
God, for his mercy endureth for ever."*

* This excellent man has gone to render his own account to the
tribunal which he describes. A few days after he gave me a copy
of this correspondence, I parted with him apparently in excellent
health, and in a green old age. When I returned to Philadelphia in
April 1840, he had just died. He was esteemed and beloved by men
of all sects and parties in his native country, and I cannot withhold
my feeble tribute of respect to his excellent qualities.

CHAPTER V

(223)

CHAPTER V

Phrenology—The Banks—Spring—Fires—Fraud Detected—Massachusetts' Temperance Law—Objections to Infant Schools—A Firemen's Fight—Effects of Democracy—Moyamensing Prison—The Dangers of Riches—The Maine War—Pennsylvania University—Black-Foot Indians—Dr Morton's Crania Americana—Phrenology—International Law of Copyright—Spring—Pavements—Queen Victoria—The American Phrenological Journal—Phrenology—The Insane Poor of Pennsylvania—New York—New York Civic Election—General Winfield Scott—Phrenology—Maine War—Sing-Sing State Prison—Auburn State Prison—The Election—Sunday—Dr Channing's Answer to Mr Clay's Speech—Universalists—Tit for Tat—The Chartists—Licentiousness of the Press—The Park Theatre—High Prices of Provisions—Female Seminary for Education—Should British Dissenting Clergymen emigrate to America?—Extension of New York City—American Judges—Spring—The Cause of the High Prices of Provisions—The Asylum for Coloured Orphans—General Washington's First Presidency.

1839.

April 6. Ther. 53°. *Phrenology.*—I met Dr ——, and by pointing out to him how to trace the superior longitudinal commissure of the brain, described by Mr Solly, which lies above the *corpus callosum,* and brings the anterior lobe into communication with the upper portions of the middle and posterior lobes, he succeeded in unfolding it very satisfactorily. The brain was in excellent condition. We tried to trace the superficial fibres described by Mr Solly as passing from the motory track, below the *corpora pyramidalia,* to the cerebellum, but were not so successful.

In the evening I delivered the last lecture of my

second course. The resolutions passed are printed in the Appendix, No. III.

I have received an invitation to deliver a second course of lectures in the Stuyvesant Institute, New York, and have agreed to do so.

The Banks.—The banks in the south-western States have suspended cash payments, and rumours are afloat that the banks in Philadelphia will follow their example. Stocks have fallen very much, and there is great commercial embarrassment. The cry for war about the Maine boundary has aggravated the evil, by creating distrust in the continuance of pacific relations with England. The next news from London are looked for with anxiety and alarm.

April 7. Ther. 53°. *Spring.*—This day is agreeably warm. The apricot trees are in full blossom ; the weeping willows, which abound in the public squares, are in full leaf, and the buds of the other trees are rapidly swelling ; the grass, from dark russet, has become green. The stoves with which the boxes of the police-watchmen are furnished are no longer used. Every thing indicates the dawn of summer.

Fires.—The fire-engines were out this morning at seven, again at 2 P. M., and now, at 10 P. M., the State house-bell is announcing a third fire in the south-west part of the city. We see the sky red and lurid, and the engines are rushing and roaring past our windows. The words " roaring" or " braying" scarcely convey an idea of the hideous noise which the leader of an engine makes through a

brass or tin trumpet as he advances. It is intended
to sound an alarm, and to give notice to clear the
streets for the passage of the procession.

April 8. Ther. 50°. *Fraud Detected.*—One of the
judges mentioned to me a curious detection of a fraud
which had occurred in his experience on the Bench.
The judge himself has been in the practice of writing his private notes in the Greek character, although
in the English language. Those notes have occasionally fallen into the hands of persons who have
taken them for Greek, and they gave him a reputation, which he was far from claiming, of being a
great Greek scholar. On one occasion a German
Jew was brought into Court charged with fraudulent
bankruptcy. The judge asked to see his books.
" Oh," said the counsel for the Jew, " you need not
take any trouble about them, for they are all written
in Hebrew, and nobody can understand them." He,
however, insisted on seeing them. They were produced, and were written in the Hebrew character
certainly ; but, judging from his own practice, it
struck him that they might nevertheless be in the
German language. He called forward a man whom
he saw in court who spoke the same dialect of German as the Jew did, and made the Jew read aloud
his own entries in the books. The German understood every word of them. The books were unravel-
led, and the fraud completely exposed.

Massachusetts' Temperance Law.—" A bill licens-
ing the sale of spirits and wine in quantities over
three gallons, and also allowing travellers to buy it

by the glass, recently passed the Senate of Massachusetts, and was sent down to the House of Assembly. The house promptly killed it by refusing it a second reading. This vote was afterwards reconsidered, 206 to 142. The bill was then ordered to a second reading. Mr Cushman, of Bernardston, moved to amend the bill by striking out ' three' gallons, and inserting ' one' gallon. Carried. The bill was then rejected by—yeas 115, nays 230."

Objections to Infant Schools.—One of the directors of the common schools informed me that he perceived the advantage of teaching by objects, and that he had laboured to introduce cabinets of natural history and philosophical apparatus into the common schools, but that he met with great difficulties. The infant schools had been given up because the children were found not to be prepared by them for the higher schools. Their instruction needed to be begun anew. Although they could multiply twenty by twenty by the aid of Wilderspin's board, yet when they came into the higher school where no board was used, they could not multiply six by six. Although they could name a lion from its figure in a picture, and narrate its natural history very learnedly, they could neither spell nor read its name. I offered two hypothetical explanations of these facts : First, It may have happened that the infant school teachers were themselves imperfectly informed and trained, which I considered highly probable, because I had not been able to discover a single copy of Wilderspin's work on infant schools in the city of Philadelphia. If so, the teachers may have omitted to instruct the children in words as well as objects, which is a complete departure from the true principles of infant teaching. Or, secondly, The masters in the higher schools may have taught words so exclusively, that children who had been trained to connect an idea with every word may have been completely at a loss when words were presented to them *without* ideas.   He said, that his own experience had led him to the conclusion that the great obstacle to the success of infant and other schools for teaching objects, was the want of trained and capable teachers.   Some of the teachers are appointed through political influence, and have no ideas to communicate.   I repeated to him the great services that Mr Wilderspin had rendered to this branch of education in Britain, and urged him to use means for obtaining his assistance.

I find that most of the directors of the public schools are men engaged in business, who mean well towards education, but who do not understand the subject.   Besides, they have not sufficient time to devote to the schools.   They see that their own district receives its proper proportion of the fund appropriated to education (for Philadelphia above $200,000 annually), and that it is expended on schools ; but this is nearly all they can accomplish.   It is, nominally, the duty of the Secretary of the Commonwealth to superintend all the public schools, but as it is impossible that he can discharge this duty, he scarcely attempts to do so.   *Party* enters so largely into every appointment in Pennsylvania, that there is some danger that, if a secretary for public instruction were appointed, the office might be conferred, not in consideration of capacity to discharge its duties, but as a reward for political exertions. The ignorance of the people constitutes a serious obstacle to the improvement of education in this State ; and to me it was curious to see the same impediments to this great cause arising here from popular ignorance, which in England flow from the hostility of the Church and the aristocracy !

April 9. Ther. 55°. *A Firemen's Fight.*—The newspapers to-day contain a report of a trial on cross bills by individuals of rival fire companies, who fought for possession of a fire-plug or station, and each has prosecuted the other for an assault !

April 10. Ther. 35°. *Effects of Democracy.*— One accustomed to European cities detects subordinate influences of the democratic principle in the American cities, which probably escape the observation of natives. The carriage way in the streets in Philadelphia is paved with round water-worn stones, apparently gathered from rivers, and is consequently rough. The foot-way is beautifully paved with brick, and is very smooth. The whole traffic of the town, carried on in wheel-barrows, proceeds on the foot-pavement. Even in the best streets, the citizen must give way to the wheel-barrow. The foot-pavement is raised 6 or 8 inches above the carriage-way, and the barrows have a little wheel fixed on a sort of out-rigging in front, to enable them to mount up to the side-pavement after each crossing. In European cities, all vehicles are generally confined to the carriage-way.

Moyamensing Prison.—This is the name of the prison for the county of Philadelphia.—It is a modern structure, and consists of solitary cells in corridors 280 feet long and three storeys high. It is conducted on the same principles with the Eastern Penitentiary. The physician who kindly accompanied me in my visit assured me that the treatment pursued in these two prisons is not injurious to health. There are no baths, cold or warm, for the prisoners, and no yard for exercise. I should imagine a warm bath once a-week would produce, both morally and physically, a beneficial influence on these convicts. Their cells are thoroughly ventilated. There is an aperture in the wall on the level of the floor, communicating directly with the external atmosphere, for allowing the air to enter, and a hole in the opposite wall, just below the ceiling, for allowing it to escape into a ventilating chimney, which goes to the roof. The prisoners, however, on the different floors, contrive to converse and communicate through these lower openings. This prison also has a kind of water-closet in each cell.

Nothing has struck me more than the extensive want of this accommodation in the American cities. Every reproach ever heaped on Scotland for its barbarism in this respect, may now be transferred to the United States. Very few of the best hotels can boast of civilization in this particular ; and in Philadelphia, where there is abundance of water, there are sad deficien-

cies even in genteel houses. This want must be enumerated among the efficient and even important causes
of bad health. The most refined and sensitive individuals of both sexes suffer great inconvenience rather
than travel from twenty to fifty yards in the open air,
when the thermometer is at zero, or very little above
it; and to those who are labouring under intestinal
affections, exposure in these frozen regions is fraught
with the greatest dangers. I have heard physicians
of great experience lamenting the extent of suffering
that may be traced to this cause; yet they hesitate to
urge publicly means for removing it, through dread of
giving offence.

The Dangers of Riches.—In this city, refined, easy,
social intercourse, for the sake of relaxation and enjoyment, is rather limited. The dinner hour is two
or three o'clock. A hasty meal is swallowed, and the
merchant returns to his counting-house, the lawyer
to his briefs, and the physician to his routine of visits. Digestion is interrupted by this sudden return
to mental and bodily exertion, and dyspepsy extensively prevails. These various persons return home
to tea; but they have neither vivacity, ideas, nor feelings, for passing the evening in easy conversation.
They are pressed down in mind by a load of business
which they cannot throw off, or exhausted by labour
and bad digestion, so as to have little enjoyment in
society. There is no idle class to cultivate society
as an object. One family tried to have an easy party
once a-week, to keep open-house in the evening, but
the attempt was unsuccessful. For several weeks, a

few were induced to come, then they left off coming,
and so the experiment failed.   Some would not go,
just because it was an innovation, and because, by
staying away, they could disappoint the innovators,
and prevent them from establishing a practice which
every one might not be disposed to adopt.   If a young
man inherit a fortune and follow no profession, it generally happens that in less than ten years he ruins
his fortune in low pursuits.   In a few years more
his health is equally reduced with his estate, and he
is banished from society, or admitted only on suffe-
rance.   These young men are pitied, their fate is pre-
dicted, and the prophecies are too generally realized.
There is no class to sustain them in the condition
of idlers, and no sinecure offices for them in the institutions of the country.   The few who form exceptions to this rule are men of natural taste and refinement, who engage in literature or science as a pursuit.   These are esteemed happy.

April 11.   Ther. 60°.   *The Maine War.*—The
Monongahela packet-ship has just arrived at Philadelphia, and brings the " Liverpool Standard" of the
8th March.   This is the only communication from
England since the news of the vote of 50,000 volunteers reached that country, and the paper is read with
intense interest.   It ascribes the war to the Whig
ministry, and depicts to the Americans the certainty
of *their ruin,* if they go to war, just as the American
papers have been, for some time, exulting in the ruin
of England, as the consequence of hostilities.   It is
lamentable to see the two freest and most enlightened

nations of the world thus gloating over the prospect of each other's destruction, in consequence of a dispute about a piece of waste-land, which is not worth more in fee-simple than the value of two line-of-battle ships. It is said here that a million and a half of dollars would purchase the disputed territory out and out! The anxiety for the arrival of the Great Western, with official despatches, is great. Already the derangement in business, the fall of stocks and property, and the apprehensions of another bank-suspension in this city, have cast a gloom over society, and war is already deprecated by the multitude as earnestly as, a few weeks ago, it was invoked.

Pennsylvania University.—This University has published a catalogue of its students for the session 1838–9. In the Collegiate department it numbers 105 ; Medical 402 ; Academical 169 ; Charity (English) schools 128,—total 804.

Black-Foot Indians.—Mr Catlin has kindly presented me with two skulls of Black-Foot Indians, from the base of the Rocky Mountains, sent to him by Mr Mackenzie. They approach pretty closely to the Caucasian variety in form, but they are smaller than the skulls of the Anglo-Saxon race. The organs of Combativeness and Destructiveness are very large. The organs of Firmness and Veneration are large, while those of Benevolence and Conscientiousness are small. The anterior lobe devoted to intellect is pretty well developed. This combination indicates a ferocious, cruel, warlike disposition, the more formidable that the intellectual capacity is greater than in many of the Indian races. Dr Morton has not seen any of the skulls of this tribe, and I have lent them to him to be drawn for his work.

Dr Morton's Crania Americana.—Dr Morton shewed me the measurements of the coronal regions of a number of his skulls, taken by means of mercury by him and Mr Phillips. The points of Cautiousness and Causality had been correctly selected in all of them except one, and in it the two points of ossification of the frontal bone stood on different levels, and they had taken the lowest, thereby increasing the size of the coronal region. The organs of Self-Esteem and Love of Approbation are, of necessity, included in the measurements of the coronal region in all of them, because they could devise no means of cutting off the locality of these organs when they poured the mercury into the coronal region. Some of the skulls, which are very large at the organs of Self-Esteem, Love of Approbation, Veneration, and Firmness, but very deficient at the organs of Conscientiousness and Benevolence, shew, by measurement, an extraordinarily large size of the coronal region. The general measurement would lead to the inference of a pretty high development of the moral organs generally, while an inspection of the skulls shews that the large size proceeds from Self-Esteem, Love of Approbation, Veneration, and Firmness, which organs, acting with small Conscientiousness and small Benevolence, tend to increase the features of barbarism instead of diminishing them. In the skulls, the organs of Benevolence and Conscientiousness are almost uniformly shewn to be deficient. On the whole, however, the measurements, as reported, give a very fair idea, corresponding to that communicated by the eye, of the general magnitude of the coronal region. The eye detects the specific organs which are large or small, while the measurements give the aggregate only.

Phrenology.—Dr M'Clellan and his patient, mentioned in vol. i. p. 335, called on me to-day. The latter is now robust and in full health. The integuments of his head have united, all except a small point in the centre, into which a few hairs have grown. I felt the extent of the wound, and now perceived that the bone had been removed as far forward as near the anterior edge of Firmness, over the whole of Self-Esteem, and over great part of both organs of Love of Approbation. The tumour was not so extensive; but Dr M'Clellan says, that the skull was disorganized to this extent, and it was necessary to remove it. The integuments are very thick at present, and the young man says that the only inconvenience which he feels is that of a weight pressing on his head at that place. He mentioned that he was formerly bold and confident, but is now diffident and timid. He went lately to an artist to have a cast of his head taken, and shook with fear at the prospect of the process; yet he never felt alarm, and never winced, during the operation. He added, that he can still imitate and ventriloquize by himself, but he has not confidence to do so before any one. Is this change owing to any peculiar affection of the organs of Self-Esteem and Firmness, or is it the result of general nervous debility remaining after so severe an operation ? He confirmed what has already been stated,—that his self-confidence left him, as the tumour increased, before coming to Philadelphia, to have the operation performed.

International Law of Copyright.—The " New Yorker" of 30th March contains an able article on this subject. It shews pretty clearly that American authors can never expect to receive adequate remuneration for their works, as long as publishers are at liberty to pillage English literature at their discretion. It asserts what I know to be true, that if an extensive American publisher has stereotyped the first edition of a popular English work, he prevents the Americans from reading improved editions.*

Farther, the New Yorker acknowledges that the complaints of British authors are well founded, when they assert that " the works published in this country (the United States) under their names frequently are not, in reality, their proper works ; that their sentiments are often suppressed, their language modi-

---

* It was only after I had threatened to reprint the seventh English edition of Dr A. Combe's " Physiology applied to Health and Education," at my own expense, that Messrs Harper agreed to reprint it, and they then offered $100 to the author for the new matter, and also as a compensation for past, present, and all future sales of the work, of which offer the author accepted. I was assured that the sales of the first edition had exceeded 15,000 copies before I applied to them The New York newspapers are constantly celebrating their liberality to British authors, and no doubt this *was* an act of liberality, as they lay under no legal obligation to make any recompense whatever ; but the *magnitude* of it was not a matter to boast of.

fied, and that even that portion which is given to the public is so deformed by typographical inaccuracies as to prove seriously injurious to their reputation. These charges have not been denied, and for the best of reasons, because the truth is so notorious that the denial would be met by instant proof of the facts. Literary men are not ignorant of this, and, for their own security, will never quote from an American reprint, if the original work is to be had. Such are the works, often the mere husks of literature, that are presented to the American public.*

Spring.—The horse-chestnut trees are now in full leaf.

Pavements. — In Chestnut Street, the great thoroughfare of Philadelphia, part of the street has been Macadamised. At the end of the frost it stood in waves, from the unequal expansion of the ground in thawing. This is assigned by the Americans as their reason for not Macadamising their roads in general. At a subsequent date I visited Canada, and saw admirable Macadamised roads in the neighbourhood of Montreal and Quebec, and asked how they stood the thawing in spring? " Perfectly well." " How do you prevent them from being thrown up when the thaw

* This practice of mutilating books by American publishers is not confined to reprints of English works. In the " Memoirs of Benjamin Franklin," published by Messrs Harper in 1840, they have omitted three paragraphs of his autobiography, which appear in the English editions between the third and fourth paragraphs on page 61 of vol. i. of their work. The apology probably may be offered that their edition is part of their " Family Library," and that the passages suppressed relate to the amours'of Ralph and Franklin; but they should have given notice that an omission had been made.

comes?" " By laying the stones six or eight inches thicker than in England; so thick that the frost does not penetrate to the soft soil below." What is done in Canada, may be accomplished in the United States. Wooden pavement has also been tried in Chestnut Street. It answers extremely well; but the expense of it is complained of, as it is said to wear out in four years.

Queen Victoria.—The Amerians take a great interest in Queen Victoria, and forgive her royalty in consideration of her youth and sex. The print shops display the finest engravings of her imported from London; and an exhibition of a picture of her in Philadelphia (not Sully's) has attracted crowds of visiters for several weeks. It is the portrait of a pretty young woman, richly attired, with the insignia of royalty lying on a table beside her; but it has no other resemblance to the Queen. All the anecdotes about her Majesty are carefully copied from the English papers, and circulated by the press in the United States.

The American Phrenological Journal.—This periodical is published monthly in Philadelphia; each number consists of 32 pages 8vo, making a volume of 384 pages per annum. It was commenced on 1st October 1838, and has all along been ably conducted. It now boasts of a circulation of nearly 1200 copies. The editor is a native of New England, a man of talent, industry, and high moral character, and he has impressed these qualities on his work. He is now studying medicine in this city. The Journal is doing great service to the cause of Phrenology in the United States.*

Phrenology.—In Philadelphia, New York, and Boston, there are shops in which Phrenological casts are extensively sold. Messrs Fowler are in the United States what Mr Deville is in London. They have devoted themselves to the practical department of the science, and have large and valuable collections for sale, both in New York and Philadelphia.

The Insane Poor of Pennsylvania.—A committee of the House of Representatives, to whom were referred the petitions relative to an asylum for the insane poor, have reported that, by information derived from about half the counties in the State, it was ascertained, that, in a population of about 800,000, there are upwards of 1100 insane persons, including congenital idiots and those rendered fatuous by disease ; whence it is inferred, that in Pennsylvania at large, there is a total of 2300 insane and idiotic poor. Nearly two-thirds of this number are in the worst circumstances ; " and probably not less than a thousand of those unfortunates are kept in county poor-houses and prisons, or in families at auction-prices.† Not being subjected to medical or moral treatment, recovery under these circumstances is very rare, from

* The price of this Journal in Philadelphia is $ 2 per annum for one copy, or $ 5 for three copies. It may be ordered in London through Messrs Wiley and Putnam, American booksellers, Paternoster Row; but it must in all cases be *prepaid.* There is a small additional charge for the conveyance to London.

† This means, that the poor are boarded out at so much a year to those who will take them at the cheapest rate.

five to eight in a hundred being an extremely favourable estimate."

The following extracts from the committee's report shew the hardships to which these unhappy
beings are exposed :—

" In one county, of forty persons more or less deranged, seven
are confined in cells, which are nearly if not quite under ground.
They may be seen from without through iron bars in the cellar
windows.   Among them is a German girl, twenty years old,
seemingly in perfect health of body, with beautiful teeth and
hair, and without any symptoms of malignity, who has been in
such a cell five months, and considered as incurable.   This interesting case, under treatment for a few months in a proper
insane hospital, would probably result in a complete restoration
to reason and liberty.

" Several other like cases are described, and all these, we are
told, ' are shut up under bolts and bars, neglected and almost
forgotten, with no friendly voice to break the silence of their
solitude ; and presented, one and all, the same revolting picture
of suffering.'

" In another county ' a man, thirty-five years old, had been confined for years in a miserable shed ; when the bolt was drawn
and the door opened, he was lying on the floor among straw, no
bed was to be seen though it was cold weather, and we had to
plunge through snow which had fallen the day previous to get
to his wretched abode.'

" ' In another county a woman of thirty-five was confined in
like manner till she raved herself to death.'

" While decided testimony is given to the good keeping and
treatment of paupers generally, it is added that ' the poor lunatics are found with the feet chained together, or chained by the
body to iron weights, logs of wood, or to the trunks of trees, or,
what is more common, under ground, without ventilation, and
breathing an air loaded with intolerable stench.' "

Frightful as this picture is, I am old enough to

recollect a parallel to it existing in the city of Edinburgh; but Scotland has now wiped off this stain from her moral reputation. Dr Dunglisson, and other medical writers, have laboured zealously to free Pennsylvania from the disgrace of such scenes, and the committee have reported a bill for the erection of a proper asylum at the expense of the Commonwealth.*

April 12. *New York.*—I went to New York to-day to prepare for my second course of lectures in that city. The new railroad by Trenton is now open. The cars started at half-past eight, and at three P.M. we arrived at New York without detention or accident. The cars from Philadelphia to Trenton had apertures at the top for ventilation; those from Trenton to Jersey city carried fifty passengers each, and had no provision for ventilation. A window on my left side was opened. In consequence of the exposure to the stream of cold air which it admitted, and which was indispensable to breathing, I lost the power of hearing in my left ear, and did not recover it for six months.

New York Civic Election.—The election of mayor and councillors for the city of New York has just terminated. The democratic party have turned the

* The bill passed both houses of the Legislature, but in the beginning of 1840 it was negatived by Governor Porter from dire necessity. The State had not means to pay the expenses of its own government and the interest of its debt, and he regarded these as more urgent claims than the building of an asylum. It is hoped that Pennsylvania will speedily recover from this depression, and that this asylum will not be forgotten.

whigs out of office, and are now celebrating their triumph. This is a revolution in public sentiment which has excited great astonishment.

April 13. The election is the universal subject of conversation. The "Morning Herald," a whig news-paper conducted by James Gordon Bennett, a Scots-man, characterized by great talent, but of about the same standing in moral reputation with "The Age" in London, thus describes the closing scene. The description, although coarse and caricatured, repre-sents correctly the *spirit* of the party, and Bennett's usual style of writing :—

" The locofocos are triumphant at every point, laughing at every corner of their infernal mouths, and shaking their sides till they almost shake the ' duds' off their limbs. At the close of the polls on Thursday night, the devil, knowing what he had been about, also began to rejoice, and accordingly let out one of the prettiest north-eastern rain storms that ever gave hundreds the consumption, and thousands the *ennui* and blue devils. But what cared the locofocos for rain, or getting wet ? When they get to their comfortable quarters in another region hereafter, they will have time to dry their ragged, dripping breeches before the flames of the fire that never dies. Tammany Hall, and all the neighbourhood, never was in such an ecstasy of delight. The whole myriads of locofocos, as numerous as the locusts of Egypt, were in perfect ecstasies throughout the city yesterday. ' Rain, blow, pelt,' cried they, ' who cares ? we have licked the damned whigs, and that's enough.' "

There, is a general admission that, on this occasion, disgraceful means have been resorted to by both par-ties to gain the election. There is no registry of voters in this city, and the title of every one who claims to vote is determined at the poll. Citizenship and residence are the chief qualifications. It is said that great numbers of foreigners have been admitted to the franchise, by one of the courts of law, without the legal qualifications.   It is even asserted that the emigrants by their votes govern the city, to the exclusion of the natives; and a longer residence is insisted on as a title to citizenship.   Frauds have been committed also on the law which requires residence in a *ward* as a qualification to vote.   When a party has had a supernumerary strength of legal voters in one ward, but been weak in another it has removed a portion of its numbers from the strong ward to sleep a single night in the weak ward; they have appeared at the polls in this ward the next day, have sworn that they were residents in it, voted, and immediately returned home.   This violated the spirit, but not the letter of the law, and is named " colonizing."   The virtuous men of both parties admit that there must be an end of all this fraud, or the ballot-box will be a mere farce; they say that, otherwise, " he who can cheat most, raise the most money, buy and colonize most, will carry the day."   There are strong calls for a registry law.

These contests, conducted without reference to moral principle demoralize all classes, and inflict a lasting injury on a republic which has no anchorage for its institutions except the virtue of its citizens. To act immorally in elections is to commit treason against the country.   Indeed it is almost the only form in which an American can commit this crime.*

* While I thus severely condemn these republican immoralities, I must at the same time do justice to the American institutions, and mention that, before the subsequent election, a very stringent law was passed to cure these evils, and that both parties admitted that

General Winfield Scott.—This officer gave the most unequivocal proofs of courage and military talents in the last war with England on the Canadian frontier. He is a man of an active mind and commanding presence, and crowns all these accomplishments by dispositions remarkably humane and just. He has been selected by the President to make a temporary arrangement with Sir John Harvey for preserving peace on the Maine boundary, until the resolutions of the British and American Governments shall be finally taken. He has succeeded in this mission. His correspondence with Sir John Harvey has been published, and is distinguished by business talent and a fine moral tone. This adjustment has given much satisfaction in New York. Some of General Scott's admirers insist on his being put in nomination for the Presidentship. Judging from the principles on which he acts, and his power of carrying other minds into his measures by means of reason and moral suasion, he certainly possesses in a high degree some of the qualities which should adorn an American President. At a subsequent period, I had the pleasure of being introduced to him, and all my prepossessions in his favour were confirmed by the personal interview. Many individuals and newspapers, that had not moral courage to

it had produced the desired effect: Farther, before I left the United States, a registry law was passed for the city of New York, which will render a recurrence of them impossible. Thus, while we lament the aberrations of the Americans, we must not shut our eyes to their tendency to rectify their own errors, and correct their own derelictions of duty.

advocate peace directly, did so indirectly by their high eulogiums on General Scott's pacific dispositions and talents for adjusting disputes by frank honesty and reason.

Phrenology.—I gave the first lecture of my second course this evening in the Stuyvesant Institute.

April 15. *Maine War.*—The Great Western, which sailed from Bristol on 23d March, has arrived after a long and very rough passage. The English have taken the belligerent demonstrations of the Americans very coolly, and do not return the threats of war. This has caused great joy here, and stocks have risen. The news, however, of the act of Congress authorizing the enlistment of 50,000 volunteers had not reached London when the Great Western sailed, and there is still some anxiety to learn the effect of that measure on John Bull.

April 18. Ther. 45°. The weather is cold and rainy. Vegetation is from ten to fourteen days later in New York than in Philadelphia.

Sing-Sing State Prison.—A report of a committee of the Legislature on this prison has been printed. It discloses great abuses. The inspectors have neglected their duty, and the superintendent is said to have erected his will into a law, to have jobbed the supply of provisions, and the sales of the products of the convicts' labour for his own benefit, applied the scourge abundantly, and rendered the prison a scene of tyranny and peculation. He, however, has published a letter in which he designates the investigation as having been *secret and inquisitorial ;* charges the witnesses with perjury, and announces that he has petitioned the Legislature to send a committee to re-examine the charges *openly*, giving him an opportunity of confronting the witnesses.

Auburn State Prison.—Similar charges are made against the management of this prison. Louis Von Eck, a convict, has died in it, and a coroner's inquest has been held on his body. The following facts are reported in the Auburn Journal and Advertiser.

" Von Eck was born in Germany, and after having received a liberal education, he took a medical degree at the University of Gottingen. He then proceeded to Cuba, where he for some time practised his profession ; and at length removed to one of the southern states, and married the daughter of Colonel ———, of the U. S. army. Thus far all things had gone comparatively well with him—but behold a change. Travelling north a few months ago, he fell into company with a set of blacklegs and sharpers, by whom he was induced to present a counterfeit check at the counter of one of the Buffalo banks. His old associates turned witnesses against him, and the poor fellow, who but a short time before was able to look upon every thing as bright and cheering, was now doomed to the habitation of a dreary cell, under circumstances the most trying and most humiliating. He was, we believe, about 28 years of age."

The verdict of the inquest is as follows :—" The jury being sworn and charged to inquire, on the part of the people of the said State, when, where, how, and after what manner the said Louis Von Eck came to his death, do say upon their oaths aforesaid, that the said Louis Von Eck, a convict in the Auburn State Prison, and a German by birth, came to his death on Monday, the 8th day of April inst., while in the prison hospital, from disease ; the fatal termination of which was hastened by flogging, labour, and general harsh treatment, imposed by the agent, Elam Lynds, and Galen O. Weed, one of the keepers, and also by inexcusable neglect and want of proper care on the part of the physician, Lansingh Briggs, who reported him from time to time as well, when actually sick."*

April 19. Ther. 48°. *The Election.*—This evening the democratic party celebrated its triumph with processions, banners, transparencies, illuminations, squibs and crackers. Every thing passed off without disorder.

April 21. Ther. 37°. *Sunday.*—I heard the Rev. Mr Dewey preach an excellent sermon, in which he spoke freely and decidedly against the late manifestations of the national spirit for war, and reproved the corruptions practised at the last election. He depicted the immorality of war; but said that, when a people is absorbed in a sordid love of gain,—when its political institutions are defiled by perjury and bribery,—war, with all its horrors, will be a less evil than the natural fruits of such a social condition. This is a striking proof that, under the voluntary system, a preacher is not necessarily led to gloss over the imperfections of his flock.

Dr Channing's Answer to Mr Clay's Speech.—Dr Channing has addressed and published a letter to Jonathan Phillips, Esq., in answer to Mr Clay's speech on slavery. It is exciting much attention, and is an admirable production. It is full of the eloquence and energy of the moral sentiments. He introduces a powerful rebuke of the Philadelphians for burning Pennsylvania Hall because abolition meet-

* Before I left the United States, the officers of Sing-Sing and Auburn prisons, implicated in these charges, had either "resigned" or been removed,—another proof of the speedy remedies applied to public abuses under this Government.

ings were held in it.   The Philadelphians are beginning to be ashamed of that outrage.

April 22.   Ther. 43°.   *Universalists.*—The Rev.
Mr Ballou, a Universalist minister from Boston,
preached here yesterday, and denied the existence
of the devil, and of eternal punishment.   Bennett's
newspaper deprecates such doctrines as extremely
dangerous ; for, if they be believed, there will be no
check on the " Loco Focos," and the Wall Street
brokers !

April 23.   Ther. 51°.   *Tit for Tat.—The Chartists.*
—As a set-off against the charges made by the English
press against the Americans for their mob atrocities,
the papers here are recording the precautions of the
British Ministry against the Chartists.   It is said
that large bodies of horse, foot, and artillery, and a
rocket brigade, have been sent into the manufacturing
districts of England to prevent an expected appeal
to arms by these men.   In the United States no
risings of the people in arms are necessary to obtain a redress of grievances.   They accomplish their
sovereign will quietly through the ballot-boxes.   In
England the masses are so untrained to freedom
that universal suffrage would lead to revolution ; but
their entire exclusion from all control over the Government is attended with great evils.   British legislation is partial to the higher and middle classes,
and, in many particulars, unjust to the people.   If
the latter were allowed to send fifty representatives to the House of Commons, their grievances
would be proclaimed and remedied.   They might be

authorized to elect delegates by whom the direct nomination of the representatives should be effected.
By some such machinery, they might be permitted to
wield a reasonable degree of influence over the Legislature without introducing the evils of universal suffrage. The chief recommendation of universal suffrage in America is its effect in forcing the more enlightened members of the community to exert themselves earnestly to instruct and improve the masses
for their own protection. We want such an influence
in Britain very much; and a limited and indirect representation of the people would be more effectual,
and far more desirable, than armed insurrections.
The latter probably will never cease until the former be granted.

The Licentiousness of the Press.—The following
paragraph, taken from " The Boston Transcript," is
another example of reprisals :—" We had heard and read
much of the licentiousness of the public press of London, but
had no adequate idea of its infamous extent, until we received a
short time since, from a friend in London, who sent them to us
to enlighten our ignorance, six or seven copies each of ' The
Crim. Con. Gazette,' and ' The Bon Ton Gazette,' papers which
are sold openly in the streets for a penny a copy, and of which
thousands are circulated daily. The contents of these papers
are so disgusting, that we found it next to impossible to read
them. We do not believe that we could have made, from the
whole lot, half a column of extracts, that any Boston publisher
or editor would dare to lay before his readers. And this is the
garbage on which the minds of tens of thousands of the inhabitants of London feed daily."

The Park Theatre.—When we arrived in New
York in September last, the public gave Mr Wallack,

the manager of the Park Theatre, a complimentary benefit at $3 for each ticket to all parts of the house. On the 19th of April, they gave him another benefit at the same rate, and on both occasions the theatre is reported to have been crowded.

April 24.   Ther. 56°.   *High Prices of Provisions.* There are great complaints in the eastern cities of the high prices of provisions, particularly of beef. In Philadelphia it costs from 8d. to 9d. a pound, and in New York from 9d. to 10d.   Various causes are assigned for this unusual state of the markets. It is said by some that in 1836–7 the mania for speculation had so completely seized all classes, that even the farmers were affected by it, and abandoned tillage for trafficking in shares and lots, in consequence of which there is now a real scarcity of farm produce. Others say that, for many years past, cattle were reared and fattened in the west, then sent to the Atlantic cities, and sold cheaper there than they could be reared on the eastern border ; that this led to the neglect of grazing in the east ; that the west has now become so densely peopled that it consumes all its own câttle, and that this is the cause of the scarcity in the eastern cities.

April 25.   Ther. 58°.   *Female Seminary for Education.*—I had the pleasure of meeting a lady who is well known in this and the neighbouring States for her success in female education.   She mentioned that Dr A. Combe's " Physiology applied to Health and Education," and my work on " The Constitution of Man," have been regularly taught by her to her pupils for some years ; and that, with a few expla-

nations, they readily understand both, and take a
great interest in them. The young ladies range from
nine to fifteen years of age.

*Should British Dissenting Clergymen Emigrate to
America ?*—This question is often put by letters to
the American clergy, and personally to individuals
who have visited the United States. My advice to
them is to let well alone, and stay in their own country, if they can obtain a decent livelihood. A clergyman must be born and " reared" in the United
States to fit him for his situation and duties. The
deficiency of domestic service,—the high rents and
exorbitant prices of most manufactured and imported
articles in the cities,—the limited extent of social
habits,—the arduous labour,—the strict surveillance
exercised by society over official persons,—and the
overwhelming force of public opinion,—render the
United States no paradise to well educated men accustomed to social life in Britain.

April 26. Ther. 57°. *Extension of New York
City*.—The speculative mania which seized this
people in 1836 has left traces which it will require
several years to obliterate. Large tracts of ground
cleared and levelled for building lie waste at the
north end of the city, waiting for the extension of
the population. It is probable that more money has
been lost and won in speculation on these " lots,"
than would have sufficed to cover them all with buildings. There is a substratum of truth in Cooper's descriptions of the scenes that occurred at that time,
in his novel, " Home as Found:"—" ' Can you tell us the
history of this particular piece of property, Mr Hammer ?' said

John Effingham to one of the most considerable auctioneers.
' With great pleasure, Mr Effingham ; we know you have means,
and hope you may be induced to purchase. This was the farm
of old Volkert Van Brunt,—five years' since,—off which he and
his family had made a livelihood for more than a century, by
selling milk. Two years since, the sons sold it to Peter Feeler
for a hundred dollars an acre ; or for the total sum of 5000 dollars. The next spring Mr Feeler sold it to John Search, as keen
a one as we have, for 25,000. Search sold it at private sale to Na-
thaniel Rise for 50,000 the next week, and Rise had parted with
it to a company, before the purchase, for 112,000 cash. The map
ought to be taken down, for it is now eight months since we sold
it out in lots, at auction, for the gross sum of 300,000 dollars.'
*   *   *   ' And on what is this enormous increase in value
founded ?   Does the town extend to these fields ?'—' It goes
much farther, Sir ; that is to say, on paper. In the way of
houses, it is still some miles short of them. A good deal depends on what you *call* a thing in this market. Now, if old Volkert Van Brunt's property had been still called a farm, it would
have brought a farm price ; but as soon as it was surveyed into
lots, and mapped——' —' Mapped !'—' Yes, Sir, brought into
visible lines, with feet and inches. As soon as it was properly
mapped, it rose to its just value. We have a good deal of the
bottom of the sea that brings fair prices in consequence of being
well mapped.' "

I was long puzzled to discover what this last statement, about selling " the bottom of the sea" at fair
prices, alluded to, until I saw a large map of Man-
hattan Island in an apartment of the State House,
New York ; and sure enough a number of lots appear
on it extended into the sea, at New York city, Brook-
lyn and Haerlem.   These are intended for wharves,
and were favourite subjects of speculation under the
name of " water lots."

We may laugh at the Americans for these follies,

but in 1814–15 they were equalled in Leith in sugar speculations, and in Edinburgh in 1824 in building and joint-stock company adventures.

American Judges.—This evening I had the pleasure of meeting with three distinguished men who have held, or now hold, the office of judges, and they seemed to me to be well qualified to command respect in any country.   One of them told me that the abolition of imprisonment for debt for small sums had produced excellent effects in the State of New York ; that subsequently the measure had been extended to all sums, and he thought that the abolition, when thus extended, had encouraged gambling speculations and fraud.

Spring.—We had a drive to-day into the country on the middle road, and returned by the Bloomingdale road.   The fruit trees are in full blossom, and the forest trees are fast bursting.   Spring proceeds with extraordinary rapidity, but I miss the sweet carolling of the lark which cheers the British spring. Here the groves are silent ; but the plumage of the feathered race is strikingly beautiful in its colours.

The Cause of the High Prices of Provisions.—The editor of " The Pennsylvanian" says that the disease of America " is the credit system."   " We have become a nation of speculators.   The whole mass of society is affected with the gambling spirit ; and in the pursuit of a royal road to wealth, while the head works, the hands are idle.   Men will not stay to dig and to delve when impressed with the conviction that city loans or new lands will convert them into nabobs." " The disease must work out its own cure." " When men find that all cannot be rich, that speculation and this massive emigration are merely a feverish mania, and that farming and grazing for the supply of large cities, form a sure and profitable business, then, and probably not till then, will provisions be sold at reasonable rates, and preserve some degree of steadiness." This, as already mentioned, is a democratic paper, but in no country could the press address the people in bolder or sounder terms than these. The heat of last summer (1838) was excessive in the United States, which rendered provender deficient in quantity, and this also must have had a great effect on the supply, and consequently on the price, of cattle.

April 28. Ther. 60°. I heard the Rev. Dr Hawkes, Episcopalian, preach a highly evangelical discourse to a large and genteel congregation.

April 29. Ther. 55°. *The Asylum for Coloured Orphans.*—To-day we visited the Asylum in Twelfth Street for coloured orphan children. It was opened in July 1837, and is managed by ladies. It contains between fifty and sixty negro children, of both sexes, from five or six to twelve or thirteen years of age. They are clothed, fed, boarded, and taught ; and although the building is too small for so great a number, it is kept in excellent order. The children are taught on the infant school system, and performed their exercises well. They have play-ground behind, and are encouraged to take abundance of exercise. One little child, born in slavery, and recently liberated

and sent to the asylum, presented a more stupid
aspect than the others sprung from free parents.
This may have been the result of its condition in
slavery, without intelligent companions, or other stimulants to its mental faculties.   In the course of my
inquiries, I learned that a considerable number of
deaths had occurred within the first two years.   The
disease in a majority of cases was scrofula in one or
other of its varied forms.   It was ascribed to the
scanty and improper diet of the children before admission, and to the insufficiency of nutriment contained in the regular but light food supplied in the
asylum.   For some time no animal food was allowed,
and Indian corn, meal, and brown bread made of rye
and unbolted wheaten flour, were among other things
largely used.   One of the consequences of this kind
of diet was inordinate irritation of the mucous mem-
brane of the bowels, and almost constant diarrhœa.
The orphans were so enfeebled, that many sunk under the acute and epidemic, or contagious diseases
peculiar to childhood, which more robust children
would have passed through in safety.   Both the managers and physician became convinced of the necessity of improving the diet of the establishment.
A change was accordingly made in this respect, as
well as in others of equal importance, and was followed by a remarkable improvement in the health of
the children.   Animal food is now used four times
a week in a solid form, and twice in soup.   White
bread, rice and milk, the vegetables of the season,
&c. are abundantly supplied.   It is now a year since

there has been a death in the asylum, where no less than fifteen deaths occurred during the preceding eighteen months. This extraordinary exemption from mortality is not ascribed to change of diet only, but to this and other ameliorations of perhaps greater importance, introduced by the enlightened and bene-volent managers of the asylum. The experiment, however, has been repeatedly made of going back from the better to the poorer kinds of food, and uni-formly with injurious consequences.*

* These particulars are extracted from a letter dated 19th May 1840, addressed to me by Dr James Macdonald, the physician to the asylum, who kindly permitted me to publish them, as they may prove useful to the managers of similar institutions in other parts of the United States. In Britain also they will not be uninstructive. In-deed I perceive that they confirm the views taken of the subject in two instructive articles published in Chambers's Edinburgh Journal on 2d and 19th February 1839. In 1838 fifty of the children in St Cuthbert's Charity Workhouse, Edinburgh, or nearly one-fourth of the whole number, were seized with severe and intractable ophthal-mia, which in several cases ended in impaired vision. From November 1837 till June 1838, seventeen died of pulmonary consumption ; se-venty were seized with hooping-cough, and there were thirty-six cases of fever. In June seventeen were " afflicted with numerous scro-fulous ulcers." Two eminent physicians reported that " the general aspect of a great number of the children not labouring under actual disease is not satisfactory, but is indicative of a feeble, unhealthy state of the constitution, which may lay the foundation of disease in after life." They traced the evil to scanty diet and deficient cloth-ing. Messrs Chambers justly remark that " the want of variety is a prevalent error in public asylums. The managers of such institutions might effect a great improvement in this respect with little or no ad-dition to the expense." 'In St Cuthbert's Charity Workhouse an im-provement in the diet was followed by a diminished mortality among the inmates. In England an opposite error has been committed. In the workhouse of St Lawrence the paupers become ill from too high feeding. This error is likely to be committed in the United States, where provisions are cheap.

April 30. Ther. 54°. *General Washington's first Presidency.*—This day the Historical Society of New York celebrated the fiftieth anniversary of the inauguration of General Washington as President of the United States, on 30th April 1789. Deputations of learned men assembled from various parts of the Union to attend the ceremony. The meeting, which was held in the middle Dutch church, was opened with prayer ; an ode written by Mr Bryant was sung by the choir, and then Mr John Quincy Adams delivered an " oration." By a very proper arrangement, ladies and the gentlemen who accompanied them were admitted first, and afterwards the doors were opened to gentlemen. Being unaccompanied by a lady, I obtained a place only in the second pew from the front of the gallery, far from the speaker. A young American, with a quid of tobacco in his cheek, who sat before me, put his feet on the seat of the pew, and sat on the board that holds the bibles, in front of the gallery, and effectually cut off every possibility of my seeing Mr Adams, and the distance prevented me from hearing him. I sat upwards of an hour without having caught one sentence of the " oration," which, from its effects on the audience, appeared to be eloquent. Mr Bryant's ode was as follows :—

> " Great were the hearts, and strong the minds
> Of those who framed, in high debate,
> The immortal league of love that binds
> Our fair broad empire State with State.
>
> " And ever hallowed be the hour,
> When, as the auspicious task was done,

A nation's gift, the sword of power,
  Was given to Glory's unspoiled son.

" That noble race is gone ; the suns
  Of fifty years have risen and set ;
The holy links these mighty ones
  Had forged and knit, are brighter yet.

" Wide—as our own free race increase—
  Wide shall it stretch the elastic chain ;
And bind in everlasting peace,
  State after State, a mighty train."

The day was concluded by a grand public dinner of the Historical Society.

From the reports of the oration, I afterwards discovered that it was essentially a historical *resumé* of the political history of the United States.

" Never," says Mr Adams, " since the creation of the globe, has such a continuous scene of prosperity and glory blessed any people as was conferred by the constitution. Yet it was most obstinately and pertinaciously contested. Never did human foresight so completely fail as in the doubts entertained of its success. Nor Washington nor Hamilton dared to hope that it would act so well in practice as it has done. Between the 4th of March and 14th of April 1789, Washington wrote thus to Knox :—' This delay is to me in the light of a reprieve ; my feelings are like those of a culprit going to the place of execution. Without the requisite political skill, to be taken thus in the evening of life from the quiet scenes of domestic felicity, and required to take the helm of affairs and guide this untried and doubtful machine, leaves me small hope of success. I am embarking my good name in a shallow bark on an unknown and tempestuous sea ; but be the voyage long or short, two things, my integrity and firmness, shall never forsake me. Whether I succeed or fail, please or displease upon other points, these the world can never deprive me of.'

" Opposed to him and his principles were many eminent patriots of the Revolution. They rallied under the flag of State rights; their cry was for unlimited state sovereignty, and un-limited state independency, not amenable to the Union. These denounced the best men of the day, with Washington at their head, as federalists and tories. He was embarking upon this troublous sea a good name, unparalleled in the annals of history. In his Diary he says, ' About 10 o'clock I bade adieu to Mount Vernon, to private life and domestic felicity.' Yet he was deceived. His progress from Mount Vernon to New York was one continuous triumphant procession. All ages, both sexes, all conditions of persons, turned out to greet their friend and preserver, and demonstrate their enthusiastic admiration of him. In passing over the Schuylkill bridge a wreath of flowers was, unconsciously to himself, dropped on his head by a bloom-ing boy placed in a triumphal arch above him. At Trenton a band of aged matrons turned out to welcome and thank him for his defence of their property, their persons, their all—thirteen years before. The virgin daughters of those mothers strewed his path with flowers, and with a song as sublime as that of Miriam hailed him as their protector who had been the defender of their mothers.

" It is delightful to look back upon the long vista of fifty years, and see all the bright visions of hope formed by those good men more than realized; and all their despondency and doubts more than dispelled."

CHAPTER VI.

1839.

May 1. Ther. 61°. *Judge Darlington.*—The 29th
of April was fixed for giving judgment in the action
of *quo warranto* at the instance of Mr Johnson, the
Attorney-General of Pennsylvania, against Judge Darlington, for the purpose of trying the validity of his
renewed commission, mentioned on p. 177 of this volume ; but he died on the 27th of April ; and the action has dropped !

Rent and Taxes in New York.—A comfortable
family-house, of about twenty-five feet in front, and
from forty to forty-five feet in depth, consisting of
kitchen, dining-room, drawing-room, and bed-room
floors, in a medium situation, lets at $800, or L.160
of rent, and pays about $80 per annum of taxes.

The Erie Canal.—This Canal, which connects Lake Erie with New York, through the medium of the Hudson River, although only begun in 1817, has already proved too small for the extent of trade which passes through it, and a vivid discussion is proceeding in the Legislature about widening and deepening it, and constructing double sets of locks, so that the stream of boats may never be interrupted except by frost. This extraordinary increase of traffic has been caused by the rapid development of the population and resources of the western parts of the State of New York, consisting of a vast extent of rich alluvial soil now nearly all cleared and settled; and also by the rapid advance in wealth and population of the states which border on the great western Lakes. The town of Buffalo, in the State of New York, is situated at the terminus of the canal where it enters Lake Erie. It has a spacious harbour, in which may be seen three-masted vessels, brigs, schooners, and from fifteen to twenty large steam-boats, all plying an active trade.

" The property from other States passing into the Erie Canal by Buffalo increased as follows in the last four years :

1835............22,124 tons.	1837,............42,229 tons.
1836,............36,273 ...	1838,.......... 98,187 ...

" The merchandise passing to the West from Buffalo, was

1835,............18,466 tons.	1837,............22,236 tons.
1836,............30,874 ...	1838,............32,087 ...

" The amount of wheat and flour, those great articles of Western produce, increased steadily from 15,935 tons, in 1835, to 57,979 tons in 1838."*

* Report by Mr Verplanck to the Senate of New York State.

It is only by contemplating such facts as these that one can form a conception of the extraordinary rapidity with which the Western States are rising in population, industry, and wealth.

Female Lecturer on Physiology.—Mrs Gove, a lady belonging to the Society of Friends, impressed with the great importance to the female sex of instruction in anatomy and physiology, pursued a regular course of study in these subjects, under the Professors of Boston, and then commenced lecturing on them to ladies. She was well received in Boston, and has recently lectured in New York. She is a lady of unquestioned character, and her lectures were attended by most respectable persons of her own sex in this city. No gentlemen were admitted. The advantages of this instruction are self-evident, and every real friend to human welfare must wish her success ; Bennett's " Morning Herald," however, to its own deep disgrace, has published what he pretends to be reports of her lectures, pandering to the grovelling feelings of the men, and alarming the delicacy of the ladies,—an effectual way, in this country, to stifle any new attempt at improvement. I have inquired into the character of the lectures, of ladies who heard them, and they declare Bennett's report to be scandalous caricatures, misrepresentations, and inventions.

May 2. Ther. 65°. *Dr Channing on War.*—One of the excellent qualities of Dr Channing is his moral intrepidity. There never was a more sincere devotee

to truth than this excellent man ; and not content
with enjoying it himself, he comes forth to apply it to
practical use, on all occasions when legitimate opportunities occur. No one who has not visited the United
States, and witnessed the prostration even of powerful minds before public opinion, can form an adequate conception of the extent of Dr Channing's moral courage. Generally, when the public mind goes
farthest wrong, it burns with the intensest vivacity,
and displays the most formidable unanimity. Its
ordinary leaders shrink from addressing it when thus
excited. Dr Channing, on the contrary, on such occasions comes forth in dauntless might. He has
just published a sermon on war, delivered in the beginning of last year, with a preface adapting it to the
present crisis. It is calculated to have the best effect in bringing the minds of the people to reason,
and amply supports Dr Channing's high reputation.
He rebukes the war-spirit of the Americans in the
following forcible language. " Can we hope that liberal
principles and institutions, unsanctioned, unsustained by the
Christian spirit, will ensure peace ? What teaches our own experience ? Because free, have we no wars ? What indeed is the
free spirit of which we so much boast ? Is it not much more a
jealousy of our own rights, than a reverence for the rights of
all ? Does it not consist with the infliction of gross wrongs ?
Does it not spoil the Indian ? Does it not enslave the African ? Is it not anxious to spread bondage over new regions ?
Who can look on this free country, distracted by parties, rent
by local jealousies, in some districts administering justice by
mobs, and silencing speech and the press by conflagration and
bloodshed ; who can see this free country, and say, that liberal
opinions and institutions are of themselves to banish war ? No-

where are the just, impartial, disinterested principles of Christianity so much needed as in a free state. Nowhere are there more elements of strife to be composed, more passions to be curbed, more threatened wrongs to be repressed. Freedom has its perils as well as inestimable blessings. In loosening outward restraints, it demands that justice and love be enthroned within man's soul. Without Christian principle, freedom may swell the tide of tumults and war," p. 30.

Lord Brougham on the Maine Boundary.—Lord Brougham, in his place in the House of Peers and in reference to the Maine boundary dispute, is reported to have said, " He had the consolation of believing, of being convinced, that we were undeniably, clearly, and manifestly in the wrong ; and when a man or a nation was in the wrong, to acknowledge error did not make the case of either worse." The Americans are highly commending this acknowledgment. In a company to-day, I heard the speech discussed, when a sagacious old gentleman said, " I wish that an honester man had said so, and it would have served us more !" This remark terminated the conversation.

May 4. Ther. 43°. *Spring.*—The peach, pear, and apple trees, are profusely covered with blossoms ; the foliage of the forest trees is partially unfolded, but there are no " gowans" to deck the ground in this country.

Protection to Negroes.—The House of Assembly has passed a bill to secure a trial by jury to " alleged fugitives from service in other States,"—*anglice*, slaves, before being delivered up to their masters. The claimant must prove to the satisfaction of the jury, " the identity and escape of the alleged fugitive," who shall " be defended by counsel at the expense of the State." The bill enacts, that " the alleged fugitive shall be entitled to subpœnas for his witnesses without any charge ; constables serving the same shall have their fees from the county ;" and " every witness summoned shall be bound to attend without fees, as in criminal cases. No claimant shall have a writ to arrest a fugitive from labour, until he shall have filed, in the office of the county clerk, a bond in the penalty of $ 1000, with two sureties, conditioned to pay all costs and expenses legally chargeable against him ; also the sum of $ 2 per week for the support of the fugitive while in custody ; also all expenses of the fugitive in case the decision shall be against the claimant ; and also the sum of $ 100 to the alleged fugitive and his damages." The bond may be prosecuted " by any person claiming benefit from its provisions, in the name of the people ; but the people shall not be liable to costs in such suit."

This bill does credit to the House of Assembly of New York.

Public Defaulters.—The newspapers teem with instances of cashiers, tellers, and directors of banks committing enormous frauds, embezzling funds, sending false certificates of deposit into circulation, and so forth. While we were in Philadelphia, Dr Dyott was tried, found guilty, and sentenced to the Moyamensing prison for fraudulent bankruptcy, committed by him on a gigantic scale as a banker. A committee of the Legislature of Michigan has just investigated the affairs of the bank of Ypsilanti, and reported, " that they consider the failure of the bank an instance of as glaring a fraud as was ever perpetrated in this or any other community"—and, in conclusion, report a bill for the repeal of the charter of the said bank.

Slavery, Emancipation, and Colonization.—A correspondence has appeared in the New York Journal of Commerce, between the Rev. Benjamin Tappan

of Augusta, Maine, and F. S. Key, Esq., a lawyer of
Washington, on the subjects of Slavery, Colonization, and Emancipation. The letters are written in
an excellent spirit, and Mr Key describes the state
of slavery in impartial terms. They should be read
by every one who desires to form a correct idea of
the difficulties which beset slave-owners, even of the
most humane and upright dispositions, in accomplishing abolition. I regard them as so important that
I print them in the Appendix, No. V. Mr Key mentions that in Maryland slave-labour has ceased to
be profitable, because free-labour from Pennsylvania
flows over into it, and is better and cheaper. The
Legislature has repeatedly contemplated abolishing
slavery, and at no distant period will do so. Slavery
cannot permanently exist in a State bordering on a
free State. When Maryland has freed her slaves,
Virginia, after a few years, will be compelled to follow her example, by two causes, 1st, The slaves will
escape easily ; and 2dly, Free-labour will come in and
displace them. He contemplates the irresistible advance of freedom by this process. He is a warm advocate of colonization, because the negroes prosper
in Africa ; while, in the United States, emancipated
slaves become immoral and wretched. The greater
number of slaves whom he has seen set free have
perished miserably from incapacity to maintain themselves. As a lawyer, he has assisted many slaves to
obtain freedom ; but very few indeed have improved
their condition by liberty. If the men in the north
would receive the slaves, and provide for them as
freemen, there are a great number of slave-hold-

ers in Maryland who would willingly emancipate their negroes and send them to the north. The exertions of the abolitionists are said to have retarded emancipation and injured the slaves. A man loses caste who *deals* in slaves, or who treats them harshly.

These are a few of the topics touched on in Mr Key's letter, and I believe that his representations contain much truth. It may be remarked, however, that there are two causes for the unsatisfactory conduct and condition of emancipated slaves *in slave States :* 1st, A life spent in slavery deprives the individual of self-will and self-reliance, and of those intellectual resources which are indispensable to successful exertion. 2dly, In such a society there is no legitimate place for liberated slaves. Every thing is cast in the mould of slavery, and free negroes are unwelcome residents among slaves and their masters. The masters regard their presence as calculated to render the slaves discontented, and are disposed to throw impediments in the way of their success rather than remove them. General abolition would be unattended by these causes of failure, particularly if the slaves were previously prepared by education for freedom.

A Travelling-House.—This day a wooden house, supported on large beams, mounted on four wheels, and drawn by horses, passed our windows in Broadway, in its progress from one situation in the city to another.

" *The Church of the Messiah.*"—A handsome new Unitarian church, for the Rev. Mr Dewey, has just been opened in Broadway. It is built of stone, and is of Gothic architecture.   It has a gallery, and altogether is seated for 1500 persons, and is said to have cost $100,000.   The pews are lined with dove-coloured damask; they have stuffed backs, and cushions for the seats.   It has a very chaste and elegant appearance.   The " Morning Herald" reports that Dr Skinner, who has a Presbyterian church in the near neighbourhood, preached a sermon, on the occasion, on the text, " Dagon appeared alongside of the ark of the covenant," and warned his congregation against the Unitarians.

May 6.   Ther. 53°.   *National Academy of Design.*—We visited the fourteenth annual exhibition of the National Academy of Design.   The pictures consist chiefly of portraits and landscapes.   A feeling for art, and a power of colouring, are conspicuous in the works; but with the exception of the pictures of Mr Sully, Mr Ingham, and a few others, the portraits stand low in the scale of excellence.   In many of them the drawing of the heads is bad, the attitudes are stiff, and the countenances staring.   The subjects look as if they were sitting for their pictures. They have put on a face for the occasion, and in many of them the expression is so full of Self-Esteem and Love of Approbation (intended for character and smartness) that the pictures are almost ludicrous.

The scheme adopted for the encouragement of art in Scotland, and which has been successful, is much wanted in the United States.   A society was formed, each member of which paid at least L.1 ($5) per annum.   A committee of the subscribers laid out the money in purchasing the best pictures offered for sale by living artists at each annual exhibition. The pictures were formed into lots, and distributed among the subscribers, whose names were drawn from an urn. These pictures are now spread over all Scotland, and have increased the general taste of the people for works of art. The sum paid for pictures has in some seasons exceeded L.3000, and this has afforded encouragement to the artists in the best possible form, —that of remuneration for their talents and labour.

The United States are at present in a condition analogous to that of Scotland. There is no general taste for the fine arts among the people ; no rich aristocracy to purchase statuary and pictures, and, therefore, no adequate encouragement to artists. Yet there are many thousands of persons who, from a favourable feeling towards art, and from the hope of gaining a prize, would willingly subscribe $5 per annum to such a society as I have described. If the Americans will try the plan, it can scarcely fail to succeed. They have both the temperament and development of brain that will produce excellence in the fine arts, if they will only enable artists to live.

May 7. Ther. 56°. *The Causes of Fires in New York.*—The commissioners appointed to examine into the origin of fires in New York have reported as follows :—

" The total number of fires from 1st February to 30th April 1839, was　.　.　.　.　.　.　64
" The amount insured was　.　.　.　$ 112,000

" The amount paid,　.　.　.　.　$ 34,434
" Amount of property destroyed not insured,　.　$ 34,752

" Total loss,　$ 69,186

" The causes of the fires enumerated are :—

" By incendiaries, ...   19

"From defects in chimneys, stove-pipes, lighted candles,
cigars, deposits of ashes, sparks from chimneys,
and accidents, ...   29

" Causes unknown, ...   16

                                                                " Total,   .   64"

The commissioners comment on the recklessness
and immorality which these causes imply, and observe, that in one instance " the design evidently was
to destroy the family of a person residing in the upper part of the building," between whom and the
perpetrator " a quarrel had for a considerable time
previously existed."

Duel at Vicksburg.—Two editors in Vicksburg,
Dr Hagan of " The Sentinel" and Major McArdle of
" The Whig," quarrelled ; a challenge ensued, and as
the parties were reputed to be excellent shots, and
the challenge was publicly known, a number of bets
were made on the result.

" On Wednesday last they met on the Louisiana shore, opposite Vicksburg, at ten o'clock, when two shots were exchanged
with pistols at ten paces without effect ; a suspension of hostilities was agreed to, and the parties returned to town. We learn
that not less than a thousand persons were present to witness
the duel. In the afternoon, McArdle seemed to think he was
not satisfied, and it was soon arranged to have another meeting.
Accordingly, at four o'clock, the belligerents were again on the
field. One shot was exchanged, and the ball of the Sentinel editor took effect in the fleshy part of the thigh of the Whig editor.
This put a stop to the fighting a second time. Whether it will
again be renewed we have not learned.

" The above items are gleaned from a private letter from Vicks-

burg, received by a friend in this city, who politely furnished us
with its perusal.   The same letter says : ' They are beginning
to fight here pretty fast now.   Three at this place yesterday, and
one at Manchester.   Thermometer 93° to 96°.   Nobody killed
yet."—*New York Commercial Advertiser* 7*th May.*

Presbyterian Church Case.—The opinion of the
judges sitting in bank on the appeal in this case has
been published.   It was delivered by Chief-Justice
Gibson.   The decision in favour of the New School
is reversed.   The leading grounds of the decision on
appeal are these : The " Union" between the Presbyterians and the Congregationalists in 1801 was a
measure of a mere temporary nature.   It was intended to accommodate the " new settlements, by
suffering those who were yet too few and too poor
for the maintenance of a minister temporarily to call
to their assistance the members of a sect (the Congregationalists) who differed from them in principles,
not of faith, but of ecclesiastical government." " This
was not intended to outlast the inability of the re-
spective sects to provide separately for themselves,
or to perpetuate the innovations on Presbyterial government which it was calculated to introduce."
" The Assembly is a homogeneous body, uniting in
itself, without separation of parts, the legislative,
executive, and judicial functions of the government."
The plan of the " Union," viewed as a temporary
expedient, acquired the force of a law by the mere
act of the Assembly, without the ratification of the
Presbyteries, which it never obtained.   " The people
embraced it with all its defeasible properties plainly
put before them ; and the power which constituted

it might fairly repeal it whenever the good of the Church should seem to require it." The exscinded synods were created under the " Union ;" their existence, therefore, like that of the Union itself, was a temporary arrangement, liable to be discontinued at any time. These synods, created by a legislative act of the Assembly, could be legally dissolved in no other way than by another legislative act of the same body. Having been so dissolved, the delegates from them were not entitled to take their places in the General Assembly. The Old School, therefore, constituted the only true Assembly, and the votes of the New School, followed by their secession and subsequent meetings as another General Assembly, were altogether inept. The judges, therefore, decided that the Old School formed the legitimate General Assembly, and that the trustees nominated by them are legally entitled to hold the property of the Presbyterian Church. The opinion of Judge Rogers, who presided at the former trial, " remained unchanged on all the points ruled at the trial."

Phrenology in the Family.—The Rev. Joseph A. Warne, A. M., an Evangelical clergyman, and pastor of the church near the Museum in George Street, Philadelphia, has published " Phrenology in the Family," 18mo, pp. 290 ; a work intended to assist parents in the education of the *feelings*. It points out the character and legitimate uses of each primitive feeling, the ordinary forms in which it is liable to be abused by children, and the best means of training it to proper modes of action. It is calculated to be highly useful in domestic education.

May 7. Ther. 56°. *Benevolent and Religious Societies.*—The annual meetings of the great benevolent and religious societies of the Union are now
taking place in New York, and they present striking
evidence that, however active the acquisitive and ambitious propensities of this people may be, their benevolent and religious sentiments are far from being
dormant. The crowds of persons in attendance, and
the large sums of money contributed, bespeak a vigorous and general activity of the moral faculties.

" *American Anti-Slavery Society.*—An abstract of the annual report was read by one of the secretaries of the society. By this
document it appears that the present number of abolition societies is 1650—of which 304 are new societies, formed since the
last anniversary. The number of presses devoted or open to
the discussion of slavery has increased, and now amounts to 9
weekly, 1 semi-monthly, and 2 monthly publications, from which
are issued 25,000 sheets weekly, and for the support of which
$ 40,000 are annually received from subscribers.

" The receipts into the treasury for the year shew a handsome
increase over those of the previous year. The total of the publications by the society, for the year, amounts to 724,862, of
which about 213,000 were copies of the Emancipator, 148,000 of
Human Rights, 19,958 bound volumes, the remainder tracts, &c.

" A considerable portion of the abstract is devoted to the discussion of the emancipation of the slaves in the West Indies.
It is assumed that the experiment has been successful there,
and thence is drawn the inference that it must be successful
here.

" The abstract recommends pressing the subject of abolition to
the ballot-box, cites various instances in which it has been done
with effect during the past year, and avows the opinion that the
time is not far distant when the influence of political abolition
will be more strongly felt.

" *American Tract Society.*—The fourteenth annual report states,
that during the year 1833 new publications have been stereo-

typed, making the whole number of the society's publications 944, of which 58 are volumes. In addition to these, 672 works, including 50 volumes, have been approved for publication abroad. Of some tracts more than 100,000 copies have been printed within the year ; and of one 184,000 copies. Total printed during the year, 356,000 volumes; 3,657,000 publications ; 124,744,000 pages.

" Circulated during the year, volumes, 299,166—publications, 4,099,170—pages, 119,733,356. Total circulation since the formation of the society,—volumes, 1,153,390—publications, 57,039,678 —pages, 917,983,578.

" The number of volumes circulated exceeds that of any preceding year by 65,000 ; the number of pages that of any preceding year by more than 22,000,000.

" The gratuitous distributions, in 422 distinct grants, including nearly 2,000,000 pages for foreign lands, amount to 8,257,266 pages.

" *Receipts* during the year, $ 131,295.40, of which $ 55,852.81, were donations, including $ 28,100.62 for foreign distribution, and $ 3,461.06 for volume circulation.

" *American Bible Society.*—Abraham Keyser, Esq. the Treasurer, read his annual report. The receipts during the year were $ 95,126.62, and the expenditures $ 98,205.31. The Rev. John C. Brigham, the corresponding secretary, announced a donation by James Douglas, Esq. of Cavers, in Scotland, to the Society, of L.1000 Sterling. The report next alludes to the calls for supplies of the holy Scriptures in various parts of the world, to the amount of $ 50,000. During the past year the issues were 134,937 copies, and the total number 2,588,235. These copies were in seventeen different languages."

The names of some of the other Societies of which meetings are announced for this week, are the New York Marine Bible Society ; the New York Female Moral Reform Society ; the American Seamen's Friend Society ; the New York and American Sunday-School Union ; the Foreign Evangelical Association ; American Tract Society ; Second American

Health Convention ; American Home Missionary Society; New York Colonization Society; Central American Education Society : American Moral Reform Society; New York City Temperance Society; American Board of Foreign Missions ; New York Academy of Sacred Music.

Travelling Houses.—To-day I saw another wooden house of two storeys, bearing on one corner ." Washington Place," and on another " Greene Street," travelling to a new site. Planks were laid down before it on the carriage-way, rollers were placed on the planks, and the house was dragged forward on them. The motive power was applied thus : Large iron bolts were driven deep into the ground eighty or one hundred yards in advance of the house ; the bolts supported a windlass, to which was attached a strong cable, the other end of which was fastened to the house by pulleys and a hook. A horse, by turning round the windlass, wound up the cable, and the house slowly advanced on the rollers. When it was brought up to the windlass, the latter was carried forward another 100 yards, fastened to the ground, and the same operations were repeated.

The Maine War.—The Liverpool steam-ship has arrived and brought English news to the 20th of April. The threats of the Americans have excited little interest, and no apprehension of a war is entertained in Britain. The Americans are very glad at this result, but a little surprised that they should have been so warm and John Bull so cool. The legislature of Maine authorized the Governor to borrow $800,000 to prepare for the war. It is currently reported that he sent an agent to New York to borrow the money in Wall Street; that the bankers told him that he must go to England to sell his bonds, and that he has returned home without being able to raise a dollar!

May 9. Ther. 56°. *Paterson Village.*—This is a manufacturing village in New Jersey, eighteen miles from New York. We visited it by a railroad. It is built on the banks of the Passaic River, near a large fall, which supplies water-power for several important manufactories. The scenery is picturesque. We visited Mr Colt's manufactory of rifles, which discharge eight balls in succession, with one loading, also of pistols that discharge four balls. There are these numbers of barrels, which can be turned round to the same lock: Of course, when once discharged, there must be a corresponding extent of reloading; but in the Indian wars, and in cases of attack by robbers, these rifles are like loaded batteries in the hands of the assailed. The workmanship appeared to be excellent, and the number sold is said to be large.

May 12. Ther. 56°. *Religion.*—I heard the Reverend Mr Bellowes preach. He said that the vulgar notions of heaven being a place where men stand through all eternity doing nothing but singing psalms, and of hell consisting in flames, and darts, and devils, are altogether unworthy of an enlightened age. Heaven consists in the highest activity of our faculties directed to proper objects, which confers the highest delight; Hell in the abuse of our faculties, with the consequent misery. I heard this discourse

criticised by some persons as too free ; others approved of it, and said that preaching in general is
far behind the enlightenment of the age ; and that
there is a greater desire for liberal, rational, and
practical sermons, in the United States, than I could
infer from the character of the sermons which I
usually hear.

An advertisement has appeared in the following
terms :—

" *Christian Liberty.*—The Association for the Promotion of
Christian Liberty will hold its first anniversary at the Stuyvesant Institute, on Friday evening, at half-past seven o'clock.
The cardinal principle of the association is, that ' American
Christians, in their religious associations, are entitled to as
much liberty as they enjoy in their political associations as
American citizens.' Persons disposed to unite with the association, and the public generally, are respectfully invited to attend.

" DAVID HALE,	
LEONARD CROCKER,	
WM. C. REDFIELD,	
S. F. B. MORSE,	*Committee.*"
GEO. R. HASWELL,	
SETH B. HUNT,	
May 9. 1839. WM. T. CUTTER,	

The meeting was held, but, as few persons came
forward to join the association, it was adjourned.

Sale of Pews.—The pews in the " Church of the
Messiah" have been sold by auction, and their prices
are reported in the newspapers.

There are 196 pews in the church, and they were
valued at $97,373. Of these seventy-four in the
body of the church were sold at prices varying from

$1200 to $401, according to the size and the situation, and twenty-two in the gallery at prices ranging from $475 to $125. There are still 100 pews left unsold, valued at $39,475, making with those sold, a total of $101,298, being $3924 above the estimated values. These sums are applied in defraying the expense of building the church. The owners of the pews contribute annually towards keeping the church in repair, supporting the minister and the choir, and defraying all other necessary expenses. The salary paid to the Reverend Mr Dewey was stated by one of the congregation to be $4000 per annum, with leave of absence for nine weeks, during which the congregation pays for supplying the pulpit. This is the only church about which I have been able to obtain so much information, but I presume that the Evangelical congregations are equally liberal to their pastors. The sums paid annually by individuals for church accommodation appear to be much larger in this country than in Britain.

Election Law.—On 7th May the Legislature of the State of New York passed a law to remedy the abuses complained of at the elections. It enacts that any person swearing falsely as to his qualification shall be guilty of perjury, and persons wilfully procuring others to swear falsely shall be guilty of subornation of perjury; and both shall be punished accordingly. Persons attempting to influence or deter an elector in giving his vote shall pay a fine not exceeding $500, or suffer imprisonment not longer

than one year, or both.   Persons voting or offering
to vote in a ward in which they do not reside, or
more than once at an election, shall be punished by
fine and imprisonment, or by both.   Persons ad-
vising or assisting others not duly qualified to vote,
shall suffer the same punishment.   Any inhabitant
of another State voting or offering to vote in this
State shall be guilty of felony, and shall be confined
in the State prison not more than one year, &c.

If the republican form of government be fertile in
abuses, it is gratifying to observe the promptitude
and energy with which checks and remedies are applied to mitigate or remove them.

May 14. Ther. 66°. *Police of New York City.*—
I have more than once made remarks on the imperfections of the police system in New York, and perceive that the evil is attracting public attention.
The "Journal of Commerce" contains a letter describing New York as the dirtiest city in Christen-
dom.   It complains of the huge dirty swine peram-
bulating the foot pavements, one of which ran against
the writer of the letter.   They, however, he says,
do great service to the city, for they eat up the animal and vegetable matter thrown out into the streets,
which otherwise would breed a pestilence,—in fact,
they are the chief scavengers.   The sting of this
representation lies in its essential truth.

It is no part of the public duty of the police officers of this city to trace out and apprehend thieves
and robbers who have committed depredations on
private persons.   A number of them exercise this

vocation on the employment of the persons who are pillaged, and who either pay them fees, or engage to give them a certain proportion of the stolen property if they recover it. The police magistrates do not concern themselves in the matter until the thief be detected and brought before them for judgment, and there is no other functionary whose duty it is to superintend the efforts of the officers to bring delinquents to justice. In short, in New York an experiment seems to be in progress to ascertain with how little of government a great city can possibly exist. I do not think that it has great cause, at present, to boast of its success.

May 15. Ther. 66°. *Phrenology.*—This day I was introduced to James J. Mapes, Esq., a scientific gentleman, residing in 461 Broadway, New York. His daughter fell from a window when she was about four years of age ; her head struck against the iron-bar which extended from the railing to the wall, and the skull was extensively fractured, but without rupturing the pia mater or doing any serious injury to the brain. She was attended by Dr Mott ; a part of the skull was removed from the superior-posterior portion of the head, the integuments were drawn over the wound, and the child recovered. The part of the skull removed was that which covers the organs of Self-Esteem and Love of Approbation. She does not wear any plate over the wound ; but the hair over it, like that on the other parts of the head, is fine, and is kept short. Immediately after the wound was closed, her father was struck with the

variety of movements in the brain, and its great mo-
bility during mental excitement, producing, as he
said, a sensation in the hand when placed on the integuments, as if one were feeling, through a silk hand-
kerchief, the motions of a confined leech. He felt
as if there was a drawing together, swelling out, and
a vermicular kind of motion in the brain; and this
motion was felt in one place and became impercep-
tible in another, according as different impressions
were made on the child's mind: but not being minutely acquainted with phrenology, he could not describe either the feelings or the precise localities in
which the movements occurred. He observed also,
that when the child's intellectual faculties were exerted, the brain under the wound was drawn inwards.

The child was introduced to me; she is now eight
years of age, healthy and intelligent; and no external trace of the injury is visible to the eye. The
form of her head is that of a superior female child:
It is long, and moderately broad at the base; Secretiveness, Love of Approbation, Self-Esteem, Cautiousness, and Firmness, are all large. Benevolence
and Veneration are well developed, and the anterior
lobe is large. I saw the pieces of the skull which
had been removed. They may be three and a half
by three inches in superficial extent. The skull has
not been replaced. On applying my hand, I felt the
brain rising and falling with the respiration, and distinctly ascertained that the organs of Self-Esteem
and Love of Approbation were denuded of the skull;
also a small part of Conscientiousness, and the poste-

rior margin of Firmness. Her father mentioned that, before the accident, he considered her rather dull; but her mother (whom also I had the pleasure of seeing) did not concur in this opinion; both, however, agreed that since her recovery she had been acute, and fully equal to children of her own age in point of ability.

With the permission of her father and mother, I kept my hand for some minutes gently pressing on the external integuments over the site of the injury, and distinctly felt a considerable movement, a swelling up and pulsation, in the organs of Self-Esteem; and the same movements, but in a less degree,. in those of Love of Approbation. When I began to talk to the child, she was shy and bashful, and at first would scarcely speak.* The vivid movements in Self-Esteem indicated that amidst her extreme bashfulness this organ was active. As I continued to converse with her, and succeeded in putting her at her ease, the movements in Self-Esteem decreased, while those in Love of Approbation continued. I spoke to her about her lessons and attainments, not in flattering terms, but with the design of exciting Self-Esteem; and the movements increased. Again I soothed her, and they diminished. This was repeated, and the same results ensued. Her father gave her several questions in mental arithmetic to solve: she was

* " Bashfulness is the result of the fear of not acquitting one's self to advantage, and of thereby compromising one's personal dignity." System of Phrenology, 4th edition, p. 702.

puzzled, and made an intellectual effort, and the peculiar movements in the organs of Self-Esteem and Love of Approbation ceased; only a gentle and equal pulsation was felt. She solved the question, and we praised her : the peculiar movements in Self-Esteem and Love of Approbation returned and increased. This experiment was repeated at least four times, with the same results. I took out a piece of paper and began to write down notes, in pencil, of what had occurred. She looked at my writing; and as all attention was now withdrawn from herself, and her mind was occupied intellectually in observing what I was doing, I placed my hand on the integuments, and only the gentle and regular pulsations of the arterial system were perceptible.

I am much indebted to Mr Mapes, the father of the child, for permitting me not only to see this very interesting case, but to publish his name and residence, so that my remarks may be verified, or corrected if I have erred.

This case is replete with instruction in practical education. It tends, so far as one example can go, to prove that, by exercising the intellectual faculties, we do not necessarily excite the feelings; and also that each feeling must be addressed by objects related to itself before it can be called into action.*

* Some years ago a similar case was reported by Mr John Grattan of Belfast in the Phrenological Journal, vol. ix. p. 473, and vol. x. p. 11. Two fissures, having the appearance of the fontanels in children, and which looked as if there had been an absorption of the bone, had existed for at least six years in the head of a gentleman aged fifty-six.

Shipwrecks.—A gentleman called on me to-day, who said that he did so in consequence of having read the observations on shipwrecks in storms contained in the " Constitution of Man." He stated that he had been bred to the sea ; had served as mate, and subsequently, for four years, as master of a merchant-vessel ; and had, in the course of his own experience, come to the conclusion that not above one shipwreck in twenty was excusable, and that nineteen vessels out of every twenty were lost through ignorance, incapacity, or carelessness in the masters, or through avarice in the owners, who sent them to sea in an improper condition. When mate of a vessel, his captain became tipsy, and, in the very gathering of a storm, ordered the crew to set more sails. My informant took the responsibility upon himself of assuming the command of the vessel, ordered the captain below, took in all the sails except one, and trimmed the ship with the utmost expedition. He had scarcely finished, when the rising storm became

So far as Mr Grattan could learn from mere description, they were situated,—the one on the left nearly over Veneration and part of Firmness, and that on the right across part of Conscientiousness and Hope ; " and I am positively assured," says Mr G., " by his daughter, that his clerks could at any time tell when he was angry, without hearing him speak or seeing his face, but simply from the great *depression* which on such occasions occurred in those fissures, or, as they termed it, ' the holes that would appear in his head ;' and that she has at different times observed the same phenomenon herself." The lady states farther, that " the depressions remained so long as he was under the influence of passion ; and, as it subsided, the depressions gradually disappeared." See other cases in my System of Phrenology, 4th edit. p. 16.

a tempest; he laid the ship to, and she rode it out well. In the middle of the tempest the captain reappeared on deck, having slept himself sober. He was astounded at the sea and the wind, and recommended that even the one sail should be taken in, but he was persuaded to allow it to stand. The captain never forgave him for having "mutinied," as he termed it; and my informant left the ship when she made her destined port in the Mediterranean.

The Franklin Fund.—I was introduced to-day to a gentleman in extensive business as a dial-plate maker; and he mentioned that the beginning of his elevation in the world was a loan of $250 from the Franklin Fund. He speaks with great gratitude and respect of Franklin's provident generosity.

May 16. Ther. 66°. *Physical Geography of America.*—A very intelligent friend, lately a member of the House of Assembly in the Legislature of New York, told me that he had read with great interest an article in the Encyclopædia Britannica, by Charles Maclaren, Esq., of Edinburgh, on the physical geography, &c. of America. He regarded it as a masterly view of the physical features of this country. I told him that Mr Maclaren had never been in America; when he remarked that few readers would have discovered this to be the case.

Haerlem.—We visited some friends a few miles beyond Haerlem, in a beautiful situation overlooking the East River. The strawberries and green pease are in full blossom, and the gooseberries ready for tarts.

May 17. Ther. 63°. *Staten Island.*—We visited this lovely island, and had a drive to the old fortification and signal port, New Brighton, &c. Staten Island is the quarantine station in the bay of New York. About a quarter of a mile from the shore strong posts have been driven into the bottom of the sea, and a large platform erected on them, partly covered with a roof. Emigrants are transferred to this platform from their ships, and inspected by the health officer before being permitted to land. We saw a multitude of them on it like sheep in a pen.

May 18. Ther. 64°. *Phrenology.*—This evening I completed my second course of lectures in New York, and a committee was appointed to present resolutions.

May 19. Ther. 63°. *Dr Channing.*—We heard the Rev. Dr Channing preach in the Church of the Messiah on the text " Blessed are the peace-makers." The church was crowded in every part. The sermon was replete with moral beauty, and the delivery was gentle, earnest, and touching. He gave a graphic view of the present state of the social, religious, and political struggles of this country. He regarded them as only the natural workings of the human mind groping its way to freedom ; and anticipated that they will lead to universal love and justice, which alone can form the basis of universal peace. Civilization is progressive, and it cannot attain to its highest condition until peace, based on benevolence and justice, prevail. The discourse was listened to with the profoundest attention, and much spoken of afterwards.

Twenty years ago, no congregation in New York would admit Dr Channing into its pulpit. His first sermon in this city was delivered in a private house, and his second in an anatomical lecture-room. Now, the Unitarians have two handsome churches, well attended by highly respectable congregations.

I perceive that the liberality of the different sects towards each other increases in proportion to the number and standing in society of the adherents of each. In Boston, the Unitarians are numerous, and belong to the first class. There I could discover no ostensible prejudice against them. The Governor of the State and the Secretary of State were Unitarians; and among the magistrates and school directors, they were found co-operating with Calvinists and men of other sects in all public duties, without dissension or disrespect on any side. In New York, where the Unitarians have only two congregations, and are of comparatively recent origin, the prejudices entertained against them by the orthodox sects are stronger; and in Philadelphia, where they are still more recent, and have only one church, the dislike of them is still more conspicuously manifested. It has been remarked that sectarian hatred increases in proportion as the differences in opinion between the partisans diminish. The animosity, for instance, expressed by Calvinists against Jews is far less than that manifested against Unitarians.*

* In Scotland, where both the Church and the Dissenters are almost all Calvinists, intolerance reaches its maximum; and the reli-

May 20. Ther. 66°. *Phrenology.*—The committee of my class presented a series of elegant and complimentary resolutions, and requested me to sit to an artist for a model of my head, to be embossed on a silver vase which the individuals who have heard my lectures intend to present to me in token of their esteem. The resolutions are printed in the Appendix, No. VI. Nothing can exceed the kindness with which my lectures have been received in this country, and only the fear of being charged with indulging my own vanity prevents me from expressing how deeply I feel every mark of their approbation. I may remark that in the resolutions of the *second* classes, both in Philadelphia and New York, the foundation of phrenology in natural truth is recognised.

Fast Driving.—The thermometer stood at 83° in the shade this evening, and at this temperature innumerable gigs and carriages of all sorts were driving on the Bloomingdale road at the rate of from ten to fifteen miles an hour, amidst clouds of dust which obscured vision at the distance of a hundred yards. They were filled with parties driving for pleasure !

May 31. Ther. 63°. *A Flat-headed Indian.*—I was introduced to the Reverend Jason Lee, who has been a missionary among the Indians, two thousand

gious public are far from manifesting that liberal and Christian spirit which, while it holds fast by that which it regards as right, recognises its own fallibility, and admits the privilege of other men to do the same, without offering disparagement to their characters in thought, word, or deed.

miles beyond the Rocky Mountains. He was accompanied by Thomas Adams, an Indian of about

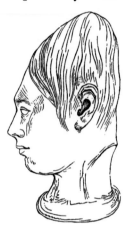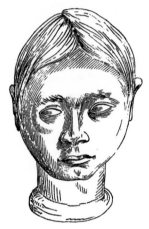

twenty years of age, of the Cloughewallah tribe, lo-
cated at the falls of the Wahlamette River (the Mul-
tuomah of the maps), about twenty-five miles from its
junction with the Columbia River. This tribe presses
the heads of their children by boards and hair cushions,
applied to the forehead and occiput. This young
man's head had been pressed. It was broader from
side to side above the ears (from Secretiveness to Secretiveness) than it was long from front to back (from
Individuality to Philoprogenitiveness). The spinous
process of the occipital bone was as high as the top of
the ear. The head appeared as if it had been tilted
up behind, in such a manner that the forehead, although deficient in the reflecting organs, was made
to stand much nearer the perpendicular than other-

wise it would have done. So far as could be judged in a case of such distortion, the organs of Destructiveness, Acquisitiveness, Secretiveness, Self-Esteem, Love of Approbation, and Firmness, were very large ; those of Combativeness, Philoprogenitiveness, and Adhesiveness, deficient. It was difficult to estimate the size of the moral organs, they were so displaced. The organs of the observing, faculties, lying on the superciliary ridge, were fully developed; the brain at the reflecting organs was shallow and deficient, but on the left side, the organ of Causality was pretty distinctly marked. The organs of Form and Language were large.

The young man spoke English well, and had practised speaking it for two years. He was intelligent in his conversation, and said that he liked the Indian and American modes of life equally well. His face was exceedingly broad, full, and lymphatic. The predominant expression was that of Love of Approbation. There were no traces of thought in his smooth fat cheeks, but his eye was dark and mild ; and, when he smiled, the countenance was pleasing. I endeavoured to direct the conversation so as to ascertain, if possible, the extent of his intellectual powers. On all subjects that fell within the scope of the faculties of observation (the organs of which are fairly developed) he was intelligent, ready, and fluent ; but on others which required the aid of Comparison and Causality, he was dull, unintelligent, and destitute equally of ideas and of language. Thinking that probably he

did not understand the words used on these topics,
I tried to explain them ; but found an obtuseness of
comprehension that rendered the attempt unsuccessful.   I found those intellectual powers to be of toler-
able strength whose organs were fairly developed,
and those to be deficient whose organs were small.
Mr Lee said that he was warm-tempered and touchy.

I explained to Mr Lee that the convolutions of
the brain in this youth might have been displaced,
but not destroyed or entirely impeded in their growth,
as the spinal marrow exists and performs its functions
in persons afflicted with hunchbacks, although bent
out of its usual direction.   I requested him to carry
a cast of a normal European brain with him, when
he returned to his station, and to beg the medical
officer of the Fur Company, who lives in his neighbourhood, to examine carefully the brains of these
Flat-headed Indians after death, and report minutely
the differences in the size and distribution of the
convolutions.   Mr Lee mentioned that the tribe
called by the English Flat-headed Indians do not
compress the heads of their children, and that they
are not flat-headed.   The name is erroneously bestowed.   The tribe to which this youth belongs do
compress the skull in infancy.

Having no means of discovering the condition of
the feelings in this young man, I requested my friend
Mr Samuel W. Dewey, who had procured this interview, to use every means of observation in his
power, and to report to me on this subject.   He did

so, and two letters with which he favoured me are published in the Phrenological Journal for January 1841. They are highly instructive, and shew that those propensities and sentiments were most active (so far as Mr Dewey had the means of observation) the organs of which were largest in the brain.*

Mr Lee spoke confidently of the success of missionary efforts among the Indians, and mentioned several who had been reclaimed to agriculture and Christianity. A man, he says, cannot be a Christian who is a wanderer in his habits; and he recommends that missionaries should teach the useful arts and Christianity simultaneously.

Colony of Liberia.—Mr Matthias, the missionary of the Colonization Society to Liberia, in Africa, was present; and he assured me that this settlement and another of the same description are doing well. The Africans are increasing in numbers; they support all the civilization which they carried out with them; live in peace, and maintain law and justice. They

---

* After I left New York I saw an announcement of the death, in that city, of the companion of this Flat-headed Indian, who was ill at the time of this conference. I was told that Dr Rees attended him as his physician. This gentleman had previously published " The Humbugs of New York," among which he included phrenology; but he allowed this young man to be buried without examining his brain, or at least without reporting on it, or calling in the aid of phrenologists to do so. It is strange that those who are so confident that phrenology is a " humbug" should be so averse to producing evidence by which alone it can be proved to be so. The condition of the brain in a Flat-headed Indian is an interesting and unknown fact in physiology, and any medical man who has the means of throwing light on it, and neglects to use them, is no friend to his own profession or to general science.

are not attacked by the surrounding tribes. He remarked that the negroes improve in America when
free, and that they improve still more in Africa when
they become their own masters. I mentioned to him
my estimate of the difference between them and the
American Indians (vol. ii. p. 77), and he acquiesced
in my observations in regard to the qualities of the
Africans.

Natural Language of Secretiveness.—In describing
the head of Col. Aaron Burr (vol. i. p. 231), I adverted to the large size of the organ of Secretiveness,
and the deficiency of that of Conscientiousness. A
writer in the " New York Mirror," in describing
him, says, " He glided rather than walked ; his foot
had that quiet, stealthy movement which involuntarily makes one think of treachery ; and, in the
course of a long life, I have never met with a frank
and honourable man to whom such a step was habitual." This is an excellent description of the natural language of large Secretiveness and deficient
Conscientiousness, as expressed in the gait. The
writer's observation is correct, that no frank and honourable man—that is, no man in whom Benevolence
and Conscientiousness are larger than Secretiveness
—will be found characterized by that kind of motion.

May 22. Ther. 60°. *Fire.*—The House of Refuge
was burned to the ground this forenoon. It was a
stirring but melancholy sight to see the whole engines of New York city, amply supplied by water
from ponds outside the walls, playing for hours on
the burning mass with the greatest energy, but with-

out effect.   The building was old, and its loss is not much regretted, except for the immediate inconvenience which it occasions.

Anti-Abolition Meeting.—The town of Newark in New Jersey was taunted with manufacturing the whips with which the slaves are flogged in the south ! It replied that it manufactures whips in general, and that carters use the article alleged to be employed in scourging the slaves.   The inhabitants have held a meeting, James Millar, Esq., the mayor, in the chair, at which violent resolutions were passed, the last of which declares " that the subject of slavery appertains to the slave States alone—that the question of its duration or abolition belongs exclusively to them —and that the meddling interference of others is uncalled for by any considerations of public justice or of public policy."   The opinion expressed in this resolution prevails generally in the United States.

CHAPTER VII.

1839.

May 24. Ther. 60°. *West Point.*—My phrenological labours being now terminated for the season, we resolved to visit Lake George, Niagara, and Canada, and this morning at seven o'clock embarked on board the " Avon" for West Point, where we landed at quarter before eleven, the distance being 50 miles. The military academy belonging to the United States stands here on a platform of land elevated several hundred feet above the Hudson River, and surrounded by hills clothed to the summit with wood. No situation can be more lovely. There are at present about 240 cadets in the establishment. They are maintained and educated in civil and military engineering at the public expense for four years, on condition that they serve the State, if called on, for four years after the expiry of their time. On the hill which rises to the west of the plateau, there is an ancient fort (Fort Putnam) in ruins, which is a picturesque object, and repays the labour of ascending to it. There are monuments to Kosciusko, to Lieut.-Col. Wood, who was killed in September 1814 leading a charge at Fort Erie, and to a pupil who was accidentally killed by a gun in his exercises. These objects, although all simple in themselves, being placed in appropriate situations, add to the interest of the scene. There is an excellent hotel for the accommodation of visiters; but it has been let this year by the Government on the condition of total abstinence by the guests from all liquors containing alcohol in any form. Not a drop even of beer is sold. It has, in consequence, been difficult to find a tenant, and the house is now only in the course of being fitted up. We, however, obtained a good bed-room, and dined at an excellent ordinary kept for a few officers of the establishment. Major Leslie politely conducted us through the public buildings, which are extensive and commodious; but here also the want of ventilation in the apartments forced itself upon our notice by the disagreeable effects of vitiated air. So careless are the students and attendants on this point, that I found every window close in several class-rooms which had been vacated for the day, and which were full of carbonic acid gas and the effluvia of the human body. I used the freedom to open them for my own comfort while passing through them, for which I hope to be forgiven by the students. The habit of chewing tobacco, and spitting, prevails in the hotel to a distressing extent.

May 25. Ther. 63°. *Phrenology.*—This morning

we had a storm of thunder and lightning, which had
a sublime effect among the mountains. It cleared
off at nine o'clock, and at eleven we embarked on
board of the " Champlain" for Albany. In this
boat an amusing incident occurred. One of the passengers accosted me, without any preface or introduction. " You have just finished a course of lectures in New York ?" " Yes, sir." " How long is it
since you lectured in Syracuse ?" " I was never in
Syracuse in my life." The gentleman was surprised
and walked away to the other end of the boat ;
and on his return he renewed his interrogation.
" Have you any of your books with you ?" " No—
they are all the property of booksellers, and I take
no charge of the sales." " Have any of them been
printed in Europe ?" " Yes, they were all printed
there first." This answer caused him to turn and
take another walk to a distant part of the deck. He
returned, still apparently greatly puzzled. " I read
your book and I have made observations, and am disposed to believe in Phrenology." " Observation is
the only philosophical mode of attaining conviction."
" Do you examine heads ?" " I do, for my own instruction, but not publicly, or for money." He again
looked puzzled. " Where is the very tall man that
was with you, when you travelled through Kentucky ?" " I have never been in Kentucky." " I
understood that you had a very tall man, of 7 feet
4 inches, and a very short man with you, in that
State." " I have not travelled in this country with
any man, either tall or short, and I have not even

seen any man of extraordinary stature here." At
this point, the interrogator's sagacity was completely at fault. He left me, and never resumed the conversation. I afterwards discovered the cause of his
inquiries. An itinerating phrenologist, named Fre-
derick Coombs, had travelled through the western
country examining heads, and, to add to the attrac-
tions of Phrenology, carried with him a giant and a
dwarf, whom he exhibited as a show. This gentleman mistook me for him; nor had he been unique
in this error, for a newspaper had previously been
sent to me containing an intimation that " the gentleman with the giant and the dwarf is *not* Mr
George Combe of Edinburgh!"

Politeness to Ladies.—The Americans always give
place to ladies in the stage-coaches, railroad cars, at
the public tables, and in other similar situations.
In the steam-boat, at dinner to-day, a small incident occurred which affords an illustration of this
practice. I was seated at table, with Mrs Combe
on my right hand. A gentleman, leading a lady,
saw the chair next me on the left hand unoccupied.
He placed his lady in it, and then requested me to
rise and give him my seat. I declined to do so; on
which he said, " Very well, Sir, if you are so un-
civil as not to give place to a lady, I shall certainly
seek another place at the table ;" and before I had
time to utter another word of explanation, he and
his lady were off beyond my reach. The plain meaning of the request appeared to me to be this. " Be
so good, Sir, as to leave the seat beside your lady,

and give it to me that I may sit beside my lady ;"
but I did the gentleman injustice. After dinner, he
came up to me, and said, " Sir, I owe you an apology for my remark : I did not observe that you had a
lady with you : You were quite right in retaining
your seat."

Political Economy.—I enjoyed some interesting
conversation with a gentleman who happened to be
a passenger, and who had had an opportunity of observing the evolutions of the mercantile world in
the United States for many years. On my remarking that many mercantile men in the great cities of
the Union appeared to me to conduct their business
too much in the spirit of speculation, without taking
accurate and comprehensive views of causes obviously in operation, which would as certainly affect
the value of their commodities, as the sun would
ripen the crop in autumn, he acquiesced in the cor-
rectness of the observation, and added that many
merchants dash at every thing as a speculation, and
talk of " the chance" much more than of the principle in nature by which the supposed " chance" must
be ruled. I described to him the effects which I
had observed in Scotland to flow from too free an
emission of paper money. Men were tempted by it
to manufacture, and also to import goods, far beyond
the demand for consumption ; a rapid rise in the
price of the raw material and in wages occurred ;
and prices of manufactured articles rose for a few
months. This was called " prosperity;" but speedily
the foreign exchanges became unfavourable to Bri-

tain ; gold was demanded from the Bank of England to
pay for the excess of imported goods ; the bank, finding her coffers drained, contracted the currency ; the
resources of the Scotch banks in London were circum-
scribed; they took the alarm, lessened their discounts,
called in their loans, and realized the debts due to
them. The direct consequences of this were, that
those individuals who had manufactured or imported
on the " credit system" were forced to sell at any
sacrifice in price, in order to raise funds to meet
their engagements; prices fell ruinously low; trade
became stagnant; the " credit" men declared themselves bankrupt; and a period of great suffering ensued. He said that in the United States the same
system prevailed to an inconceivable extent; and
that as one phantom vanished, another was conjured
up. Certain speculators now hold cotton in ———,
to the value of three millions of dollars, waiting
for a rise. The basis of the adventure was the
known fact, that last year's crop had been considerably short of an average ; and, in the face of a falling
market, they held on, convinced that the prices *must*
rise. They acted on this single fact, without taking
into consideration collateral circumstances. I remarked that the high price of provisions in Britain
is a most important element in such a speculation ;
for it must influence the price of cotton. The mass
of the British people are very important consumers
of cotton fabrics ; when they are forced to expend
all their money in purchasing food, they must wear
their old clothes, and give up buying new. They

will go in rags rather than starve. He said that this very circumstance might account to some extent for the fall in the price of cotton, although the last crop was short, and that a few more incidental circumstances might entirely counteract the consequences of the short produce; but that these collateral influences were rarely considered by those whose fortunes were at stake.

Condition of New York City.—I made some remarks on the condition of the city of New York; when a gentleman observed that the cause of the disorder of the streets, pavements, police, and many other things in New York, is the aversion of the lower classes to be taxed, and the subjection of the politicians to them. At the present time, the democratic party of that city is engaged in expelling every public officer of the whig party, and substituting their own men; this they could not do, if they offended the people by taxing them. A *moral* party is much wanted—one which should advocate what is right, and care nothing about votes. Such a party would rally round it the sound portion of the people, and do great good. At first they would fail; but if they had courage to persevere, they would acquire such strength that they would be in a condition to dictate terms to both of the political parties. At present, no leading man has courage to encounter the opposition of both; and the substantial interests of the country suffer.

We arrived at Albany at half-past six, where we were kindly received by my brother and his wife.

Nothing could exceed the beauty of the scenery through which we have passed.

May 26. Ther. 43°. *The Niskayuna Shakers.*— We drove to this Shaker settlement, situated about half way between Troy and Schenectady. The grounds are not naturally fertile, but are remarkably well cultivated. The settlement presents a number of plain-looking buildings, one of which is used as a church. In size and appearance it resembles an ordinary school-house of one storey. This being Sunday, there was a large number of strangers in attendance, who came in carriages of various kinds. The female Shakers entered the church by one door, and the men by another; and the strangers were forced to follow the same rule. We were provided with benches to sit on. At ten o'clock the Shakers appeared. The women were dressed something like Sisters of Charity; the men wore the ordinary dress of male Quakers, only their coats and hats were of the colour of dust, broader in the skirts and brims, and of a coarser fabric than those usually worn by other Quakers. The women occupied one end of the floor, and the men the other. The apartment had neither pews, pulpit, desk, nor any other appendage of a church. An aged, sensible-looking man, one of their number, addressed the visiters. He told them that the Shakers are " a peculiar people;" that they were now met to worship God; that the whole human race were interested in what they were doing, and would, in God's good time, be benefited by it; that, in the mean while, their mode of worship and

their manners appeared to the world to be strange;
that although they knew this to be the case, they
opened their doors to every visiter, and all that they
required in return was that visiters should behave
with common decency, and forbear from whispering
and laughing. "We have provided," he continued,
" spit-boxes for those who spit, or at least as many
as we could, and we hope that they will try to sit
near them ;—if not, we beg that they will not put
more tobacco in their mouths, so as to render it
necessary for them to spit, and that they will not
dirty the floor. Chewing tobacco is a practice not
followed by ourselves, and we wish to be protected
from its effects."

The service began by one of the men delivering
some sensible moral precepts; after which, as the
day was warm, the men stripped off their coats and
laid aside their hats; while the women took off their
shawls and bonnets. They then commenced singing and dancing; at the same time waving their
hands, which they held in the attitude of the fore-
feet of the kangaroo. While singing, they knelt occasionally; and, at other times, several of them took
their station in the middle of the floor and sung,
while the rest danced round them. Their tunes
were merry measures, with strongly marked time,
such as are played in farces and pantomimes. By-
and-by some of them began to bend their bodies
forwards, to shake from side to side and to whirl
round. A favourite motion was to let the trunk of
the body drop downwards, with a sudden jerk, to

one side, care being always taken to recover the perpendicular before the equilibrium was lost. The head and trunk were drawn up by another jerk. In all their shakings and contortions they never lost the step in their dance, nor ran against each other.

During these gesticulations some of the strangers laughed. One of the male Shakers, singling out a young lady whom he had observed committing this breach of decorum, addressed her thus: " Young woman, you laugh too much. We are a-worshipin' God: we want you to be quiet; that's all we desire."

The Shakers trace back their origin to the days of Oliver Cromwell; but the testimony was lost for many years, and revived in 1747 under James Wardley, a tailor, and Jane, his wife, in Bolton and Manchester, in England. They believe that the second appearance of Christ is at hand, and, in accordance with this doctrine, they enforce a total separation between the sexes. No children are born in their institution.* In 1770, Anna Leese became a distinguished leader of the sect, and declared herself to be " the Elect Lady," the woman " spoken of in Rev. xii., and the mother of all the Elect." In 1774, she, and a number of her followers, left Manchester, complaining of persecution, and came to New York. Being joined by others of their own faith, they settled at this place, then called Nisqueunia, near Albany, where they have spread their opinions, and in-

* I observed in the newspapers mention made of a Bill depending before the Legislature of New York State, to provide for the wives and children of men who had become Shakers; but its terms were not published.

creased to a considerable number.   They have also a
large settlement near New Lebanon, twenty-five
miles to the east of Albany.   " They are neither
Trinitarians nor Satisfactionists.   They deny the
imputation of Adam's sin to his posterity, the doctrine of election and reprobation, as well as the eternity of future punishment."   They deny also " the
resuscitation of the body," and " reject the celebra-
tion of water baptism and the Lord's Supper."*

They admit freely all who wish to join them, and
subject them to probation.   I was told that they receive numerous recruits from among destitute Irish
mothers with families, whose husbands have died or
deserted them.   They cultivate the ground, and manufacture a variety of articles, which they sell in the
towns.   The community is prosperous and rich.

About half a dozen of the men whom we saw were
past the middle period of life : they had large, round,
portly figures, with regularly-formed and well-developed brains, and the external aspect of good sense.
They were obviously the leaders.   The rest presented
heads such as one generally sees in Lunatic Asylums,
characterized by excessive predominance of some organs, and great deficiency of others.   The organs of
the domestic affections were strikingly deficient in
some of them, but not in all.   In several, Self-Esteem and Firmness were exceedingly large, combined
with a narrow base of the brain, and an expression
of countenance in the highest degree fanatical, dog-
matical, and inflexible.   In these men the nose was

* Adam's Dictionary of all Religions.

disproportionately long. In many the brain was below an average in size, and the men looked silly.

The heads of the women were covered by their caps; but the general size and outline could be seen through the thin muslin. The great majority of them had well-developed foreheads; but in some the head was small. Some were pretty. I distinctly remarked that those who shook, jerked, whirled round, or otherwise gave marks of being possessed, had small heads, and the expression of their countenances was maniacal or fatuous. Those individuals who had large well-shaped brains never manifested contortion, but danced, and sang, and waved their hands, and knelt and rose, all with the most perfect composure. One boy of twelve or thirteen, with a small head, but enormously large Secretiveness, jerked incessantly, so that it became fatiguing to look at him; he was in excellent health, and there was no expression of fanatical emotion in his countenance. He appeared to me to be acting a part. One man whose brain indicated a close approximation to idiocy. rolled his head, and shook incessantly. After the meeting, he continued shaking on the road home to his residence, till one of the brethren gave him a good shake, which had the effect of quieting him. The women were the greatest shakers; and their pale faces, wild looks, and flabby condition, indicated at once a low state of health, and irregular nervous excitement.

The oddly formed brains indicate bizarre minds, and these produce strange actions. The sincere members of the community appeared to me to be monomaniacs on the point of their religion. In other respects they are said to be rational, honest, benevolent, and industrious. From the large development of Self-Esteem and Firmness, they would in other days have endured martyrdom without hesitation; but here these feelings are manifested chiefly in pretending to exclusive salvation, and setting at nought the opinions and practices of the world.

May 27. Ther. 62°. *Forfeitures for Taxes.*—I attended a great sale of lands, building-lots, and houses, lying in all parts of the State of New York, brought to the hammer for non-payment of taxes. The sale was held in the State-House, Albany, and purchasers from great distances were in attendance. The catalogue, printed in double columns, formed a pretty thick pamphlet. A sale of this kind takes place every two years. If I rightly understood the proceedings and the explanations of them given by a friend, the whole property is put up to auction at the sum due on it for taxes and costs, and the bidding is backwards : that is to say, if the property extends to 50 acres, and the taxes to $50, one bidder will engage to pay the sum named for 30 acres of it ; another for 20 ; another for 10 ; and so on, until no one will go lower. The lowest is the purchaser. The State conveys to him his portion, which is now specially marked off; and the remainder continues the property of the original owner. It is a common practice, when the title to a property becomes confused or irregular, to allow it to be forfeited to the

State for taxes, and to buy it in : the State gives a new title, which it guarantees to the purchaser. The property is redeemable by the forfeiting owner, if he pay up the sum advanced with interest at ten per cent. to the purchaser, within two years of the sale. After two years, it is irredeemable.

Napoleon Bonaparte.—When Napoleon granted licenses to American ships, on certain conditions, to touch at English ports, on their way to France, they were all subscribed by himself. He had no faith in the officers of his government, that they would not take the money and grant the licenses, all for their own advantage. The gentleman who mentioned this fact to me, had seen a license which bore date " The field of battle at Wilna." When ships were loaded under these licenses at New York, the French Consul sent a description of the cargo in cypher to Napoleon ; and in his possession alone was the key to the cypher. The custom-house officers reported the cargo to him, on the arrival of the vessel in a French port ; he had it compared with the consul's report, and it was only when the two agreed, that the ship was safe. An eminent merchant in New York had a large quantity of goods seized by the French at Antwerp. He complained to Napoleon, proved that they were truly American property, and solicited compensation ; but in vain. He went to Paris, and laid the case before Talleyrand, whom he had known when a refugee in America, and who mentioned it to the Emperor, on an occasion which he thought to be favourable. Napoleon listened to his statement, turned

round to him, and said, " How much of the compen-
sation-money are you to receive for this agency?"
Talleyrand made no reply ; but reported this answer
to his American friend, and no compensation was
ever given.   These two anecdotes I believe to be essentially authentic, and they are examples of the absence of conscientiousness as a sentiment, and as a
principle of action, in Napoleon and in those who administered his government.   This appears to me to
have been the greatest defect in Napoleon's mind ;
and one to which the downfall, as well as the rise of
his empire, may in part be ascribed.   He outraged
justice, till Europe, in moral indignation, cast him
forth as a mischievous being from its soil.

   Rate of Board in Albany.—In winter the members of the Legislature assemble from all parts of
the State, and hold their sessions here.   They live
chiefly in boarding-houses and hotels.   The rate for
a bed room and board, with the use of a public dining-
room and reading-room, is from $3, to $8, $12, and
$ 14 a-week, according to the style of the house.
Albany looks very beautiful at this season.

   May 29. Ther. 63°. *Glen's Falls and Caldwell.*—
Yesterday, we went by the railroad to Saratoga,
which is now interesting.   It has a clean and fresh
appearance, and the air is aromatic from a profusion
of blooming lilacs. To-day, we travelled by a very bad
road, to Glen's Falls, a village on the banks of the
Hudson, where there is a great abundance of water-
power, derived from a fall of 63 feet in the river.
There were nine passengers inside the stage, and

one on the " deck," as the top is called in this country. One of the passengers mentioned that " Mr
—— of New York had sold to a friend of his a lot
of 100 acres up in this country, at $3½ per acre. His
friend bought it by a map and description. When
he came to take possession, he found the lot composed
entirely of rocks and stones, and lying so high, and
so deeply buried in an impenetrable forest, that " even
a bird could scarcely have got to it."   He left it, considering himself completely cheated of his money.

At Glen's Falls, there is an old crazy bridge over
the river, so unsafe that the passengers were requested to leave the stage and walk along it.   The
country from Saratoga to Glen's Falls is pretty well
cleared and settled ; but the soil is white and sandy.
Many stumps of trees stand with crops growing round
them.   In other places, the stumps have been pulled
up by a machine, like teeth drawn from a jaw, and
now form substantial and picturesque fences.

The next stage brought us to *Caldwell,* a village
on the shore of Lake George.   This part of the road
runs between hills, most of which are in a state of
nature.   We left Saratoga at 1 P.M. after dinner,
and arrived at Caldwell at 8 P.M., the distance being
27 miles.   We passed a rock where Colonel Williams was killed by the Indians during the French
war, and a small insignificant pool, by the roadside,
3 miles from Lake George, named " Bloody Pond,"
from its having received the slain of a battle fought
near it in 1755.   The hotel at Caldwell proved good.
It is clean and completely prepared for a rush of sum-

mer visiters.   The situation is extremely beautiful, overlooking the lake.

May 30.   Ther. 47°.   *Lake George.*—At 7 A.M. we embarked on board the " William Caldwell," a handsome new steam-boat of fifty-horse power, low pressure ; and sailed down Lake George.   It is 34 miles long, and in its general features remarkably like Loch Lomond in Scotland.   The breadth, varying from 1 to 4 miles, is the same ; the distribution of small and large islands is similar ; the hills which rise from the margin of the lake are of corresponding heights ; with the exception of the highest peak, which at Loch Lomond is 3260 feet, and here 2200 feet, and with the farther difference, that the American hills are clothed with trees to the summit, while the Scottish mountains are dark and bare.

We reached the north-eastern extremity of the lake at half-past ten ; entered a coach that was in waiting ; and passed along the banks of the Cecilia River, which, rising from Lake George, empties itself, at the distance of a few miles, into Lake Champlain.   We reached the ruins of Fort Ticonderago on Lake Champlain ; surveyed them leisurely, admired the beauty of the scenery, and listened to the stories of the battles which had here been fought between the French and the English, and latterly between the English and Americans.   Afterwards, we dined at an inn in the neighbourhood of the Fort, and returned by the same road and the same steam-boat in the evening to the hotel at Caldwell, highly gratified with our day's excursion.

Emancipation in Jamaica.—Few passengers were
yet travelling by this route to Canada; but we met
one English gentleman who had just come from Jamaica, where he had resided for several months,
thence he had proceeded to New Orleans, where he
entered a steam-boat and came up the Mississippi
and Ohio to Wheeling; and he was now on his way
to Canada. He mentioned that the reports which
are circulated in the United States about the effects
of emancipation in Jamaica are partly true and partly
false. It is true that many of the negroes may be
seen idle ; but it is not true that the lands in general are left uncultivated. If an estate required the
labour of three hundred slaves to cultivate it successfully, free-negroes labour so much more energetically,
that from one hundred and fifty to two hundred of
them actually accomplish the same work within the
same time. The remaining hundred or hundred and
fifty are still on the estate, and take their turn in labour. The practical arrangement is this,—one-half
or two-thirds of the whole labour the first three days
of the week, and the remainder the other three days.
The negroes enjoy the pleasures of mere existence
highly ; they bask in the sun surrounded by their
wives and children, and are happy. The wages paid
to them for three days' labour, added to the produce
of their grounds, suffice to supply all their wants, and
they have not yet contracted artificial tastes, which
would call for extra labour to procure the means of
their gratification. One or two plantations may be
seen uncultivated and covered with weeds ; but these

belong to individuals who used their slaves and apprentices so cruelly, that nearly all their negroes left them or refused to labour the moment emancipation took effect. Even on these estates, however, a few acres may be seen cultivated—the work of some domestics who were not ill treated while slaves, and whose gratitude induces them, when free, to remain in the service even of these masters, and to raise provision for their maintenance. I have seen this account confirmed in its essential features by subsequent published reports.

The beautiful scenery through which we have travelled to-day has been the theatre of many a bloody strife, and graves are still pointed out which contain the bones of hundreds of fallen warriors. It is painful to reflect that to these spots came the flower of France and England in the hey-day of life and enjoyment, and in maddened fury terminated each other's existence. In looking on a battle-field, I cannot help thinking of the mothers who there lost their sons, the wives bereaved of their husbands, and the children whose fathers were cut off; contemplated in such a spirit, the scene appears like an arena in which madmen have come together and indulged their phrenzied passions.

May 31. Ther. 46°. It has again become extremely cold. The Indian corn is just appearing above the ground.

June 1. Ther. 53°. *The Law.*—In all our travels in the United States, we have met with abundant evidence of the activity of the law. Lawyers abound, and courts of justice are held often, and in every locality.   To-day we found a vast concourse of lawyers, doctors, and ordinary citizens, at the village of Ballston Spa, near Saratoga, attending the trial, before Judge Willard, of a young man of some fortune accused of murder.   After a long trial, he was found guilty of manslaughter in the second degree.

Schenectady.—After leaving Ballston Spa by the railroad, the locomotive engine became unserviceable, and the train quietly stood still.   Every car poured forth its company in alarm, like bees issuing from their hive on a serious assault.   The passengers pushed the whole train backwards about a third of a mile, to a passing station, when the engine was run off the track, and a messenger was despatched to Ballston, three miles distant, for aid.   After waiting an hour, *one horse* appeared, and we proceeded forward at a snail's pace.   The evening was fine, and nature fresh and young, which made the detention less tedious.   Independently of such alleviations, however, the Americans are certainly remarkable for good temper ; for although there was ground for provocation in the slender supply of horse power when the engine failed, the numerous company displayed the most exemplary patience and good humour.   After advancing four miles with one single horse, we obtained three, and at last arrived after dark at Schenectady.   We went to the hotel near the railroad office, one of large dimensions, and of good reputation.   The first thing to be done on entering an American hotel, is to go to the bar and inscribe your name in the book of arrivals, adding the name of every individual in your party. When a number of travellers arrive at the same time, the bar-keeper consults with the chamber-maid, and distributes the bed-rooms according to their estimate of the condition of their guests. Single gentlemen are worst served, ladies and married persons best. I do not know whether it was observed that we were foreigners, and whether any extra attention was paid to us on this account ; but in general we experienced the most unexceptionable treatment at the inns, and our accommodations were seldom otherwise than good. On the present occasion we waited longer than usual before any person came to shew us to a room. At last the landlady of the house appeared; she mentioned that the chamber-maids " had gone to the circus," apologised for the delay, and did the honours herself in a very pleasing manner.

In Boston, New York, and Philadelphia, excellent gas is burned in the houses, but in the hotels visited by us since we left New York, oil lamps are extensively used. I have observed that they form a pretty accurate index to the general economy of the house. If they are clean, well trimmed, and burning brightly, the house is well kept throughout. The least neglect shews itself in them. The superintending mind which maintains a discipline that reaches them, does not allow higher objects to be neglected, or to be treated in a slovenly manner. In travelling we find the hours advertised for the starting of coaches and railroad cars to be very ill observed. A de-

tention of half an hour is common, sometimes of a
whole hour. While we waited for the starting of a
train, C—— read a letter from London which the
post had just delivered. A female passenger looked
over her shoulder, and attempted to read it. The
hand was too cramp for her to make it out, and she
turned to her companion and said aloud, " I wanted
to see whether that letter was full !"

June 2. Ther. 55°. *Road to Utica.*—We started
by a railroad train this morning at ten o'clock for
Utica. The distance is seventy-seven miles. The
railroad follows the valley of the Mohawk River.
This valley in general is not above a mile broad. On
the right bank of the Mohawk runs the Erie Canal,
and on the left bank are the high road and the railroad, all nearly parallel to each other. The valley is
inclosed on both sides by hills, apparently of 500
or 600 feet in height, partly cultivated, and partly
bearing the primeval forest. The railroad consists
of a single track, and no inclined plane occurs.
It was commenced in 1834, and completed in 1836,
at a cost of $1,540,000, or $20,000 per mile. It
forms the second link in the great chain by railroad
from Albany to Buffalo and the Falls of Niagara.
The annual dividends are generally ten per cent.*
In the car with us were two Canada Quakers, and
a person whose appearance and manners led us to
suppose him to be a journeyman tradesman. For
three hours they discussed the subject of a gene-

* Tanner's Description of the Canals and Railroads of the United
States. New York, 1840, p. 78.

ral or particular providence with good temper, and some considerable ingenuity. The mechanic maintained the doctrine, that " whatever is, is right," which the Quakers denied ; but as the subject puzzled Milton's Devils in Pandemonium, it was no disparagement to the talents of my fellow-travellers that they did not succeed in throwing much additional light on its obscurities. We arrived safely at Utica at 3 P. M., and found excellent accommodation in Mr Baggs's hotel. The geology of the Mohawk valleys is described in the second annual report of the Geological Survey of the Third District of the State of New York, by Mr Lardner Vanuxem, in the Assembly paper, No. 200, Feb. 20. 1838.*

* " The valley of the Mohawk," says he, " forms an important geological line of division. A high and abrupt elevation, caused by the appearance of the northern edges of the rocks of which it is formed, characterizes the southern side of the valley ; whilst the northern side, being in general formed of the inclined planes of the surfaces of the rocks which pass under and support those of the great escarpment, presents nothing in common with its southern border. The rocks, whose appearance commences in the bottom of the valley, and which extend north, are black shale (with its overlying green shale and sandstone), the Trenton limestone, the Birdseye limestone, the calciferous sand rock, and the gneiss, the arrangement being in the descending order ; thus the black shale, relatively to the four other rocks, is invariably the upper one, while gneiss is as invariably the lowest.

" Along the borders of the Mohawk, from the eastern end of Montgomery to the eastern part of Oneida county, there exists a series of parallel *uplifts* extending but a short distance *south* of the river ; their effect in that direction being confined altogether to the valley. To the *north* the uplifts extend for some distance, but are finally lost in the mass of primary rock, of which gneiss, the lowest member of the uplift, seems to form the greater part. The general direction of the uplifts is north and south."

June 3. Ther. 54°. The weather is cool and showery. Blossoms are still visible on the apple and pear trees; the oats and barley do not yet cover the ground so thickly as to obscure the soil; and altogether vegetation is fully later than it is at Edinburgh in ordinary seasons at the same period of the year.

Trenton Falls.—We hired a carriage with grasshopper springs and two horses to drive us to Trenton Falls, fifteen miles distant from Utica. No words can describe the horrible condition of the road, and yet it was a turnpike, on which toll was levied both going and returning. It runs, however, through a beautiful and fertile country, crosses a ridge ot hills from which delightful views are obtained of Utica and of the valley in which the Trenton Falls are situated. The houses are neat; much of the country is cleared, and the fields are well cultivated. All seems civilized except the roads. The rural population will scarcely expend a dollar on a road which will not present them with half-yearly dividends and a saleable stock. The waste of labour, destruction of vehicles, and loss of time, are taxes which they seem not to appreciate, or rather which they evade, by using the roads only during winter snows and midsummer droughts, when nature renders them passable.

The falls of the Trenton are very picturesque. The river, " the West Canada Creek," is about the same in size as the Clyde at Lanark in Scotland; its bed is cut deep into limestone, and its banks are thickly wooded. There are six falls: in the upper-

most the water is precipitated eighteen or twenty
feet down an abrupt ledge into a spacious basin.   In
another the perpendicular descent is forty-eight feet,
and in a third it is thirty-seven feet.   In the others
the fall is broken.   The entire descent in less than
five miles is 387 feet.   The proprietor has cut walks,
erected stairs, thrown a bridge across the river, built
sheds and seats for resting and taking refreshments,
excavated paths in the rock to admit the visiter to
the best points of view, secured dangerous paths by
chains, and established an excellent hotel; so that, altogether, the visit to the Falls is rendered highly interesting and inviting.   The scenery is full of loveliness and
beauty, approaching in some points to grandeur.   The
lime rock abounds in organic remains, and specimens
of ammonites, trilobites, &c., along with rock-crys-
tals, are exhibited at the inn.   In the hotel, we found
residing for a few days one of the most estimable and
distinguished men of the United States, with whom
we had previously become acquainted, along with several members of his family.   We enjoyed the pleasure of their society; and altogether this has been a
day of great gratification.

   Utica.—This was the site of the old Fort Schuyler.
The first settlement took place in 1789.   In 1798 a
village charter was granted, and in 1832 the place
was incorporated into a city.   It contains now nearly
10,000 inhabitants.   It is regularly laid out, the
streets are of good width and mostly paved, but it
has no lamps.   It has sixteen churches, a lyceum, an
academy, a high school, a female institute, a museum,

and an institution called the Young Men's Association, in which there is a library and reading-room, which are gratuitously open for the use of strangers. It contains also three banks, an insurance company, and from six to eight newspaper establishments. We found several phrenologists in the city, from whom we received much attention. They drove us to see the new Lunatic Asylum now in the course of erection by the State of New York, about a mile and a half from the town. The foundations of this institution are laid, and on a large scale. It is in the form of a square, and will inclose eleven acres of ground within its area. It is calculated to accommodate 1000 patients, paupers, and also persons who pay. Attached to it is a farm of 130 acres. The building stands on an eminence sixty-eight feet above the level of the Erie Canal, and commands a beautiful view of the surrounding country. The erection of this asylum is intrusted to commissioners, and so searching is the spirit of party, that even the management of charities cannot escape from its influence. Francis E. Spinner and Elam Lynds have been dismissed, and Anson Dart and Willett H. Shearman have been appointed commissioners in their stead, purely, it is said, on party grounds; but Captain W. Clarke, the most active of the commissioners, has in the mean time been spared. We enjoyed much hospitality and excellent society during our stay at Utica. I observed, in a newspaper there, an advertisement by Mr Crowley, 42 Geneseo Street, intimating that he professes Practical Phrenology,—

that he will give lessons in it on one or two evenings in every week, and that he examines heads for a fee. I did not see him.

June 5. Ther. 54°. *Journey to Syracuse.*—A railroad is in the course of construction between Utica and Syracuse, but not yet serviceable. The road was described as very bad, and we were advised by our friends to travel by the boat on the Erie Canal. We started at eight o'clock in the morning, and proceeded at the rate of five miles an hour. The distance is fifty-three miles, and the canal runs for a part of the way through a low, marshy, unsettled, and uninteresting country. It rained the most of the day. After dinner, a brisk young man entered the boat, and in a loud voice asked if any lady or gentleman wanted to have " corns cured." He was asked his terms, and said they were half a dollar for one corn, and less for each additional. He offered to remove the corn by the root instantly, without pain, and engaged that it should never grow again. After a great deal of bargaining and bad wit, one passenger made an agreement with him to have one corn extirpated, for which he was to pay 25 cents (1s. sterling). The operator, who was dubbed by the passengers " the Doctor," pulled out a bottle, borrowed a penknife, applied some sulphuric acid to the corn, received his 25 cents, paid 18 cents for his fare, and left the boat. The lent knife was destroyed by the acid, but " the Doctor" was fairly beyond reach before its owner made this discovery. The best piece of wit elicited on the occasion was a remark that this

was in every sense "a toe-boat." The master of the
boat told me that "the Doctor" had done a small
business to-day, but that yesterday he had cleared
$9 in the boat going east.

In most of the public conveyances, very little attention is paid to the safety of the passengers' luggage. In this boat two men were returning to Ro-
chester, whence they had come yesterday, to inquire
after their portmanteaus, which they had missed on
arriving at Utica. The owners of all the public conveyances give notice that they will not be responsible
for luggage ; but the supreme courts in different
States have decided that no individual can set aside
the common law, which enforces this liability, and
that the public notice is of no avail. As this rule of
law is interesting to travellers in general, I subjoin
in the Appendix, No. VII. a report of the decisions·
They have, in some instances, led to the adoption of
a regular plan for securing the effects of passengers,
which is at once simple and effectual. Long straps
of leather are used, having at their extremities loop-
holes, to which are attached pieces of tin-plate bearing numbers from one to two or three hundred. The
same number is stamped on the tin-plates attached
to each end of these straps. When a passenger presents his luggage, one of the plates is slipped off the
strap and given to him as his voucher ; and the strap
itself, bearing the other plate, is attached to his port-
manteau. This is repeated with every piece of his
luggage. At the end of the journey, the baggage
master reads aloud the numbers attached to the

packages, as he takes them out of the boat, car, or
coach ; and the owner, on producing the check-plate
bearing the same number, receives the package, but
not otherwise.   There is no lock on the canal from
Utica till within one mile of Syracuse, where three
descending locks occur.   We arrived at Syracuse at
half-past eight o'clock, and found very comfortable
accommodation in the Syracuse Hotel, close beside
the wharf.*

Syracuse.—We were again greeted by several
highly respectable citizens of Syracuse who have
embraced phrenology, and have formed a phrenological society.   One of them kindly drove us in an
open carriage to Salina, a village in the neighbourhood, which has received its name from its salt
springs.   These have all been reserved by the State,
and they yield a large revenue, applicable to the expenses of the Erie Canal.   The spring was known to
the Indians, and was discovered by the resort of the
wild animals to drink the water.   It lies near the
Onondaga Lake, which is fresh to the bottom.   The

---

* Before we left the United States, the Syracuse and Utica Railroad
was completed.   It is a continuation of the Utica and Schenectady
Railroad.   It passes up the south acclivity of the Mohawk, near to,
and parallel with, the Erie Canal.   Its length is fifty-three miles.
The capital stock is ₰800,000.   According to a statement of the President, the company received for tolls in five months ₰117,614, equal
to twelve per cent. on its cost, or thirty per cent. per annum.   The
revenue of these railroads is derived from passengers alone.   Their
charters prohibit them from carrying goods, the monopoly of which
the State, as proprietor of the Erie Canal, reserves to itself.   In September 1840, this stock sold in the New York market at ₰117 per
share of ₰100.—*Tanner's Canals and Railroads,* p. 78.

well at Salina, which was opened twelve or thirteen years since, is seventy feet in depth, and from it brine is raised, by means of forcing pumps worked by a water-wheel, to a reservoir eighty-five feet above the Oswego Canal. It is distributed to a great number of salt-works. In the month of July 1837 these pumps raised 482 gallons of brine in a minute, or 28,920 gallons in an hour. Its temperature during its passage from the pumps into the reservoir is 50° F. Its specific gravity is 1.11060 at 60° F. It is said that for a period of thirty-six years its strength has undergone no change. One thousand grains evaporated to a perfect dryness by heat, left a residuum of 146.50 grains. The following is the result of an analysis of this quantity of the water :—

Carbonate of lime,	.	.	.	0.17
Sulphate of lime,	.	.	.	4.72
Chloride of calcium,	.	.	.	1.04
Chloride of magnesium,		.	.	0.51
Chloride of sodium, or common salt,			.	140.02
Oxide of iron, with a minute portion of silica and carbonate of lime,	.	.	.	0.04
Carbonic acid, holding in solution the carbonate of lime and oxide of iron,		.	.	0.09
Water, with a trace of organic matter and bromine,				853.41
				1000.00

This brine contains 1130 grains of pure and perfectly dry chloride of sodium in a wine pint, and 9045 grains, or 1.29 lb. avoirdupois in a gallon. It therefore requires 43½ of these gallons to yield a bushel of salt weighing 56 lb. But as salt made by boiling usually contains not less than five per cent. of water,

41½ of these gallons will yield a bushel of salt of mercantile quality.*

There are wells also at Syracuse, Geddes, and Liverpool, and in 1835 the quantity of salt manufactured from them all amounted to 2,222,694 bushels.
The individuals who manufacture the salt pay a tax
to the State for the use of the springs.

In the Appendix, No. VIII., I present a table exhibiting " the relative strength of the different brines
from which salt is manufactured in the United States,"
and a table " shewing the composition of the various
specimens of Onondaga and foreign salt in 1000
parts."

Dr Hoyt mentioned, that in the men who superintend the boiling of the salt, the *venous* blood is
nearly as florid red as the arterial blood in other
men. He bled one yesterday, and but for the continuous flow, he might have believed that he had
punctured an artery. These men are remarkably
healthy, and if sober, are rarely affected with any
ailment.

Syracuse is the capital of Onondaga county. It contains about 800 houses and stores, several churches,
two banks, a court-house, and a jail. It appears to
carry on an extensive business. We saw two Onondaga Indians, a man and woman, in the street. They
have a settlement seven miles distant. These two
were poorly clothed, dirty, and forlorn in their appearance ; like the most abject of European beggars,
only dark in the complexion. They spoke English

* Abridged from *Report by Dr Lewis C. Beck to the Governor of the
State of New York.* Assembly Paper, No. 200, p. 25.—20.h Feb. 1838.

Phrenology.—In the evening the Phrenological Society of Syracuse held a meeting in the Presbyterian church. I had positively declined to deliver a lecture, or to make any public exhibition, but agreed to take a part, incidentally, in the proceedings of any meeting of the society. I insisted that the public notices of the meeting should be so expressed, and they were so. On entering the church, which was filled, the president of the Society led me at once to the pulpit ; and announced that I would address the audience. I told him that he must begin with the ordinary business of the Society : he then said, that they had no business that evening except to hear me. I was thus unexpectedly forced to extemporize without either a theme or preparation. I spoke for an hour and twenty minutes, and the people listened. The phrenologists were so much satisfied, that next morning I found that they had come to the inn, and as a mark of respect, proposed to the landlord to settle my bill. This intended courtesy I respectfully declined, and we parted friends.

June 7. Ther. 58°. *Railroad from Syracuse to Auburn.*—This railroad was opened only on 5th June, and we travelled on it the third morning of its operation. It was not inclosed, and the domestic animals along the line had not yet become accustomed to the appearance of the locomotive engines and trains. It was a curious study to mark the effects of our train upon them, as it rushed past. The horses in the fields generally ran away, carrying their heads erect, and their ears bent downwards and backwards ; and they turned their heads alternately to the one side and the other to catch a glimpse of the dreaded enemy behind. One horse, however, turned round to us, and presented a bold and inquiring front. He erected his ears and turned them towards us, stood firm on his legs, and looked as if he would " defy the devil." The sheep and lambs fled in terrible agitation and confusion. The swine early took alarm, and tried to run from before us. When we overtook them, they endeavoured, in an ecstasy of fear, to push themselves through the fences, if there happened to be any, or into the banks. The cows fled, but were speedily breathless, and gave up in despair. A huge breeding hen rose suddenly from her brood, and put herself in an attitude of defence, without moving a step. Another hen, without a brood, flew straight up into the air, in a paroxysm of fright. Fortunately none of these animals ventured on the railroad, and we arrived at Auburn, distance 26 miles, in one hour and ten minutes, without accident or detention. In a separate car were two stout, rascally-looking convicts, chained together, under charge of an officer, going to Auburn State-Prison. They were merry and reckless, and came out at the half-way station to have their last supply of tobacco and whisky, before entering on the life of temperance that awaited them in jail.

Auburn State-Prison.—We visited this prison, accompanied by his Excellency Governor Seward (to whom we carried letters of introduction), and saw its whole economy. It was commenced in 1816, and is built on the plan of a hollow square, inclosed by four walls each 500 feet long. The convicts labour during day in large workshops, under the close surveillance of the officers of the prison, to prevent them from conversing. After work hours, they are locked up in separate cells. They move to and from their cells, and to and from the hall in which they receive their meals, in the lock-step, and are never allowed to communicate with each other. The system of treatment is essentially the same as that pursued at Boston and Blackwell's Island, already described. Here, however, the sleeping cells are lower in the roof, and have no ventilating chimneys communicating with the open air. The convicts dined during our visit, and we saw 650 of them in a large apartment, seated at narrow tables arranged like the seats in a theatre, so that the convicts at one table looked on the backs of those at the table before. The keepers were stationed in the open passages to watch them. Their heads presented the usual development of criminals, viz., deficiency of size in many, deficiency of the moral organs in the great majority, deficiency of intellect in many, with large organs of the propensities in nearly all. One exception struck me. A man apparently above sixty presented an ample coronal region, with a good intellectual development, such as one very rarely sees in confirmed criminals. I mentioned the fact to Governor Seward, and he very obligingly made inquiries into his history. He learned that the man had been a " root doctor ;" but in consequence of the removal of the late agent of the prison, and the recent appointment of Dr Palmer in his place, no information could be obtained concerning the offence for which he had been convicted. Among the convicts was a man in respectable circumstances, who, under religious delusions, had chastised his son, a child, to such an extent that he died. He is sentenced to seven years' confinement. His intellectual organs appeared to be of average size; those of Combativeness and Destructiveness to be large; and the moral organs rather shallow and deficient. In the hospital we saw a convict who, six days before, had voluntarily chopped off his left hand. Governor Seward asked him why he had done so. " Because," said he, " it had offended against God and man, and it was borne in upon me, that if I cut it off, as commanded by the Scripture, God would forgive me, and man also." In the hospital we saw likewise an interesting man, Mr Rathbun of Buffalo, acting in the capacity of steward. He had been engaged in gigantic building speculations in the town of Buffalo, and at Niagara Falls, and failing in resources, he was a participator in forgeries, to the extent, as we were told, of nearly a million of dollars. He was a man of great talent, and of highly popular manners, and so bold in his undertakings, that he was a general favourite with the people. It was with great difficulty that the jury could be induced to find him guilty, although the evidence was overwhelmingly clear, and the frauds enormous in their extent. At last, however, they returned a verdict against him, and he was sentenced to five years' imprisonment. He has been appointed steward of the hospital as an act of grace. He obeys the prison rules, does not presume on his former station, discharges his duties, but keeps himself quite aloof from his fellow-convicts.

Captain Lynds, the late agent of the prison, is described as having been a brave officer of the army, and the father of this convict-system. He had also managed the prison at Sing-Sing. He entertained the opinion that convicts were sent to prison to be punished, and that discipline could be maintained only by the lash. He acted on these views, and his proceedings had been so much at variance with the spirit of the age, that there arose a great public excitement on the subject, in consequence of which he had retired. Dr Palmer had succeeded him, and the social dinner, which we saw has been instituted since his appointment. I have already, vol. ii. p. 16, expressed my opinion of the relative merits of the Auburn and Philadelphia systems.

Auburn.—After dinner, we hired a carriage and drove along the shores of the Owasco Lake, two miles from the town, and, but for an execrable road, would have enjoyed the scenery highly. Although its banks are low, the landscape of the lake is exceedingly beautiful, and at this season in its prime. We visited Judge Conklin of the Supreme Court, who has a residence near the lake, and enjoyed much interesting conversation with him and his family. The more I see of the American judges, the higher becomes my estimate of their powers, activity, and attainments. I spoke to Judge Conklin of the nearly universal want of ventilation in the American courts He acknowledged it to be a very great evil, and mentioned that he had suffered severely from it a few years ago, when trying an important cause in a neighbouring town. It was mid-winter, and the trial lasted eight days. The court-room was crowded to excess, and there was no cranny for ventilation. He suffered so excessively from the bad air, that he opened the window directly at his back, and sat with it open during the whole days of the trial. He then drove home in an open carriage, the only one he could procure; the thermometer being at zero. He was seized with a cold which nearly proved fatal, and which did not leave him for many months.

We returned to Auburn in the evening. It is one of the most pleasing little towns we have seen, even in this land of pretty villages, and shews evident marks of prosperity. It has numerous mills and manufactories, driven by the stream which issues from the Owasco Lake. Its population now amounts to 6000. There are seven churches, an academy, a Presbyterian theological seminary, a museum, two banks, a court-house, and a jail.

I made inquiry into the system of repairing the roads here, and was told that they are maintained by so many days' labour assessed on each proprietor. It is performed in this month. The ruts are filled up with mud, and this is all that is done till the subsequent year. We saw them using the plough to mend some of the bye-roads in this State.

I had the pleasure also of visiting Dr Briggs, whose name has already been mentioned in the verdict of the coroner's inquest on the body of Louis Von Eck. He mentioned that Captain Lynds was severe on small breaches of discipline, for the very purpose of preventing greater infringements of the rules and heavier punishments; that the reports circulated were greatly exaggerated; and that, if such flogging as was described had existed, he, as physician to the prison, must have known of it, which he never did.

June 8. Ther. 65°. *Geneva.*—At Auburn we met a family from Boston travelling westward, and along with them hired an " exclusive extra," or stage-coach seated for nine persons, and drawn by four horses. We started at half-past nine A. M., and found the road, although the great high-way turnpike to the west, horribly bad. Here I realized the fact of having the crown of my head rudely beaten against the top of the vehicle, so dreadful were the jolts. Seven miles west from Auburn, we crossed the Cayuga Lake on a wooden bridge, one mile and eight rods in length. This lake is thirty-eight miles long, and from one to two miles broad. It is shallow, but a steam-boat navigates it daily to Ithaca, a thriving village at its head, thirty-six miles distant from the village of Cayuga, where we crossed it. Fifteen miles farther west, we entered Geneva, a small town situated on the bank of the Seneca Lake, and distinguished for its picturesque beauty. We dined here; and started again for Canandaigua, where we arrived at eight P. M., the distance being sixteen miles. Since we left Auburn the country has presented a rich soil, well cultivated, with every external indication of great prosperity among the people. C—— was feverish when we arrived at Canandaigua, in consequence of the pain occasioned by the excessive jolting which she had sustained.

Canandaigua.—This village is situated at the distance of half a mile from a beautiful lake bearing the same name, and is itself one of that class of towns which I have seen in no country except the United States. Fifty years ago, it was in the heart of the desert ; now its principal street is two miles in length, with two broad side-walks, decorated with trees. The houses stand in enclosures at a little distance from the road, and are ornamented with trees, shrubs, and flowers. The street is a long succession of pretty villas, of pure white, gleaming through the richest verdure. The houses and offices are built chiefly of wood ; but they have a handsome appearance. In remote situations in the United States the family burying-ground may be seen, indicated by tomb-stones, in the fields or orchards, there being no general burial-place except at a great distance. The living there dwell among the dead. Even in the villages, the graveyards, as they name them, are not attached to churches ; but are enclosures set apart for this purpose, and unconnected with any buildings. In strolling abroad to-day, I passed the burial-ground of this village, and the first tomb stone that attracted my attention bore the following inscription. " If eternal happiness be the reward of tender love, unobtrusive piety, and the kindliest charity, blessed is the spirit which once animated the lovely tenant of this sepulchre." It was the monument of a young wife, erected by her husband to her and her infant daughter.

The peculiarity of American villages consists in the beauty of the dwellings and the superior manners and education of the inhabitants compared with European villages. There is, however, not much society among themselves, but to strangers they are very hospitable. A number of Scotsmen are settled here, some of them in affluent circumstances, and their condition is such that I could not bewail their change of country. Some of them complain of trouble with their " helps ;" but I strongly suspect that the meagre wages allowed to domestic servants (less than the common remuneration for labour in other departments of industry), has much to do with these annoyances. When ample remuneration is given, I am assured that the native Americans will engage in service, and prove faithful, useful, and obliging.

In visiting a Scotch gentleman in this village, I was surprised to observe a number of pictures and articles of *vertu* which I thought I had seen before. They proved to have been the property of the late Thomas Sievwright, Esq. of Meggetland, near Edinburgh, which had been brought to sale after his death. Their present owner happened to visit that city at the time of the sale, and purchased largely. It was interesting to meet with the relics of an old acquaintance in such an unexpected situation.

The land in this neighbourhood is cleared and fertile. It sells at prices varying from $30 to $50 an acre, according to quality and situation. It may be let on the following terms. If the proprietor furnish only the land, a tenant will pay him one-third of the produce in kind. If he furnish the land and the chief part of the stocking and seed, he will receive one-half of the produce; but in either case he must sell his share and turn it into money as he best can. Money-rents for land are nearly unknown. Although the soil is excellent, the cultivation is not of a superior order. The price of labour is so high, and that of produce so low (owing to the fertility and vast extent of the new lands in the west, the produce of which is brought to the eastern cities, and keeps grain cheap), that draining, manuring, and other expensive operations, are sparingly executed. A large crop of wheat yields forty bushels an acre; but this extent of produce is rare. The growth of wheat is much more rapid, and the straw stronger than in Britain; but in general the ear does not fill so thoroughly. The title to land is very simple. A printed form of conveyance is filled up with a description of the property, executed before witnesses, and registered in the county books, and the title is complete. Twenty-five years' possession on a written title gives an indefeasible right, excepting only the claims of minors, and of other persons *ab agendo*.

June 11. Ther. 58°. *Avon Springs.*—We proceeded to Avon village, a distance of twenty-five miles, and visited the Avon springs. The first spring is called

the Avon New Bath Spring, and was discovered by
the present proprietor in 1835. The depth of the
well is about thirty-six feet, and the formation
through which the water rises is the calciferous slate.
The temperature of the water is about 50° Fahr.
and the specific gravity is 1.00356. One pint of the
water contains

			Grains.
Carbonate of lime,	.	.	3.37
Sulphate of lime,	.	.	0.44
Sulphate of magnesia,	.	.	1.01
Sulphate of soda,	.	.	4.84
Chloride of sodium,	.	.	0.71
			——
			10.37

Sulphuretted hydrogen 3.91 cubic inches.

The water of this spring, when heated, assumes a
beautiful green colour; the cause of which is not ascertained.

The middle spring, situated about thirty rods east
of the former, gives a temperature of 51° Fahr., and,
according to Professor Hadley, is of the following
composition. A pint of this water contains

			Grains.
Carbonate of lime,	.	.	1.00
Sulphate of lime,	.	.	10.50
Sulphate of magnesia,	.	.	1.25
Sulphate of soda,	.	.	2.00
Chloride of sodium,	.	.	2.30
			——
			17.05

Sulphuretted hydrogen,	12.0 cubic inches.
Carbonic acid, .	5.6 do.*

Hotels and baths have been erected at these springs,

* Dr Beck's Report, No. 200, p. 66.

and there is a considerable and increasing resort to them by invalids.

June 12. Ther. 44°. *Indians.*—A party of Indians appeared in the village this morning, travelling in a waggon drawn by two shabby grey ponies. The driver was an Indian youth, apparently about sixteen or seventeen years of age, and rather good-looking, clothed in the European style, but in clothes of various colours, obviously not made for himself. The women of the party were dressed in trousers and short gowns of cotton cloth; they wore shoes, and each had a good large thick blanket with a blue border wrapt round her person. The young man wore a fur cap, but the heads of the women were uncovered; their hair was long and twisted up behind. They were dark and very plain. They came to sell their manufactured articles. Afterwards two other Indian women came into the village; their costume was the same, only their coarse black hair hung in lank locks about their heads and necks, in savage disorder and neglect. I addressed them; but they understood no English. On my presenting them with a piece of money, they expressed thanks by pleased looks and a slight curtsey.

June 13. Ther. 50°. *Geneseo.*—We proceeded to Geneseo, a thriving village on the high ground, which forms the eastern boundary of Geneseo valley. The view from it is beautiful and luxuriant. The Geneseo valley consists of a vast expanse of rich alluvial clay, nearly level, through which runs the Geneseo River, navigable for small boats to Lake

Ontario. The name means the river of the broad valley. The country is cleared as far as the eye can reach, and carries the richest crops of wheat, and other common grains. " Geneseo flour" bears a high price in the New York market ; and in all the villages in this region where there is water-power, one sees large mills erected, bearing the inscription " cash for wheat." In clearing the forest, the present proprietor has spared the finest trees and left them in the most picturesque groups. The valley, seen from the village, looks like an extensive and beautiful English park.

The village is this capital of Livingston county, and contains a high school, Episcopalian, Presbyterian, and Methodist churches, a handsome courthouse, two inns, and numerous " stores." The whole country through which we have lately passed, and also this county, lie on limestone. Beginning on the north, the rocks " are the hydraulic limestone, Onondaga and Seneca limestones, the extensive group of fossiliferous shales, succeeded by the upper black shale, the Cashaqua shale, the Gardean and Portage groups. The latter occupies only some of the high grounds in the southern part of Livingston county." For many feet in depth the Geneseo flats, as they are generally called, consist of fine sand and clay intimately mixed.*

* Report by James Hall, State Geologist, No. 50, p. 416. Mr Hall, in his report on the Physical Geography, Valleys, &c., of Western New York, remarks that " the absence of all strata superior to the coal series (if we except some small tracts of tertiary towards the

I observe, for the first time this season, barley in the ear.

June 14. Ther. 48°. June 15. Ther. 46°. The wheat begins to appear in the ear.

June 16. Ther. 50°. June 17. Ther. 52°. June 18. Ther. 71°. To-day we had the first dish of ripe cherries.

June 19. Ther. 48°. We proceeded westward to Batavia, 25 miles, in company with a highly interesting party of friends, in two " exclusive extras," and visited Batavia and Lockport. There we found a railroad which carried us to the Falls of Niagara, where we arrived on the 21st of June.

June 22. Ther. 50°. *General Scott.*—I had the pleasure of being introduced to this gentleman, whom I have formerly mentioned, vol. ii. p. 243. He has gained the admiration of the wise and good men of all parties for his successful exertions in restraining the fierce spirit of the American borderers, and preventing them from attacking the Canadian English.

eastern part of the State) in New York and Pennsylvania prove that this great area has never been submerged beneath the ocean for any length of time, since the period of these ancient depositions. We have proof, however, of the violent action of water in the denuding and excavating agency, in the production of valleys and water-courses. These phenomena may have been caused in part by a sudden submergence, and the rapid passage of a wave over the surface. The subsequent changes may have resulted from an inland sea, which, for a long period, remained in possession of a large portion of the interior of the continent, ranging at various elevations. This in its subsidence gave rise to small lakes, on the more elevated grounds, which, from accumulating waters, burst their barriers and communicated with those of a lower level, or passed off through the present water-courses to the ocean." P. 432.

He and the British officers on the Canada shore
have been, and still are, on the best terms of reciprocal intercourse. To the credit of both, it is generally acknowledged that they, the men of the sword,
have been the real peace-makers in this district during the last eighteen months. They have used
every exertion to restrain the infuriated masses on
both sides. General Scott mentioned to me that his
grandfather was a Scotchman, who fought on the
side of the Pretender at the battle of Culloden, and
subsequently fled to America. He might have returned after the amnesty, but preferred remaining
in the Colonies. We had the pleasure also of making the acquaintance of General Porter, who resides
here, and is the proprietor of Goat Island, in the St
Lawrence, through which the best access has been
made to the Falls.

The Western Country.—We met with two friends
who had just returned by the lakes from the far west,
whither they had gone on an exploratory trip for their
own information. They had suffered severely from
the ague, and saw almost every family affected with
it, many having not yet recovered from the attacks
of last autumn. They mentioned that the timber
land is generally preferred to the prairies. They
came to the conclusion that the " West" forms a
desirable place of settlement for men of small capital, great bodily strength, and youth ; but that no
educated man with a competency can settle there,
except by sacrificing for many years every advantage which these confer.

Niagara Falls.—We devoted four days to the enjoyment of this wonder of the world, and were not disappointed. The first impression, however, must differ in every individual, according to the natural endowment and habitual activity of his faculties. I confess that the first view did not awaken those profound emotions of astonishment, sublimity, and awe in me which are generally described as its effects on visiters. I had read many descriptions and seen numerous pictures of the scene, and found its general features very much those which I had expected. It excited my intellectual faculties too entirely to allow me to experience vivid emotions. The most forcible idea suggested was that of the astonishing power of gravitation. The mass of waters rushed downwards with an indescribable momentum, and seemed to reveal to the senses the awful force of this mysterious influence. Above the Falls the river runs over a bed of limestone; below them it has worn a deep channel in the rock, leaving high perpendicular walls on each side. The difference of level between the water on the upper and that on the lower beds of the rock is 158 feet 4 inches. The descending surface is perpendicular, and the whole waters of the St Lawrence are precipitated over it in unbroken masses. The fall is fourteen miles from Lake Ontario, into which the waters flow; and it is obvious to the eye that they have excavated the deep channel all this distance,* and are still engaged in the work of excavation. By observing the progress which they have made in certain spaces of

* Mr Lyell treats of this subject in his Principles of Geology, vol. i. p. 261, 3d edit.

time, data have been obtained for calculating the period which must have elapsed since the work began, and that which may be still required before they shall deepen the whole course upwards to Lake Erie, about twenty miles. I became immersed in the contemplation of these ideas, and others of a similar description, all allied to reason, and it was only by degrees that the observing faculties and the sentiments awakened and came into communion with the scene. They at last embraced it, dwelt on it, responded to it, thrilled with intense delight, and carried it off indelibly impressed upon the memory and imagination.

It would be in vain for me to attempt a description of the Falls : this has often been given by abler pens. I may mention, however, that after surveying them from the British side, the American side, and Goat Island in the middle of the stream, under the rays of the noontide sun of the 22d of June, and those of a bright full moon at night; after seeing the most perfect solar rainbows lying at our feet by day, and lunar rainbows (like the ghosts of those of the sun) by night; after listening to the legends of Indians losing command of their canoes, and being precipitated over its brow and engulfed in the whirlpool below ; after frequent crossing and recrossing the foaming stream below the cataract in boats ; and after descending by the Biddle staircase and looking up to the world of water pouring down overhead ; in short, after dwelling for days on its every feature,—I was far less impressed by its sublimity than by its beauty : it is full of grace and ma-

jesty, and emotions of pleasure were constantly predominant while I gazed on it.   The Atlantic in the
equinoctial gale of 20th September 1838, seen from
the deck of the Great Western, far surpassed Niagara Falls in terrific grandeur.   My companion accurately described them in the following words : " One
sits and gazes one's self out of all thought, and into a
delightful sort of reverie, which is interrupted only
when some new effect of clouds or sunlight rouses
one's attention.   I can only say, that I never saw
such *greens* nor such *whites* as are presented by the
rushing waters,—nor such graceful motions, nor such
delicate veils, nor such rainbows, nor listened to such
lulling sounds !   And all in the midst of more beauty
of accompaniment than Niagara usually receives credit for.   The banks of the river are high, steep,
rocky, and wooded ; and the water is a cool and lovely
green.   Goat Island is a little Eden, and all the paths
and ways leading to the Falls are judiciously laid out."
The best guide to the Falls is the admirable work of
Mr Ingraham of Boston.   He is a man of taste and
education, and passionately enamoured of the scene.
We walked several miles down the river, and visited
the " Rapids," but they merit no particular description.   About two miles and a half below the village,
the railroad approaches within a few yards of the
brink of the precipitous bank of the stream, and at that
spot, the Falls themselves and surrounding scenery
appear grouped together, and look like a living cabinet
picture of the most exquisite gracefulness and beauty.

On crossing to the Canadian side, where there was

a large and commodious hotel (since burned down), the first object that presented itself was a British sentinel of the 43d Regiment keeping guard at the landing-place. He asked no questions, and I learned afterwards that he is posted there to prevent the British soldiers from deserting. There is no danger in crossing the river even in a small boat, for the basin which receives the cataract is so deep (supposed to be 800 feet) and so wide that the turbulence soon subsides.

Lundies Lane.—This is the name of the village on the Canadian side of the Falls, and the site of a severely contested battle between the British and Americans, fought on the 25th of July 1814. About 870 men on each side were killed, wounded, or taken prisoners, and the Americans retired at night. No traces of the devastations now remain. I wished to obtain some information, and accosted a man sitting in a field. He was an Irishman, and said that he could not walk. I asked him why. His answer was in these words : " I was crazy, Sir, and the people who had the charge of me put me into a cellar, and my feet were frozen and afterwards cut off." " Where did this happen?" " In the town of Niagara, Sir." This town is on the Canadian side, near the junction of the river with Lake Ontario. What a scene of suffering and cruel neglect was embodied in this brief narrative !

June 25. Ther. 62°. *Journey to Buffalo.*—We left Niagara Falls at half-past 2 P.M., in a railroad car, and arrived at Buffalo at 4 P.M. The distance is

22 miles. Fifty years ago, it would have appeared
as incredible that we should approach to and depart
from the Falls of Niagara by railroads and locomotive
engines, as that the stream should run upwards ; and
yet this feat is accomplished. It seems so natural,
now when it is done, that only on reflection and
by contrast does it excite surprise. This railroad
runs nearly along the right bank of the Niagara
River the whole way to Buffalo, and affords admirable views of the scenery. Several islands in the
stream present themselves, the largest of which,
Navy Island, has been the theatre of some recent
contests between the Government forces and the Canadian Patriots, as they call themselves, or Rebels,
as they are named by the British. The people on
both sides of the river were strongly excited during
the late Canadian insurrection, and the subject still
continues an interesting topic of conversation. The
feeling of the two nations towards each other was
discussed in very reasonable terms by the passengers in the railway car. One of the Americans said,
" It is not true that the British hate us. I know
that they shew our people a great deal of kindness
and hospitality when they go over to the other side.
It is only the ignorant and bigoted Tories who hate
us, and they do so merely because they hate republican institutions. They have no notion what
we are. I wish we could catch a parcel of them and
parade them through our States, as they did Black
Hawk and other Indian chiefs.* It is the only

* The United States' Government from time to time invites the

way to open their eyes, and make them see that we are men." This speech called forth a loud laugh of approbation ; and it appeared to me to contain a very sensible idea. The Tories in general are kind-hearted men ; and a sight of the industry, the prosperity, the order, and attention to religion that essentially reign in this vast republic, notwithstanding its faults and imperfections, would expand their sympathies, and render them less afraid of human nature when left, unguided by kings and nobles, to fulfil its destinies. The same gentleman added, that he knew it to be a fact that the British officers of the line had done every thing possible to alleviate the sufferings of the prisoners taken in the late border troubles.

American Hotels.—The hotels in the western region of New York State are on a large scale and very good ; but only one basin, one tumbler, and one basin-stand, are allowed for two persons. On representing civilly, however, our British habits, we were always indulged with duplicates. The meals are served with amazing dispatch. We were generally first and last at table, yet only 15 minutes, by

most formidable of the Indian chiefs to visit Washington. They are received with great ceremony, conducted to all the public institutions, and afterwards invited to the large Atlantic cities, where similar honours are paid to them. Care is taken to shew them the navy yards and the ships of war, the arsenals and arms ; and also reviews of the best appointed militia regiments. The object of the Government is to send them home with a practical conviction of the colossal power of the United States contrasted with that of their warrior bands, and it is generally accomplished.

my watch, elapsed between our sitting down and rising up. Within that time 150 persons had crammed
down a breakfast. " You Europeans," said an American, " eat as if you actually enjoyed your food !"
" Assuredly we do,—and you Americans will never
escape from dyspepsia and headachs until you also
learn to enjoy your meals."

June 26. Ther. 65°. The village of Buffalo was
burned to the ground by the English in 1814. It is
now a town of 20,000 inhabitants, and carries on an
extensive trade, as the eastern port on Lake Erie.
Here the New York and Erie Canal has its terminus.
The streets are wide, the houses substantial, and the
stores numerous, of vast extent, and stocked with almost every useful and ornamental article produced by
Europe and America. The newspapers reported the
" Lake craft" in the following terms:—" There were in
harbour this morning nineteen steam-boats, two ships,
one barque, seven brigs, and sixty-one schooners : in
all ninety sail. Among these is not included the
Julia Palmer, now being converted into a steamer.
Of the steam-boats, about one-half are undergoing
repairs or being repainted, preparatory to commencing
the fall campaign,—the others are taking their regular turn in the line. The sail craft are all, or nearly
all, loading or unloading, and present a lively appearance." We counted seven large steam-boats on
the wharf, all announced as ready to sail, and containing excellent accommodation for passengers.
They have public cabins and private state-rooms, and,
from their large size, promise to be comfortable ves-

sels. One of the three-masted ships was announced as belonging to the " Mill-waukie and Chicago Line," indicating that she is one of a number of regular traders. I have already mentioned that it has been found necessary to enlarge the Erie Canal. It will be made from sixty to seventy feet wide, and seven feet deep, and have double sets of locks. We may safely anticipate, from the vast extent of country with which it communicates by means of the lakes, and the astonishing rapidity with which the population increases, that at no great distance of time even these enlarged dimensions will be too small, and that full employment will be found for the railroads also, in the transportation of goods. Buffalo is probably destined to become a city of several hundred thousand inhabitants! To a spectator on the shore of Lake Erie, every thing resembles an ocean prospect. The eye is arrested by the line where the horizon meets the water; and a few hours' sail must carry the navigator far out of sight of land.

Phrenology.—There is a phrenological society here, and the subject is well understood, and extensively cultivated. I met a number of the medical members, and privately assisted at the dissection of a brain. I was told that the phrenologists are so numerous and influential, that they would experience little difficulty in getting phrenology introduced into the public schools as the philosophy of mind, if they had a work suitable for the purpose. They have only one zealous opponent, a Presbyterian clergyman, who preached against the science. They requested him to publish his discourse; but he declined to do so. In the evening an ordinary meeting of the society was held, this being one of their regular nights. Above fifty persons, ladies and gentlemen, were present, and Dr Raymond gave an excellent demonstration of the structure of the brain. I delivered a short address, and was much gratified by the state of the science in this important place.

The Indians.—The *Seneca village*, settled by about 900 Indians, principally Senecas, with some Onondagas and Cayugas, lies from three to four miles southeast of Buffalo. They live on what is called an " Indian Reserve," extending to 49,000 acres of land. I delivered a letter of introduction to Honnondeuh, one of their chiefs, from whom I obtained some interesting information. We found him living in the same hotel with ourselves.

Honnondeuh appears to be about thirty years of age; he is well-formed, with features decidedly Indian, and a complexion probably one-fourth white. The form of his brain indicates a cross between the Indian and white. He was sent by his father, who is an Indian, to the common school at Buffalo, and afterwards to Hamilton College, where he completed a good education. At the school and college he assumed the appellation of Thomas Strong. He speaks English like an Anglo-American, and his dress and manners are those of an American gentleman. He studied law, and at present receives a salary for acting as interpreter and agent between his tribe and the United States' Government. A treaty is now proceeding for the removal of his people, and of all the other Indians in the State of New York (about 4000 in number), to a territory west of the Missouri, extending to 1,800,000 acres of prairie and woodland, purchased by the United States' Government from the Ossages Indians.

When the British first settled in America, they found the different tribes of Indians in possession of different portions of the country as common hunting-ground, but individual property in the soil was unknown. The British settlers, therefore, could not acquire legitimate individual rights from the Indians, because they had no such rights themselves. To prevent frauds, and to lay the foundation of individual titles, the English Government, at a very early date, prohibited all its subjects from purchasing land from the Indians, and entered into a treaty with them by which the chiefs bound themselves, when they wished to sell, to give the right of pre-emption to the Government. Thus it became an established principle, that the Indians had only a right of possession in common, in their own lands; that they could not sell any portion of them as individual property; and that the Government alone had the privilege of purchasing up their right of possession, and of converting the tenure of the lands into fee-simple.

After the Revolution, the United States' Government claimed this right, as come in place of the British Crown; and their whole transactions with the Indians have been founded on it since that event.

An Indian reserve means a certain tract of land

left in possession of an Indian tribe, on which no white man is allowed to settle. Not only does the American Government prohibit the Indians from selling these reserves to individuals, but it does not permit them even to divide them among themselves and convert them into fees. They must possess them in common, or give them up, and remove to the west. Farther, it refuses to allow the rights of American citizenship to an Indian in any circumstances. Honnondeuh, under his name of Thomas Strong, purchased a lot of land in the State of New York from an American who had a complete title; " but," said he, " the moment the land was conveyed to me, my blood extinguished the right." He drew up and presented a respectful petition to the Legislature of the State of New York, detailing the circumstances, and praying for an act to authorize him to acquire a legal title to the land. His petition was referred to the Committee on " Indian Affairs," and they reported that it was not expedient to comply with his desire.

" Here we are," said he, " surrounded by white men who found their prosperity on individual property in the soil, and yet they prohibit us, as a tribe, from dividing our own lands among ourselves, and laying the foundation of our own improvement. Not only so, but when we, as individuals, acquire their knowledge, and adopt their manners, they still prohibit us from owning individual property in the soil, either of our own lands or of theirs. In such circumstances, our advance in civilization is impossible.

Our people associate only with the outcasts and lowest of the whites, because all others exclude us from participation equally in their rights and in their society. We adopt their vices, because an insurmountable barrier is placed between us and their virtues. We become miserable, degraded, extinct." He delivered these words with deep earnestness, but without passion. An American gentleman who heard this exposition, remarked to me, " If you or I had been so treated, we should not have spoken so calmly of our wrongs !"

The present state of the treaty with these Indians (if I rightly apprehended the explanations given to me) is this : After the Revolution, both New York and Massachusetts claimed these Indian lands, and the dispute was adjusted by the territory being included within the limits of the State of New York, but under the condition that the right of pre-emption should be reserved to Massachusetts. By this arrangement Massachusetts was placed in the right of receiving the immediate profit which could be realized by extinguishing the Indian title, and selling the lands to white settlers ; while New York secured the lands and population to augment her wealth after they were settled. Massachusetts, not choosing to wait till she could remove the Indians, sold her right of pre-emption to Gorham and Phelps. This right has been several times transferred from them to other individuals, and parcelled out into lots. A company of fifteen or twenty persons has acquired the right of pre-emption of the 49,000 acres possessed by the

Senecas, and has employed agents to buy up the Indian right of possession. Massachusetts has sent a commissioner, General Deerborn, to see that the Indians are not cheated; and the Government of the United States lend their aid by offering new territories in the far west; and negociations are now proceeding between all these parties for the removal of the Indian tribe.

Honnondeuh has visited the proposed new territory, and is satisfied with it. He saw the surrounding Indians, and was assured of their peaceful dispositions towards his people, if they should come. The United States' Government promise to give them these lands in *fee*, with the right of holding individual property, and selling them among themselves at their pleasure. Honnondeuh and his father have voted for the removal, influenced chiefly by the advantages of this last boon. " We may live there," said he ; " here we must become extinct." One of our party asked him whether he would go with his tribe to the " far west." " Certainly," said he, " I will go with my people." He explained to us that he is chief of a clan only, and succeeded his brother in this place of honour. His father is not a chief, the right having come by his mother.

This Indian reserve approaches to within one mile of the town of Buffalo, and we saw many of the tribe in the town. Some were clothed in rags, with a tattered great coat above all, and were reeling drunk in the streets ; others were clothed like English carters, and some like respectable tradesmen. Most

of the women wore trousers, coarse cotton short-
gowns, and a large blanket adjusted as a robe. The
men wear hats or caps ; the women were bare-headed,
and often bare-footed, haggard and ugly.

Another of our party asked Honnondeuh what progress the missionaries were making among his tribe ?
" They begin at the wrong end," said he ; " they
inform us how to save our souls, but do not teach
us how we may improve our condition. We believe that our souls will be taken care of by the
Great Spirit ; we want rights, justice, civilization
first, and then we shall be glad to hear what the
missionaries can do for our souls." He added that
the missionaries have kept a school among them, and
one of the Gospels (of which he presented C——
with a copy) is printed in the Seneca language.
Great difficulty was experienced in translating it, in
consequence of the great poverty of that language. I
pursued this topic, and learned from him that his tribe
have no words to express many of the emotions and
ideas formed by means of the moral sentiments and
the reflecting faculties, especially when the emotion
or idea is a complex one, expressive of the activity
of a group of these faculties acting in combination.
These emotions and ideas themselves are unknown
to them. and the translation is accomplished only
by means of paraphrases, some of them of a very
awkward character, and which, after all that can be
done, do not suggest to the Indian the same emotions
or ideas which the English words call up in the
Anglo-American mind. In short, the translation,

to prove successful, would require in many instances not only to express the original sense, but to evoke feelings and conceptions never previously experienced by the Indian faculties.

He does not understand the language of tribes who live at a distance. There is no perceptible affinity between his speech and theirs. He repeated to us, first in his own language and afterwards in English the speech which he made to the Ossages Indians, and their answer, conveyed through three interpreters. It consisted of a series of announcements of substantive facts; of distinct propositions; and of questions founded on these. The answer consisted of direct replies, accompanied by an assurance of amity. We asked him whether Mr Henry Clay, or the best Indian orator, was the more eloquent. He replied that the ideas which they expressed, and the arguments which they used, were so utterly unlike, that no comparison could be made between them. " Our orators," said he, " could not find words to express, nor could our people conceive, the ideas which Mr Clay utters. But within our own range I have heard some of our orators as eloquent as Mr Clay." He said that they instructed some of their young men to speak as orators, or, as they called them, " interpreters."

Honnondeuh had a great deal of conversation with the ladies of our travelling party, gave them Indian names expressive of qualities, and became a great favourite with them. He acted and spoke with natural ease and dignity, and altogether conducted himself as an educated gentleman, and we treated him as such. He is not married ; but he has a sister who is educated and married to an Indian.

One of our American friends, who is deeply learned in the history, and practically acquainted with the affairs, of the United States, mentioned that he believed the account given to us by Honnondeuh to be substantially correct. He acknowledged that there is great injustice in the treatment of the Indians, but remarked that the evil originated with the English Government, and that the Indian affairs were in such a condition when the American Government succeeded to the English, that no other system could be followed. Besides, said he, the Indians joined the English in the war of the Revolution, and the United States conquered their territory. They conceived that they acted mildly towards them in pursuing the same course which the English had adopted previously to the contest.

Buffalo, as I have already remarked, is the scene of Mr Rathbun's speculations. He planned the " American Hotel," in which we now reside, and it is as magnificent as a palace. It accommodates with ease 140 travellers.

June 27. Ther. 67°. *Railroad to Lewistown.*— We left Buffalo at nine A.M. in a railroad car on our return to Niagara Falls. It thundered and rained plentifully, and the locomotive engine could not drag us forward. Its wheels continued revolving, but slipt on the wet rails, and we stood motionless. This railroad is twenty-three miles in length, and cost

$110,000. It has ascents in some places exceeding seventy feet in the mile. In order to save the expenditure of capital in levelling, the Americans construct their railroads with much higher gradients than the English, and, in this instance, the gradient has been carried so high as to render the road inefficient in wet weather. The company was incorporated in 1834. After many stops we obtained horses, and at half-past two o'clock reached Niagara Falls. We did not remain in the village, but entered a railroad train for Lewistown, situated on the right bank of the Niagara, near its junction with Lake Ontario. We arrived there at a quarter past four P.M., and immediately embarked on board of the " Great Britain" steam-ship for Kingston in Upper Canada. Opposite Lewistown is Queenstown in Canada, which the Americans burned in the war of 1814. On a height above this village a handsome column has been erected to the memory of the English general Brock, who fell there in the Battle of Queenstown. It forms an interesting feature in the landscape, which is naturally fine.*

June 28. *Oswego.—The St Lawrence.*—The steam-

---

* Before we left the United States, a disgraceful attempt was made to destroy this monument. It is a hollow pillar containing a winding stair. Some miscreants had forced open the door at the bottom, placed several barrels of gunpowder inside, closed the door, and fired the whole by a slow match. The stair was blown out at the top, and the column itself seriously rent, but not thrown from its basis. I heard the Americans express the greatest indignation against the perpetrators of this barbarity. The strictest investigations were made to discover them, but without success. The general opinion seemed to be that it was the work of one individual.

boat was large, and had excellent accommodations. We sailed all night, and at seven A.M. touched at the American town of Oswego, on the right bank of Lake Ontario. It lies at the mouth of the Oswego river, and we were told that here Mr Van Buren, the present President of the United States, laid the foundation of his fortune by a speculation in lots. He purchased 600 acres of land at $6 or $7 an acre; afterwards sold part of it for $70,000; and keeps the remainder, which is regarded as very valuable. The opening of the Oswego Canal, which branches off from the Erie Canal, and the consequent rise of the town, has caused this great advance in value. He has also obtained several liberal grants from the United States' Government to improve its harbour. It now appears to be a flourishing place.

At two P.M. we arrived at Kingston, Upper Canada. The St Lawrence commences here. When we were at Niagara Falls, General Scott mentioned to us that a plot was suspected to be hatching by the disaffected Canadians and their American allies to burn the British steam-boats on the St Lawrence; that he had communicated all the information he possessed on the subject to the British officers, and had also instructed the American officers to observe the strictest watch to defeat the scheme. At Kingston we entered another steam-boat, and soon saw that General Scott's information was acted on. We were boarded by a British sergeant and corporal, and a party of soldiers. The sergeant mustered them on the deck, gave the words " shoulder arms," " open pans," and then went along the line and examined every

lock and flint, to see that it was fit for service. The
arms were then piled on deck, and we commenced
our voyage. The river is here ten miles broad,
strewed with a thousand islands, varying from a foot
square to many hundreds of acres in extent, all covered with bushes or timber. The evening was fine,
and the scene was highly picturesque as we glided
among them. Their grouping and forms presented
a new picture every five minutes, and all graceful and
rich. At sunset the sergeant again mustered his
men, and placed three sentinels; one near the pad-
dle-box on the American side; one in the stern on
the same side, and one in the bow of the boat. It
was moonlight. We approached a large barge lying
at anchor close to the shore. " What boat, a-hoy?"
cried the soldier on the bow. No answer. We approached close to her. She was a lumber-boat with
nobody on board. We passed Ogdensburg on the
American, and Prescott on the British side, and I saw
the windmill, which a short time before had been the
scene of an attack.

June 29. Ther. 63°. June 30. Ther. 62°. July 1.
Ther. 72°. July 2. Ther. 76°. July 3. Ther. 78°.

We arrived at Montreal at 7 P.M. on the 29th of
June, having travelled 422 miles (the distance from
Lewistown), chiefly by steam-boats, but partly by
stage-coaches, in fifty hours. We remained in Montreal till eight o'clock in the evening of the 2d of
July, when we embarked in the St George, a large
and commodious steam-boat, and arrived at Quebec
next day at 2 P.M., the distance being 180 miles.

July 4. Ther. 68°. July 5. Ther. 64°. July 6.

Ther. 64°. We remained in Quebec during these days, and visited the town, the citadel, General Wolfe's monument, the Falls of Montmorenci, the Indian village of Lorette, and other objects of interest.   At 9 P. M. of 6th July we embarked again for Montreal on board of the " Canada" steam-boat, and in twenty-four hours completed our voyage, although we ascended the stream, and had a schooner in tow the whole way.

I offer no remarks on Canada for two reasons : first, Our visit to it was short, our motions were rapid, and my means of forming correct opinions therefore deficient ; secondly, The subject deeply excites party feeling in Britain, and no observations which I could offer would be of use in removing the prejudices which attend political questions.   My general impression is, that Lower Canada, compared with the United States, is like senility contrasted with manly vigour ; and that this is the result, first, of the ignorance of the French population ; and, secondly, of a provincial government.   The constitution of the United States developes, in an extraordinary degree, the faculties of its individual citizens, and the energies of its social masses ; while a provincial government, by depriving both individuals and masses of political power, and vesting the ultimate disposal of the great interests of the country in a foreign and distant legislature, paralyzes the minds of its subjects, and substitutes feelings of dependence and doubt for those of self-reliance and unhesitating confidence in distant results.

July 9. Ther. 74°. *Lake Champlain, Burlington,*

&c.—At 9 A. M. we left Montreal, crossed the river in a steam-boat to La Prairie, travelled seventeen miles on a railroad to St John's, and at one o'clock embarked on board of a large American steam-boat, named the "White Hall," ascended the River St John and Lake Champlain, and arrived at Burlington in the United States at 7 P. M., after a delightful day's travelling.

On reaching the first port above St John's, a piteous scene presented itself in a party of Irish emigrants. They were going to the head of the Lake, and the captain demanded their fare. They had no money, and the captain thrust them ashore at this place amidst cries, and tears, and prayers, and every moving appeal which Irish eloquence could command. Great commiseration was excited among the passengers, and we regretted that the expulsion was completed, and the boat pushed off, to prevent their rushing on board again, before we knew what the lamentations arose from. Our compassion, how-ever, was abated, when we were assured by the men in charge of the steam-ship that the emigrants had money, but were unwilling to part with it, and that they have a regular plan for accomplishing their pas-sage without paying a cent. They go on board and are carried to the first port, before their fare is de-manded, and before it is possible to put them ashore for refusing to pay. They are there thrust out, but wait at that port, and go on board the next boat that touches at it on its passage up the lake; they are carried by it to another port, again refuse to pay, and are again put ashore.　They wait there for a third boat, and repeat the same evolutions, protesting each time that they have no money.　At last they accomplish the whole distance, and then laugh at the captain of the vessel which has brought them to their destination, and boast of their trickery.

July 10. Ther. 72° 11. Ther. 64°. 12. Ther. 64°. 13. Ther. 64°. 14. Ther. 63°. In these days we visited Montpelier, Hanover, Littleton, and the White Mountains. Miss Martineau has so eloquently treated of the White Mountains, and other travellers have so frequently described the other features of our route, that I merely add that we were much gratified by the beauty of the country, the prosperity of the towns and villages, and the generally good accommodation which we found on the road.

In one of our walks in the valley which lies at the base of the White Mountains (which, by the way, are not white, except when covered with snow in winter), a young man carrying a gun accosted us, " Do you fear the gun ?" " No, if you do not point it at us." He fired at some object almost at his feet. It was a snake about two feet long. He blew its head off, and lifted up its body. He then joined us. " Have you been up Mount Washington ?" (the highest peak), said he. " No." " Perhaps you have been here before ?" " No, I have not." " Perhaps you come from a pretty considerable distance ?" " Yes, I do." " In what direction ?" North-east." " Is it very far down east ?" " Yes, a good way." He was preparing another question, when I added,

" I have come across the ocean."　" O, ay! you
have come from England ; that's a pretty considerable
way, as I have heard my father say."　" When did
your father come to this country ?"　" Fifty years ago."
He then asked me the rate at which agricultural labour
was paid in England.　I told him as correctly as I
could the rate in Scotland.　He continued, " Well,
I hire by the month to do farm-work with Mr Fa-
bian (the innkeeper), but I get more money than
that ; but when I go to buy clothes and shoes, and
other articles that I want, I guess that my money
does not go so far as it would do in England, and
that when we come to the point, how much we
have in hand at the end of the year, the difference is
pretty considerably less than one would at first suppose, and yet that is the main thing for a poor man
to look to."　I told him that he was right in supposing that most articles produced by labour were
cheaper in England than in the United States.
" But," said he, " they tell me that if a poor man
become sick in England, nobody will attend to him."
I explained to him that this was a mistake, and described the hospitals and dispensaries.　I added that
the greatest difference lay in this—that in England a
man was sometimes able and willing to labour, and
could get no employment ; but here there was work
always.　" Yes," said he, " that makes a great difference ; men are scarce here."

I spoke to him of the pranks performed by a tame
bear at the inn. " On the White Mountains," said he,
" I was leading my little brother, three years of age,

by the hand, when I saw two young bear cubs run up a tree. I pursued them, and caught hold of one. It cried out, and its mother appeared. My little brother was now in danger. I took off my coat, and tied it by the sleeves round the branch on which the young bear sat. I descended, got a thick stick, and commenced an attack on the mother. She retreated before me. I followed her for a mile, leading my brother all the way, and then left him at a cottage. I returned to the tree. My stratagem had taken effect. The young bear had been afraid of the coat, and had not attempted to escape. I climbed up the tree, seized it, and carried it off. The mother had now returned, and its cries brought her to its rescue ; but I shewed a bold face with my stick, and she did not attack me, but hung upon my footsteps. I proceeded to the cottage and got assistance. We used the young bear as a decoy, and captured the mother also." These are small, dark-coloured bears, and not very formidable.

I have introduced this conversation as a fair specimen of the intelligence, enterprise, and resources of the American labouring people. There was no rudeness or presumption in the manner in which this young man put his questions to me. The predominant motive was obviously the desire of information. He lived in an inquiring age, and acted in its spirit. At the same time he was quite at ease, as all the Americans are in their intercourse with strangers.

Mosquitoes.—After the summer heat fairly sets in, the pleasures of American scenery are greatly marred by the torment of mosquitoes. At the White Mountains, they are really a very formidable evil. Abroad, they assail one in thousands, and sting by every crevice through which the skin can be reached : in the house the nuisance is not abated ; and even at night, the only alternatives are to close the doors and windows and shut out both them and the fresh air, or to be stung unmercifully. Around the inn, fires of green wood were lighted to scare them away by the smoke ; but with little effect. While suffering under this affliction, we read the following story in the New York Sun, and sympathized very sincerely with the unfortunate hero of it.

" A correspondent writes us, concerning the mosquitoes of Michigan, that a man who lived near Grand River, being in the woods, was exceedingly annoyed by mosquitoes, and took shelter under an inverted potash kettle. His first emotions of joy, for his happy deliverance and secure asylum, were hardly over, when the mosquitoes, having scented him, began to drive their proboces through the kettle; fortunately he had a hammer in his pocket, and he clenched them down as fast as they came through, until at last such a host of them were fastened to the poor man's domicile, that they rose and flew away with it, leaving him shelterless !!"

July 15. Ther. 62°. 16. Ther. 62°. 17. Ther. 64°. 18. Ther. 68°. 19. Ther. 72°. 20. Ther. 72°. 21. Ther. 68°.

Portland-in-Maine.—We left the White Mountains on the 16th of July, and descended through the " Notch," highly romantic pass made by a narrow cleft in the mountains. In many parts its features are grand and awful, rising almost to the sublime.

After a few miles of rapid declivity, the valley opens, and the mountains diminish in height. The scenery, however, continues very beautiful. We reached Conway, 36 miles distant, at half-past seven P. M. We found a pleasant clean inn and attentive host. On the 17th we drove to Portland-in-Maine, 55 miles, through a gently undulating country, much of it still unsettled, and the crops so late that barley is only now coming into the ear, and oats are still less advanced. Very little wheat is sown. In the valley of the Connecticut we saw numerous maple trees, each with a little trough standing at its root, into which their sap is received for the purpose of making sugar; but we have seen few or none in Maine. Wild strawberries and wild raspberries everywhere abound, and occasionally dishes of them are presented at table in the inns. Portland is a beautiful town of 16,000 inhabitants, lying in a fine bay; it owns a great number of vessels, which are chartered out to merchants in most parts of the Union, and make voyages all over the globe. Its own commerce is not extensive; but so many of these vessels arrive for orders and repairs, that its harbour presents an array of ships, unexpected both in numbers and tonnage.

We drove to Cape Cottage, on Casco Bay, where we enjoyed sea breezes and beautiful scenery for eight of the hottest weeks of autumn.

APPENDIX.

No. I.—Referred to on p. 20.

TABLE OF THE MENTAL DISORDERS IN THE EASTERN PENITENTIARY DURING 1839.—WHITE PRISONERS.

Prisoners. No.	Age.	Country.	Health on Admission.	Diseases.	Causes.	Effects of Treatment.	Duration of Attack. Y.	M.	D.	After Imprisonment. Y.	M.	D.	Present State of each Prisoner, January 1. 1840.
947	46	Pennsylvania,	Asthma and Pleuritic Pain,	Hypochondria.	Unknown,	Cured,			4		5	9	Discharged from E. P., Sept. 17. 1839, in sound mind and health.
867	30	New York,	Dysentery and Gleet,	Do.	Do.	Relieved,			22	1	0	21	Do. do. April 13. do.
784	21	England,	Good mind and health,	Do.	Mst.	Cured,			10	1	7	5	Do. do. July 3. do.
926	39	Germany,	Plethora and pain of chest and abdomen,	Do.	Unknown,	Relieved,			24	1	1	16	Do. do. May 3. in sound mind, imperfect health.
988	40	Ireland,	Hallucinations, from mania a potu,	Hallucinations,	Intemp.	Continues,						1	A worthless prisoner, subject to violent fits of anger.
975	26	Pennsylvania,	Imperfect health, and mind disturbed,	Do.	Unknown,	Cured,			18		10	24	Discharged from E. P., Sept. 8. 1839, in sound mind and health.
1128	55	Delaware,	Good, but hard drinker and distressed,	Do.	Intemp.	Relieved,			16		7	19	At work at knitting, and continues distressed.
1069	40	Pennsylvania,	Monomania,	Monomania,	Do.	Pardoned,						1	Pardoned and sent to the Alms-house.
1039	26	Germany,	Eccentricity of mind,	Eccentricity of mind,	Do.	Relieved,			16		1	16	In 3d block of cells, picking wool, and in sound mind and health.
1055	21		Scrofula,	Dementia, acute,	Mst.	Cured,			11	1	3	0	In 7th block, at weaving, and in sound mind and health.
1062	29		Good health,	Do.	Do.	Do.			5	1	2	0	In 4th block, at shoemaking, and in sound mind and health.
673	59	Pennsylvania,	Imperfect, and mind troubled,	Do.	Unknown,	Do.			11		7	12	In 3d block, at making hickory brooms, in sound mind and health.
842	27	Holland,	Good health, disturbed mind,	Mania,	Do.	Pardoned, July 1839,	1	0	23		7	12	Sent to the Alms-house.

COLOURED PRISONERS.

Prisoners No.	Age	Country.	Health on Admission.	Diseases.	Causes.	Effects of Treatment.	Duration of Attack. Y.	M.	D.	After Imprisonment. Y.	M.	D.	Present State of each Prisoner, January 1. 1840.
492	28	Pennsylvan.	Good, mind discontented,	Hypochondria,	Mst.	Relieved,			7	3	3	10	In 4th block (Infirmary) good health, self-willed and malicious.
531	21	Maryland,	Good,	Do.	Do.	Cured,	1	9		3	3	22	In 5th block, at shoemaking, in sound mind and health.
1107	19	Delaware,	Do.	Hallucination,	Do.	Do.			13			25	In Infirmary, and wishes to go to work,
924	19	Maryland,	Gonorrhœa, wilful,	Do.	Do.	Do.			7		6	10	do. has been at spooling, but is too worthless to be continued at work.
1096	18	Pennsylvan.	Good,	Do.	Do.	Relieved,			17		6	17	Is again in Infirmary for hallucination.
746	23	Do.	Subject to vertigo,	Do.	Do.	Cured,			9		4	2	In 4th block, weaving, in sound mind and health.
845	21	N. Carolina,	Good,	Dementia, acute,	Do.	Do.	2		20	1	4	3	Discharged from E. P., Aug. 30. 1839, in sound mind and health.
588	29	New Jersey,	Typhus Pneumonia, from Arch St. Pris.	Do.	Do.	Do.	2	2		2	8	28	Discharged April 19. 1839, in sound mind and improved health.
1021	26	Virgin. a run slave, murd.	Rheumatic destructive disposition.	Deviltry,	Unknown,	Continues,					1	17	Continues to be very destructive, otherwise reasonable.
569	29	Pennsylvan.	Good,	Dementia,	Mst.	Do.				2	10	5	In good health, and mind much restored, and disposed to be at work in his own way, very pleasant and mild.
921	23	Delaware,	Syphilis,	Do.	Do.	Cured,	1	9			9	6	He died, Aug. 24. 1839, of chronic pleurisy and scrofula.
632	26	Pennsylvan.	Health good, revengeful,	Do.	Do.	Do.	1	6		2	6	14	Discharged E. P., Aug. 19. 1839, sent to Moyamensing Prison.
984	18	Philadelphia,	Good,	Do.	Do.	Do.			27		8	22	In 3d block, picking wool, in sound mind and health.

" The preceding tables shew that the cases of disordered mind have occurred in early manhood with few exceptions, that four of them happened after more than two or three years' imprisonment, but the rest within an average confinement of about seven or eight months ; that they have generally yielded to a short medical treatment ; that about sixty-one per-centage of them have been caused by self-abuse, and that there has been three per cent. more of the cases among the coloured than the white prisoners. Its physical cause is here indicated. The cephalic disorders here presented is not that insanity of mind which solitude, confinement, and oppression may produce on a cultivated intellect, and high tone and spirit. The cell of the prisoner is lighted and ventilated, its stone walls and iron door is the end of the law to him, and all the rest is only kindness ; the visits of the keepers, superintendents, warden, and inspectors, destroy the ennui of solitude, and make it only a separation from idleness and vice. He is employed in profitable work. When he is sick prompt medical aid is afforded, and nursing. Six days he labours, and on the Sabbath he rests, reads his Bible, and listens to the voice of his moral instructor, who has often visited him. There cannot be much in such solitude and confinement to induce insanity. The form of disordered mind here found is of a physical character—a brain complaint—a congestion of the cerebellum most generally. The refuse of the coloured population who, owing to our proximity to the slave States, constitute a disproportionate number of the prisoners, are here deprived of sensual indulgence, except self-abuse, and in this, therefore, they are excessive, as are also the less intelligent white prisoners ; consequently the organs of digestion become weakened, and confinement then with full animal diet, are unitedly not harmless, cephalic pains follow, disturbing dreams, depressed spirits, he continues the injurious practice, and hallucinations, violence, and incoherence follow, and if the prisoner be not properly treated, the case becomes one of chronic and incurable dementia. Separate the coloured prisoners from this institution, and the instances of disordered mind will become comparatively few."—*Extract from the Report of Dr Darrach, Physician to the Eastern Penitentiary of Pennsylvania for the year* 1839.

No. II.—Referred to on p. 60.

TABLE OF ATTENDANCE AT THE FIRST COURSE OF LECTURES
ON PHRENOLOGY IN PHILADELPHIA.

Date.	Weather.	Subjects.	No. of Sub-scribers present.	Visiters present.	Complimentary Tickets.*
1839. Jan. 4.	Clear.	The Brain a congeries of organs manifesting different mental faculties.	195	213	30
„ 7.	Do.	Size, *cæteris paribus*, a measure of Power, Temperaments, &c.	303	133	38
„ 10.	Do.	Structure of Brain and Skull, Amativeness.	386	96	31
„ 11.	Do.	Philopro. Concentrat. Comb.	395	77	33
„ 13.	Rain.	Destruc. Aliment. Love of Life, Secretiv. Acquisit.	396	64	38
„ 17.	Clear.	Construct. Self-Esteem, Love of Approb. Cautiousness.	398	69	34
„ 18.	Do.	Benev. Vener. Firmness, Conscientiousness.	355	58	28
„ 21.	Do.	Hope, Wonder, Ideality, Wit, Imitation.	427	82	32
„ 24.	Do.	Individ. Form, Size, Weight, Colouring.	428	62	38
„ 25.	Do.	Locality, Number, Order, Eventuality, Time, Tune.	410	83	41
„ 28.	Do.	Language, Comparison, Causality, Materialism.	417	129	47
„ 31.	Do.	Modes of activity of the faculties.	348	139	44
Feb. 1.	Snow.	Varieties of dispositions and talents. Moral Responsibility.	316	136	36
„ 4.	Fair.	Physical Education.	317	224	35
„ 7.	Clear.	Mental Education.	330	217	61
„ 8.	Rain.	Application of Phrenology to the present and prospective condition of United States.	294	222	54
		Which numbers (divided by 16) give an average attendance	5715	2004	620
		of subscribers, -	356		
		of visiters, -	125		
		of invited hearers,	39		
		Total average,	520		

* The Committee of Management were requested by me to present tickets
to all the gentlemen of the press and their ladies, and to as many persons
besides as were likely to be benefited by the lectures but who were unable
to pay for admission.

REMARKS ON THE PRECEDING TABLE.

The diminution in the numbers, under the head of subscribers, may appear to indicate a falling off in their attendance; but such was not the fact. Each subscriber received sixteen transferable tickets, being one for each of the sixteen lectures of which the course consisted. Many of the subscribers gave away portions of their tickets to friends to induce them to attend; others, conceiving that they should be tired long before the end of the course, gave away portions also. They, however, were interested, and attended to the close by purchasing tickets as visiters, the numbers of whom increased as those of subscribers diminished.

In this course of lectures, as in all the others, I impressed on my audience the necessity of studying Phrenology by observation before they could judge of its truth, and deprecated the idea that I wished to render them believers without grounds for philosophical conviction, which could be obtained from observation alone.

At the close of the last lecture, the following resolutions were adopted by the class, and subsequently presented by Nicholas Biddle, Esq., in name of the committee. The newspapers, in reporting the resolutions, added to the names certain notes in explanation of who the committee were, for the information of their distant readers. These I retain.

" Resolved,—That they have listened with great pleasure and mental profit to the comprehensive views of human nature, and to the elucidations of individual character set forth by Mr Combe in his lectures just completed. And that in these they recognise many important suggestions for the improvement of education and jurisprudence, and the consequent increase of the happiness of mankind.

" Resolved,—That a committee be appointed to carry to Mr Combe the preceding resolution, and a wish, on the part of this meeting that he will be induced to repeat his course of lectures on Phrenology in this city.

" The following gentlemen were appointed a committee to carry into effect the foregoing resolution, viz.:—

" 1. Nicholas Biddle, LL.D., President of the Board of Trustees of the Girard College, one of the Trustees of the University of Pennsylvania, Member of the American Philosophical Society, &c., &c.

" 2. Joseph Hartshorne, M.D., Member of the American Philosophical Society—(one of our oldest and most experienced and trusted physicians and surgeons—a practical man.)

" 3. Benjamin W. Richards, a Trustee of the University of Pennsylvania, formerly Mayor of this city, and long one of the Managers, if he is not now, of the Eastern Penitentiary, and of the Almshouse.

" 4. William Gibson, M.D., Professor of Surgery in the University of Pennsylvania (medical class this winter is 401), Surgeon to the Blockley Hospital (Almshouse Infirmary), Member of the Philosophical Society.

" 5. Thomas Harris, M.D., President of the Philadelphia Medical Society, Lecturer on the Institutes and Practice of Surgery, Member of the American Philosophical Society (a gentleman in extensive practice as surgeon and physician, author of a Life of Commodore Bainbridge.

" 6. Alexander Dallas Bache, President of the Girard College, for merly Professor of Chemistry in the Faculty of Arts of the University of Pennsylvania; after graduating at West Point (U. S. Military Academy), he taught Mathematics as a Professor in this institution— Member of the American Philosophical Society.

" 7. Rembrandt Peale, a painter of celebrity, author of ‘ Notes on Italy,’ &c.

" 8. Charles Picot, for several years the head of a seminary for young ladies, and who, by his success as a teacher, has acquired celebrity through the United States.

" 9. John Bell, M.D., Member of the American Philosophical Society, Lecturer on the Institutes of Medicine and Medical Jurisprudence, Professor of Anatomy applied to the Fine Arts, Editor of the Select Medical Library and Eclectic Journal of Medicine, one of the Editors of the Journal of Health (the initial article, with two or three exceptions, of each number of the Journal of Health is by Dr B.); author of a work on Baths and Mineral Waters, and on Health and Beauty, &c.

" That the friends of the phrenological philosophy elsewhere may know how Mr Combe has been greeted by the literary and scientific men of Philadelphia, we have added to the names of the committee given above, such information as shews their standing."

No. III.—Referred to on p. 224.

RESOLUTIONS OF THE SECOND CLASS AT PHILADELPHIA.

The average attendance at each lecture in the second course in Philadelphia was 357.

The following resolutions were adopted, and presented by a committee:—

" At the close of Mr George Combe’s second course of Lectures on Phrenology, in the Hall of the Musical Fund, April 6. 1839,

" On motion, Professor Samuel B. Wylie was called to the chair, and George M‘Clellan, M.D., appointed Secretary.

" The Rev. Chairman addressed the meeting on the propriety of making some public expression of the satisfaction which the very numerous class in attendance had derived from the lectures.

" On motion, the following resolutions, offered by Mr Thomas Fisher, were unanimously adopted :—

" Resolved,—That this class have listened with great interest to the able and highly instructive exposition of Phrenology which Mr Combe has offered us.

" Resolved,—That whatever may have been our previous acquaintance with the subject, the lectures of Mr Combe have impressed us with much respect for its practical importance, and with the kindliest feeling for the learned lecturer.

" Resolved,—That Phrenology is recognised and commended as a science founded in nature, by a large portion of the most distinguished anatomists on both sides of the Atlantic, and that we believe it to be the only adequate illustration of the existing wonderfully various manifestations of the human mind.

" Resolved,—That it will afford us pleasure, and that we believe it will be highly acceptable to this community, that Mr Combe should make it consistent with his arrangements in other cities to give, during next winter, another course in Philadelphia.

" Resolved,—That a committee of seven gentlemen be appointed to communicate to Mr Combe a copy of these resolutions.

" The following gentlemen were accordingly appointed :—

" Samuel B. Wylie, D.D.   Joseph Hartshorne, M.D.
" Samuel George Morton, M.D.   Thomas Gilpin, Esq.
" George M'Clellan, M.D.   Thomas Fisher."
" Charles S. Coxe, Esq.

No. IV.—Referred to on p. 138.

LETTER FROM JAMES P. ESPY, ESQ. IN EXPLANATION OF HIS PROPOSAL TO PRODUCE RAIN ARTIFICIALLY IN TIME OF DROUGHT.

[*From the National Gazette.*]

Messrs EDITORS,—Knowing the difficulty, if not the impossibility, of making the subject intelligible in a short newspaper article, it is with reluctance that I am now induced, after much earnest solicitation from my friends both near and remote, to give a very brief summary of the reasons and FACTS which have led me to desire that an experiment should be made to see whether *rain may be produced artificially in time of drought.*

The documents which I have collected on this subject, if they do not prove that the experiment will succeed, do at least prove that it ought to be tried; this, I trust, will most satisfactorily appear when they shall be published entire. In the mean time it has become necessary to present to the public something on the subject, lest longer silence might be construed into an abandonment of the project.

1. It is known by experiment that if air should be expanded into double the volume by diminished pressure, it would be cooled about 90° of Fahrenheit.

2. I have shewn by experiment that if air at the common dew point in the summer season in time of drought, 71°, should go up in a column to a height sufficient to expand it by diminished pressure into

double the volume, it would condense into water or visible cloud, by the cold of expansion, more than one-half of its vapour,—a quantity sufficient to produce nearly three inches of rain.

3. It is known by chemical principles, that the caloric of elasticity given out during the condensation of this vapour, would be equal to about 30,000 tons of anthracite coal burned on each square mile over which the cloud extended.

4. I have shewn by experiment (see Saturday Courier, March 18. 1837) that this caloric of elasticity would prevent the air from cooling only about half as much as it would if it had no vapour in it, or about 45° at the height assumed, which would cause the air in the cloud to be, at that height, about 45° warmer than the air on the outside of the cloud at the same height. I have shewn from these principles (See Journal of the Franklin Institute for 1836) that the barometer would fall under the cloud thus formed, in favourable circumstances, a quantity as great as it is known to fall sometimes under the middle of a dense and lofty cloud, and that consequently the air would rush in on all sides towards the centre of the cloud and upwards in the middle, and thus continue the condensation of the vapour, and the formation of cloud, and the generation of rain. (See also Journal of the Franklin Institute for September and October 1838, and for January, February, and March, and subsequent 1839.)

5. I have shewn also in the volumes quoted above, that the air does move inwards on all sides towards the centre of the space or region where a great rain is falling, and of course upwards, after it comes in under the cloud, which is so much lighter than the surrounding air ; at least, that it does so in all storms which have been investigated, which now amount to sixteen, besides several tornadoes, in all of which the trees were thrown with their tops inwards.

From the principles here established by experiment, and afterwards confirmed by observation, it follows, that if a large body of air is made to ascend in a column, a large cloud will be generated, and that that cloud will contain in itself a self-sustaining power, which may move from the place over which it was formed, and cause the air over which it passes to rise up into it, and thus form more cloud and rain, until the rain may become general ; for many storms which commence in the West Indies very narrow, are known to move from the place of beginning several thousand miles, widening out and increasing in size, until they become many hundred miles wide. (See Redfield and Reid, and the Reports of Joint Committee.)

If these principles are just, it will follow, when the air is in a favourable state, that the bursting out of a volcano ought to produce rain ; and such is known to be the fact; and I have abundant documents in my possession to prove it.

So, under very favourable circumstances, the bursting out of great fires ought to produce rain ; and I have many facts in my possession rendering it highly probable, if not certain, that great rains have sometimes been produced by great fires.

It is a general opinion in parts of the country where great fires frequently take place, that those fires produce rain. Now this opinion could hardly have originated without some circumstances besides mere coincidence attending them, such as related in the following account. Mr Dobrezhoffer, a missionary to Paraguay, speaking of the tall grass and bulrushes on fire, says—" I myself have seen clouds and lightning produced from the smoke as it is flying off *like a whirl-wind;* so that the Indians are not to blame for setting fire to the plains in order to produce rain, they having learned, that the thicker smoke turns into clouds which pour forth water."—(Account of the Abiphones, vol. iii. p. 150.)

Mr Lapice, of Louisiana, informed Dr S. Calhoun of this city, " that the conflagration of the long grass in the prairies of that State covers every thing with its cinders for miles around, and that rain follows it shortly, according to immemorial observation in that country."

" Very extensive fires in Nova Scotia, in the woods, are so generally followed by heavy floods of rain, that there is some reason to believe, that the enormous pillars of smoke have some share in producing them."—(Mag. Nat. Hist. for Dec. 1835.)

The bad philosophy of supposing that smoke was turned into cloud and produced rain, does not weaken the evidence of the main fact.

If the principle is correct, that clouds are formed by up-moving columns of air, we should expect to find, in favourable states of the air, that clouds would form over large cities and manufacturing towns where much fuel is burnt, and so we find it to be.

Extract of a letter to me from Benj. Matthias of Philadelphia:— " In the course of last winter, while in England, I visited Manchester four or five times, and on each day it rained. Several of the inhabitants assured me, that it rains in Manchester more or less every day in the year."

Extract from Ed. Mammat's Collection of Facts, concerning Ashby Coal Field. 4to. London, 1836.

" When the air is apparently stagnant in the valley of the Thames and surrounding country, a strong current is found to set in, on every side of London, along the streets leading from the country, in the morning. This current is no doubt occasioned by the rarefaction in the high chimneys, over so many thousand fires just kindled, and must be the cause of the introduction of fresh air to an immense extent, which would not otherwise flow. This rarefaction produces other phenomena, among which, when the atmosphere is in a light state, and clouds are passing at a height which does not allow them to condense and fall in rain, these accumulate in passing over London, and either remain as a dense fog, or drop in small rain all day long, scarcely clearing once ; the country at a little distance having very little rain."

The bad philosophy of supposing the air so light on these occasions as to let the clouds on passing sink down in it over London, does not invalidate the evidence of the principal fact.

From these remarkable facts alone, I think it will be acknowledged that there is some connection between great fires and rains other than mere coincidence, even if that connection remained a mystery. Humboldt acknowledged this in the case of volcanoes, when he speaks of the *mysterious* connection between volcanoes and rain, and says, that when a volcano bursts out in South America in a dry season, it sometimes changes it to a rainy one. But now, when it is demonstrated by the most decisive evidence, the evidence of experiment, that air in ascending into the atmosphere in a column, as it must do over a great fire, will cool by diminished pressure, so much that it will begin to condense its vapour into cloud, as soon as it shall rise about as many hundred yards as the temperature of the air is above the dew-point in degrees of Fahrenheit, it amounts to a very *high* probability, that great fires have *sometimes* produced rain. That great fires and even volcanoes should not *always* produce rain, is manifest from the circumstance, that as they break out accidentally, they may sometimes occur when the state of the atmosphere is unfavourable, and even adverse to rain. First, if they should break out when there is a current of air, either near the surface of the earth, or at a considerable distance above, of some strength, the up-moving column would be swept by it out of the perpendicular, before a cloud of great density could be formed, and thus rain would be prevented.

Second, They might break out when the dew-point was too low to produce rain at all; and third, there may sometimes be an upper stratum of air, containing so much caloric that its specific levity would prevent the up-moving column from rising into it far enough to cause rain.

These three things I conceive are the only circumstances which prevent great fires from producing rain at all times when they occur The first two can be ascertained without much difficulty by means of small balloons, and the dew-point—the last in the present state of science cannot always be known, and a failure on that account must be risked by the experimenter. This risk I am willing to run if Congress or the State Legislature will promise a sufficient reward *in case of success.*

It has been objected to my project, that I propose too much, and that it is utterly absurd to expect to make rain in time of drought, when there is such a scarcity of vapour in the air.

Now this objection is founded on an entire ignorance of the fact, arising from a want of due consideration. For there is *generally* more vapour in the time of summer drought than at any other time, as I know by experiments constantly made almost every day for these last ten years; and this is reasonable in itself, for the vapour is rising into the air and increasing every day of dry weather, preparing for another rain. A quiet state of the atmosphere is also more likely to occur, to great heights, in time of droughts than at any other time, for immediately after rains there are sure to be cross currents of air, produced by the inward motion of the air at the lower part of the cloud and an outward motion in the upper part, which require some time after the rain to come to rest.

If I have succeeded in shewing that there is any the least ground to hope that an attempt to produce rain might sometimes succeed under favourable circumstances, and that those favourable circumstances are more likely to occur in time of drought than at any other time, then it follows that the experiment is a highly interesting one, and ought to be immediately tried. If it should be successful, who can tell the mighty results which may follow in its train?

I have many reasons and facts which induce me to believe that if a very large cloud is once generated, the rain will become general, or at least spread over a wide extent of territory, and who can tell, *a priori*, that this will not be the case, when it is now known that an immense steam power is let loose in the formation of such a cloud,—a power which can be calculated with as much accuracy as that of the steam-engine itself, and in part on the same principles?

Gentlemen have made their puns on this project, and had their laugh, and I am sorry to see by letters which I have received, that my friends and relations at a distance are much troubled at these innocent laughs; but let them be consoled: I have laughed too, well knowing that those who laughed the most heartily would be the most willing to encourage the experiment, as soon as they discovered they had nothing to laugh at. As a proof that I was right in this anticipation, I may be permitted to say that I have lately received a letter from a highly distinguished member of the American legislature, who laughed as heartily as *any* one when my petition was presented there, containing many kind expressions, and promising me, by way of amends for his levity, " to avail himself of the earliest opportunity of being better informed on the subject of my new philosophy." Such conduct as this is all I want; I fear not the strictest scrutiny.

If I should be encouraged to go on with the experiment, I mean to have a large mass of combustibles prepared ready for use, and when I have found all the circumstances mentioned before favourable in a time of drought, I would set fire to the circumference in various places at once. Soon after the fire commences, I will expect to see clouds begin to form about as many hundred yards high as the temperature of the air is above the dew-point in degrees of Fahrenheit. I will expect to see this cloud rapidly increase in size, if its top is not swept off by a current of air at a considerable distance above the earth, until it becomes so lofty as to rain. I shall expect the cloud to move eastwardly, increasing in width as it advances, and the next day I shall expect the region to the south of where the rain fell to be visited by rain, for a reason explained in my writings.

But it is in vain to anticipate all the results which will follow, for nothing but the experiment itself can demonstrate them. If the experiments, when repeatedly tried, should fail, it would be in vain for me to say I would not be mortified, but I will not incur any disgrace—unless it is disgraceful to desire to see a great experiment made which all the knowledge we have on the subject, in the present state of science, leads us to hope will be crowned with success.

I have made this very brief, though necessarily imperfect, statement of my reasons for wishing to see the experiment tried, which can alone decide the question, to comply with the earnest and repeated solicitations of my friends. I will now, in conclusion, say a word for myself.

The present state of the science of Meteorology renders it highly important to know in what direction, and with what velocity, summer rains travel over the surface of the earth. What is their shape—round or oblong—and if oblong, in what direction their transverse diameter lies, and whether they move side foremost, or end foremost, or obliquely? Now, I request gentlemen throughout the United States, who feel interested in this subject, to keep a journal of all rains from the beginning of June till the end of September; noting their beginnings and endings, the force and direction of the winds, and also of the clouds, and send the accounts (published in some paper) as early in October as convenient, to William Hamilton, Esq., Actuary of the Franklin Institute, Philadelphia.

Finally, if any gentleman intends to clear from twenty to fifty acres of woodland this spring or early in the summer, in the western or north-western parts of Pennsylvania, will he please to inform me of the fact as soon as convenient.

Journals of the weather also for the 16th, 17th, and 18th of March 1838, kept in various parts of Virginia and North Carolina, are much desired; and if gentlemen can even tell me how the trees are thrown down, indicating the direction of the wind, the information will be highly valuable, and should not be withheld if nothing else is known or recollected.

I am, Gentlemen, yours respectfully,

JAMES P. ESPY.

Philadelphia, April 2. 1839.

No. V.—Referred to on p. 265.

CORRESPONDENCE BETWEEN MR TAPPAN[*] AND MR KEY.

[*From the African Repository for April* 1839.]

Augusta, (Me.) July 31. 1838.

MY DEAR SIR,—Some years since I had the pleasure of travelling in company with you from Philadelphia to Baltimore, and was indebted to you for the privilege of being introduced to the acquaintance and hospitality of the much beloved and respected Dr Nevins. I know not whether you will recollect the circumstance, but I must make it my apology for writing to you now with somewhat more of freedom than I would feel in addressing a stranger.

---

[*] Rev. Dr Tappan of Augusta, Maine.

The subject of slavery has frequently come up, within two or three years past, in the meetings in New England of ecclesiastical bodies, and resolutions have been passed expressing their views respecting it. At a late meeting of the General Conference of Maine (consisting of clerical and lay delegates from the county conferences of Congregational churches throughout the State), a committee was raised, of seven clergymen, to correspond with ecclesiastical bodies at the south. After some consultation, the committee were of opinion that it would be advisable, in the first place, to correspond, individually, with individuals at the south. In conformity to that opinion, I am taking the liberty, dear sir, to address this communication to you. *You*, I am persuaded, will not accuse us of intermeddling, in this matter, with that which does not belong to us. You have welcomed the aid of your fellow-citizens at the north in the colonization enterprise, in the hope (if I have not misunderstood your views) that the influence of that enterprise would be conducive to the termination of slavery. You will not, therefore, object to the inquiry, whether our influence may not be exerted at the North, as well as at the South, bearing more directly upon such a consummation.

Our first object, in the correspondence proposed, is to obtain information. Permit me, then, to request your attention to the following inquiries :

Does the opinion generally prevail among the ministers and members of southern churches that slaveholding, as practised in this country, is sanctioned by the Word of God ? If this is not their opinion, how do they justify themselves in holding slaves ?

Do professors of religion forfeit their Christian character by *buying* and *selling* slaves, as they may find it convenient ? or do they subject themselves to censure and discipline by any immorality or ill treatment of which they may be guilty towards slaves ?

Since the discussion of slavery in the Legislature of Virginia a few years since, has there been in that State any change of opinion more favourable to the continuance of the present system ? If so, to what causes is that change to be attributed ?

Is it the general belief of humane and Christian Colonizationists at the South, that slaves *ought* not to be emancipated, unless they are also sent out of the country ? If this is their opinion, on what is it founded? Were they set free, would not their labour still be needed, and might it not be rewarded on terms more advantageous to both parties than under the present arrangements ?

Is there any good reason to believe that any thing of importance will be done, generally speaking, to prepare the slaves for freedom before they are made free ?

Is there not an under-current of opinion and feeling in the South, among the more enlightened and philanthropic, and is it not widening and strengthening, against the continuance of the present system, and an increasing conviction that it may safely and advantageously be abolished ?

What will probably be the influence upon the Southern mind of the experiment now in progress in the West Indies?

What, in your opinion, has been the effect, on the whole, at the South, of the efforts of abolitionists? Were the letters, which passed the last winter between Mr Ellmore and Mr Birney, read (to any considerable extent) by Southern members of Congress? So far as they were read, what was the impression produced by the statements and reasonings of Mr Birney?

Can there be any useful co-operation between the good people at the North and South (except by means of the Colonization Society) in efforts for abolishing or meliorating the present system of slavery?

What are the present prospects of the American Colonization Society?

Have many of the officers of this Society liberated and colonized their own slaves?

Begging you to excuse the liberty which I have now taken, and requesting an answer at as early a period as you may find it convenient,—I remain, my dear Sir, very respectfully, yours,

BENJAMIN TAPPAN.

To Francis S. Key, Esq.

P.S.—It is not proposed to make any public use of your name, in connection with any facts or opinions which you may have the kindness to communicate.

MR KEY'S REPLY.

Washington, 8th October 1838.

REV. AND DEAR SIR,—A long absence from home prevented my receiving your letter till lately; and, though I could wish for more time and leisure to answer it more fully and satisfactorily, I will endeavour to do it without further delay. I well remember our meeting on the occasion you mention; though that would not be necessary to induce me to treat with all respect and attention a letter from you on any subject, and particularly on one which has long and greatly interested me. Before I answer your questions, you will excuse my saying a few words for myself—as that may shew how far I am competent to answer them, and what my answers may be worth.

I was born in Maryland, and have always lived in a slave State,—am pretty well acquainted with the middle States, and have been as far as Alabama to the South. No northern man began the world with more enthusiasm against slavery than I did. For forty years and upwards, I have felt the greatest desire to see Maryland become a free State, and the strongest conviction that she could become so. That desire and that conviction have not abated in the least—I feel sure that it will be so. I have always been endeavouring to aid in promoting that object, and do so still. I consider it now in the course of accomplishment; and, could I give you all the facts in my possession, and the results of my observation and experience for many years, I believe you would come to this conclusion—that there is now a field open for the labours of all who wish to promote emancipation, to which they should direct and confine their efforts; and that such efforts, if pursued in the right way, would accomplish more, in comparatively a few years, than has ever been yet effected : and with these great advantages—that the dissensions arising from this delicate and exciting subject would be everywhere quieted, and the condition of the slaves in the other States greatly meliorated. Had I time, I would like to go on to the North and maintain these propositions. As this cannot be the case, let me now say a word or two more about them.

You may ask why such efforts should be confined to Maryland ? I answer: because, first, they would there be readily received ; secondly, her people see the advantages of her becoming a free State ; thirdly, she is the border State, and can obtain free-labour ; fourthly, that species of labour, already prevailing in some part of the State, manifests its superiority by every sort of improvement. These, and many other causes now in full operation, shew, what experience will prove, that no slave State adjacent to a free State can continue so. The people of Maryland are satisfied of this ; and a vast majority of them are not only content, but pleased at the prospect. Her Legislature has declared these views, and, with reference to such a result, has made liberal appropriations to the scheme of Colonization.—The State has a colony of its own at Cape Palmas. Its condition is flourishing ; and, notwithstanding many difficulties, and the violent and most unreasonable opposition of the abolitionists, the coloured people have consented to remove to it as fast as their establishment there could be prudently conducted, under present circumstances. It is true that her slave population is diminishing, at the same time, by other means. Her proximity to a free State enables many to escape. Indeed, near the Pennsylvania line, there are few slaves but such as are willing to continue so. Many are also sold, and many remove with their masters to the South, where their labour is more profitable. This, I agree, is not so favourable a disposition of them as colonization ; but it cannot be helped, and it is better for them than remaining slaves in Maryland, where the unprofitableness of their labour makes it difficult for their masters to maintain them comfortably.

You may also desire to know what I mean by qualifying these efforts to be made in Maryland, by saying they must be " *pursued in the right way*,"—and you may ask if I do not mean, by this *right way*, Colonization. I answer, that it must be done in a way that the people of Maryland will agree to. Nothing can be more unreasonable than to attempt it in any other way. And if there is any way, to which they will consent, which is better for the slaves than their present condition, it ought to be acquiesced in even by those who may think that there is a better way. Now, there are some ways in which the people of Maryland will never agree to these efforts being made ; 1st, Not by abolition publications—because they are dangerous and unnecessary. It is vain to argue about their being dangerous. They know it from experience, and certainly are better judges of what is dangerous to persons in their situation than any men elsewhere can be. Further—whether better judges or not, they will be, and they

ought to be, the only judges; for the danger is to themselves. And
such efforts are proved to be unnecessary; for there are now, and always have been, more slaves ready to be emancipated than there are
means to remove from the State, that condition of removal being, as the
people of Maryland think (allowing some exceptions), indispensable.
Of this I shall speak hereafter. 2dly, They will not allow an immediate and general emancipation, deeming it ruinous both to the slaves
and themselves. And, 3dly, They require, as a condition, removal
from the State, except in particular instances, where the slaves, on
account of their good conduct and character, may be allowed to remain, on certain conditions. That such removal may be accomplished
in a way advantageous to the liberated slaves, the door of colonization has been opened. We believe (we think upon undoubted evidence) that, besides the obvious and immense advantages to Africa,
this mode of disposition is the best for them; and we are sure that
time will make this apparent to all. But, if the people of the free
States think otherwise, and are so sure that they may remain safely,
happily, and usefully in Maryland, as to be willing to receive them
into their own limits, there would be no objection to their doing so.
If there is this difference of opinion as to their remaining among the
whites, between the people of the free States and the slave States,
surely the only fair way of settling it is for those who are in favour
of their remaining to take them. It is unnecessary, therefore, to discuss this question. If ever so necessary, I am sure it would be vain;
for the people of Maryland have an experience upon the subject that
no arguments could shake. And they will believe that they are
more competent to decide it than the people of the free States can
possibly be.

I will, however, state the result of my own experience. I have
emancipated seven of my slaves. They have done pretty well, and
six of them, now alive, are supporting themselves comfortably and
creditably. Yet I cannot but see that this is all they are doing now;
and when age and infirmity come upon them, they will probably
suffer. It is to be observed, also, that these were selected individuals,
who were, with two exceptions, brought up with a view to their being so disposed of, and were made to undergo a probation of a few
years in favourable situations, and, when emancipated, were far better fitted for the duties and trials of their new condition than the
general mass of slaves. Yet I am still a slaveholder, and could not,
without the greatest inhumanity, be otherwise. I own, for instance,
an old slave, who has done no work for me for years. I pay his
board and other expenses, and cannot believe that I sin in doing so.

The laws of Maryland contain provisions of various kinds, under
which slaves, in certain circumstances, are entitled to petition the
courts for their freedom. As a lawyer, I always undertook these
cases with peculiar zeal, and have been thus instrumental in liberat-
ing several large families and many individuals. I cannot remember
more than two instances, out of this large number, in which it did not
appear that the freedom I so earnestly sought for them was their ruin.

It has been so with a very large proportion of all others I have known emancipated. A gentleman in Maryland, upwards of thirty years ago, emancipated by his will between two and three hundred negroes. They all took (as they were required to do) his name. For several years, they crowded our cities, where their vices and idleness were notorious, and their sufferings extreme. I have not seen one for many years, and am informed that there are none in the county where they were liberated. There may be some in the free States. Their name was Barnes. I do not believe there could be now found in Maryland twenty of the name.

It is in vain, in the face of facts like these, which every man I have ever spoken with upon the subject avows his knowledge of, to talk of the British West India Islands and the apprentice system—at least, it must be vain to talk of these things till they are fully tried. I shall be surprised, though gratified, if the result of these experiments differ from that of similar attempts in Maryland. I observe that, at the last anti-slavery anniversary, it was admitted that the apprentice system was all wrong, and had failed; and now, the recent accounts from Jamaica represent the deplorable state of the island, in consequence of the refusal of the negroes to work, except for wages beyond the power of the planters to give.

I will proceed now to answer your questions. This is the first:

" Does the opinion generally prevail among the ministers and members of southern churches, that slaveholding, as practised in this country, is sanctioned by the Word of God? If this is not their opinion, how do they justify themselves in holding slaves ?"

The ministers and members of southern churches will not attempt to justify themselves in any thing without the sanction of the Word of God: the latter part, therefore, of the question is unnecessary. You ask, then, if we believe that slaveholding, as practised in this country, is sanctioned by the Word of God. I answer, that they believe generally, I think, that Scripture contains neither an express sanction nor an express prohibition on the subject. It gives general rules to govern men's conduct towards each other, applicable to this and all other cases. If men cannot hold slaves without violating these rules, they must not hold them ; and, if these rules permit or require us, under any circumstances, to hold slaves, then the Word of God sanctions *such* slave-holding. Take, then, the great rule of the Gospel—" Do unto others as you would they should do unto you." This must govern all possible cases of human conduct, and bears, of course, upon this question as to slave-holding. Does it sanction slave-holding *under all circumstances?* or prohibit slave-holding *under all circumstances?* It does (and, I think, most wisely) neither—leaving it to be determined by circumstances whether this law of love authorizes or forbids it. If a Christian, then, considering whether he shall hold a slave or not, takes this rule, and applies it honestly, as in the sight of God, to his case, and comes fairly to the conclusion that he should, who shall condemn him ? All that can be said is, that he is misled by prejudice or interest, and has come to a wrong conclusion. Hundreds and thousands of Christians, shewing in their whole life undoubted evidences of the faith which they profess, have so applied this rule to their conscience, and so come to this conclusion. Their brethren at the north, knowing nothing of the peculiar circumstances under which they have acted, nor of the care and faithfulness with which they have inquired and decided, call upon them to justify themselves for violating the sanctions of God's word. This, I am willing to believe, is more owing to want of information than of charity : though, certainly, even without information, it would be only reasonable to indulge the hope and the belief that there was something of a justificatory nature in the circumstances surrounding their distant brethren, which should relieve them from such an accusation.

Consider what a proposition it is that must be maintained by those who thus denounce, in these sweeping terms, all slave-holders. It is this : A man always violates the divine precept of doing as he would be done by when he holds a slave.

Strange as this proposition would sound to any one at all acquainted with the various circumstances under which persons in a slave State become the owners and holders of slaves, yet I doubt not many honest, but heated, abolitionists are ready to maintain it. Indeed, it is often avowed in their publications. Yet I think it is easy to state a few instances in which it would seem impossible to deny that this precept not only permitted, but required, the holding of a slave ; and they are instances continually occurring.

A man becomes (sometimes by no act of his own) the owner of an old or infirm slave, when emancipation would be the basest cruelty, and there is no way of maintaining him in comfort, but by holding him as a slave ; is he to be emancipated ? So of a slave who is idle, intemperate, &c. &c. who, without wholesome restraint, would be wretched himself, and a plague to all others ; would this Christian precept require him to be emancipated ? So of all cases where the holder of slaves conscientiously believes that their condition, from the peculiar circumstances of their situation, will be made worse by freedom—worse to themselves and others.

There are, again, other instances when a benevolent man will meet in a slave community with such appeals to his charity, that he will buy and hold slaves because he wishes to do as he would be done by. Many are so bought and held. A slave may have an unkind master— may be about to be sold away from his friends or family—a family of slaves may be liable to separation : in all these cases, a man who is known to be a good master, and who has the means of employing them so as to maintain them comfortably, will be importuned to purchase them. It will be a manifest improvement in their condition. Will not this Christian precept sanction his yielding to their entreaties ? It may be said that he should buy them and liberate them. This, even if satisfied that it would be better for them, he might not be able to afford. And shall he refuse to do the lesser charity because he has not the means to do the greater ?

I therefore answer your first question thus : " Slave-holding, as practised in this country, is sanctioned by the Word of God," when it is practised, as I know it often is, in such instances as I have stated, and in many others, consistently with the Christian precep of doing as we would be done by. And " slave-holding, as practised in this country " otherwise, as when slaves are bought and held for the mere purposes of gain by traffic, or by extorting their labour without any regard to their welfare (for it must be admitted that it is so practised by some), is not sanctioned by the Word of God. So that slave-holding is right or wrong (as many other things are) according as it is practised. I have not thought it necessary to advert to some passages of Scripture which it seems hard to reconcile with the idea that slave-holding, under all circumstances, is within its prohibitions.

Your second question is as follows :—

" Do professors of religion forfeit their Christian character by buying and selling slaves, as they may find it convenient ? or do they subject themselves to censure and discipline by any immorality or ill treatment of which they might be guilty towards their slaves ?"

The persons among us who buy and sell slaves for profit are never, as I have ever heard or believe, professors of religion. Such conduct, or any immorality or ill treatment towards their slaves, would forfeit their Christian character and privileges, if their minister did his duty. And nothing more disgraces a man in general estimation than to be guilty of any immorality or ill treatment towards his slaves.

Third question—" Since the discussion of slavery in the Legislature of Virginia, a few years since, has there been in that State any change of opinion more favourable to the continuance of the present system ? If so, to what causes is that change to be attributed ?"

A considerable change of opinion has taken place in all the middle States, particularly, perhaps, in Virginia and Maryland, such as your question suggests. Some who are favourable to emancipation connected with removal now avow themselves against it altogether, and against the agitation of every thing connected with slavery, and shew less kind feeling toward the blacks. I attribute this to the publications and efforts of the abolitionists.

Fourth question—" Is it the general belief of humane and Christian colonizationists in the south, that slaves ought not to be emancipated, unless they are also sent out of the country ? If this is their opinion, on what is it founded ? Were they set free, would not their labour still be needed, and might it not be secured on terms more advantageous to both parties than under present arrangements ?"

It is, I believe, universally so thought by them. I never heard a contrary opinion, except that some conceived, some time ago, that a territory in our country, to the West, might be set apart for them But few, comparatively, adopted this idea ; and I never hear it advocated now. This opinion is founded on the conviction that their labour, however it might be needed, could not be secured but by a severer system of constraint than that of slavery—that they would constitute a distinct and inferior race of people which all experience proves to be the greatest evil that could afflict a community. I do not suppose, however, that they would object to their reception in the free States, if they chose to make preparations for their comfortable settlement among them.

Fifth question—" Is there any good reason to believe that any thing of importance, generally speaking, will be done to prepare the slaves for freedom before they are made free?"

As the colonization scheme advances, I think much will be done. Many masters will prepare their young slaves for such a change. Many, who cannot afford to emancipate altogether, will make arrangements with their slaves to go to Africa, and remit a moderate price for themselves, as they may be able to do. And if a desire to return to their father's land should become general (as I trust it will), both among the slaves and free blacks, nothing could be better calculated to improve and exalt the whole coloured race. It would encourage them to good conduct, industry, temperance, and all those efforts that men make to better their condition.

Sixth—" Is there not an under-current of opinion and feeling in the South among the enlightened and philanthropic, and is it not widening and strengthening against the continuance of the present system, and an increasing conviction that it may safely and advantageously be abolished?"

I have not seen any appearance of such a current for several years past. I think it would be difficult to find any tolerably informed individual who holds such opinions or feelings. There was formerly some feeling of this kind in favour of a gradual abolition of slavery. I think there is none now, unless connected with the condition of removal. I assure you that I never hear, though I converse with men of all sorts, slaveholders and others, who hold no slaves, any opinion favourable to emancipation, except on that condition.

Seventh—" What will probably be the influence upon the southern mind of the experiment now in progress in the West Indies?"

If the southern mind becomes calm and unheated by opposition, and that experiment should succeed, it would, I think, have great effect—Removal from the country might not then be insisted on as a condition of emancipation.

Eighth—" What in your opinion, has been the effect, on the whole, at the South, of the efforts of abolitionists? Were the letters which passed last winter between Mr Elmore and Mr Birney read (to any considerable extent) by southern members of Congress? So far as they were read, what was the impression produced by the statements and reasonings of Mr Birney?"

I think the efforts of the abolitionists have been most unfortunate. There is a great and unfavourable change of opinion and feeling in the whites towards the blacks, which, I think, cannot be otherwise accounted for; and the whole coloured race have been injured by these efforts. The free and the slaves have been both subjected to more restraint. The publications mentioned have been very little read by southern men. They would rarely take up any thing understood to be written by a prominent abolitionist.

Ninth—" Can there be any useful co-operation between good people at the North and South (except by means of the Colonization Society) in efforts for abolishing or ameliorating the present system of slavery?"

I think good men at the North, if they will fairly inquire, will, both for the sake of Africa and our own land, prefer the colonization plan to any other. They must do this soon, as they must know (what they may know now) what benefits Africa is receiving, and our colonists are enjoying, under its efforts. But, if any of our Northern brethren cannot see this, let them prepare an asylum for emancipated slaves among themselves, where they can be usefully employed and happily settled, and raise funds for their removal and settlement. I believe as many could be obtained readily as could be thus provided for. In this way, they could essentially promote emancipation.

In "meliorating the present system of slavery," they could also do much. This might be done in several ways, but more particularly in assisting in their religious improvement—a subject which now greatly occupies the minds of southern men, particularly since the Southampton insurrection, which, you may know, originated with a religious fanatic, or a hypocrite playing the fanatic. From a variety of causes, the public mind, particularly of religious professors, has been turned to this subject. The Assistant-Bishop of Virginia, a year or two ago, made a strong appeal to the churches of his diocese; and the ministers of all denominations are taking up the subject, and considerable efforts are making for their regular religious instruction. The Bishop of North Carolina told me, a year ago, of very interesting commencements of this kind introduced into that State. He stated that it was now common for two or three neighbouring planters to join in employing a minister for their slaves; and he said he had then applications for ministers for six or seven such situations, and found it impossible to supply them. I was informed, last winter, of the arrangements made by Mr Rhett, a member of Congress from South Carolina, for the instruction of his negroes. He employs a minister, who lives on his estate, and devotes himself to the improvement of his slaves, for whom he has built a church, where they have regular service. I made several inquiries of Mr Rhett, who gave me a very interesting account of his establishment, and says it has introduced order, good conduct, and happiness among his slaves to a remarkable degree, and that many of his neighbours are endeavouring to adopt similar arrangements. Now, we want ministers for all these places. The demand for them is now great and earnest; and I believe that, in every neighbourhood where there are many slaves, in the middle States, such situations will be found. Let our Northern brethren qualify their young ministers for these interesting charges—qualify them, by making them understand this delicate subject of slavery—or, keeping them pure from all the fanaticism of abolition, send them with their minds open to conviction, where they may see and judge for themselves, and where they will learn that, while many Christians are holding slaves, from the necessity of their situation, they are holding them without forgetting they are their brethren,—and where they will see slaves far happier than the labouring classes of many countries. At present, young men from the

North are excluded from these situations, because they are supposed to be under the influence of abolition principles, and slaveholders are afraid to trust them. Let this prejudice against receiving young men from the North as teachers and ministers in such situations be removed, by a more correct and charitable state of feeling and opinion at the North towards slaveholders, and a wide and most interesting field of labour will be opened to pious young men from the northern States, in which they will be able to do much for the mel.oration of the present system of slavery, and, in some situations, where it can be done with advantage to the slaves and without danger to the masters, to promote emancipation also.

I will here mention that the religious instruction of the slaves in the middle States (I speak more particularly of Maryland) has been more attended to by the Methodists than by any other denomination. I think more than three-fourths of the whole coloured population, where they have access to Methodist churches, belong to that denomination. Nor is there any prejudice against the Methodist teachers and preachers, on the part of the masters, although that sect has been always considered friendly to emancipation. A change has, however, taken place, not only in the opinions and feelings of that class of Christians, but in the discipline of their church, which it may be proper to mention. It shews how Christians, strongly prejudiced against slavery, and anxious to abolish it, have been made to learn, by their own observation and experience, that, under certain circumstances, it is perfectly consistent with Christian principles to purchase and hold slaves. Methodists formerly denounced slavery in general terms, as it is now denounced at the north. They were never allowed, and would not be now, to act as jurors in a suit for freedom. They were not allowed by their discipline to continue in the church, if they purchased and held slaves. If a member of their church purchased a slave, no matter under what circumstances, the matter was brought before the monthly conference, and it was then determined, the age and value of the slave and the price paid for him being all considered, what was a reasonable term of service to be required of him as a compensation for what his master had paid for him—that is, how many years' service, at the usual rate of hire, would reimburse the advance of the master—and he was then to be no longer a slave, but a servant for that time.

The rule of discipline is now changed; and now, when a member of their Church purchases a slave, it is brought, as before, to the consideration of the conference, and the circumstances are inquired into. If it is considered that he has bought from a mercenary motive, for gain alone, without any inducements of kindness or favour towards the slave, he is censured and suspended from his church privileges, and made to do what is thought right, or excommunicated, according to the circumstances of mitigation or aggravation that may be found in the particular case. If he has bought from kindness to the slave, to prevent the separation of a family, or in any way with the motive of bettering his condition, he is allowed to hold him, and is considered as having acted consistently with Christian principles. In this way, Methodists now buy and work slaves as other Christians do; and their church (as is the case with all other denominations) only requires that they shall treat them well. Cruelty to slaves, if charged and sustained against any man belonging to a church of any denomination, would exclude him from its privileges, and would also exclude him from all reputable society. I do not mean to say that the slaves in Maryland are maintained as well as they ought to be; in some parts of the State, I know, as I have already said, their masters are unable to do so.

It may seem strange to gentlemen unacquainted with our institutions how a man can buy a slave from mere charity; yet nothing is more common—as a very short residence in any slave neighbourhood would convince them. Perhaps I may best shew this by supposing a case—it is such a one as often occurs: To make it more apposite, I will suppose the person applied to to be a man from the North, with the strongest prejudices against slavery. He buys a farm in Maryland, which he cultivates with hired labour, both because of his opposition to slavery, and because it is, in his opinion (as in some parts of Maryland it is in fact), cheaper than slave labour. He has nothing but his farm and its stock, and it requires all its produce, with a good management and strict economy, to maintain his family. Such a man, who has lived in this way a year or two, and whom we will designate as Mr B., is applied to on a Saturday evening by Tom, a stout, hearty young negro, and the following dialogue takes place between them:—

Tom. Master, I am come to ask a very great favour.

Mr B. Well, Tom, let me hear what it is. If what you want is reasonable and in my power, I shall be glad to do it.

Tom. Master, I think it is reasonable, and I hope it will lie in your power. My wife, you know, is a free woman, and has now been in your service some time. I was hired to you last harvest, and at other times, and you know what sort of a hand I am.

Mr B. Yes, Tom, I have been well satisfied with both your wife and yourself, and you know that I offered, partly to accommodate you both, to hire you by the year, but your master thought he could not spare you.

Tom. Well, sir, he must spare me now. I am to be sold; and what I want, and what would make me and my wife happy for our whole lives, is for you to buy me.

Mr B. Tom, that is out of the question. You know I hold no slaves—I am principled against it. I will go and see your master, and hire you. Surely he will not sell you.

Tom. Sir, he can't help it. They say he has had a power of money to pay for his cousin in town, who was broke up last spring; and another debt has now gone against him, last week, at the court. So he called me into the hall yesterday, and says he, " Tom, you have been a good fellow, and so was your father before you. You'll have to be sold by the sheriff, if you can't get a master in the neighbourhood: go and see what you can do." So he gave me this note, and he gave notice to all but the old people. He said he had been to the gentleman who held the debt; and all he could do was to give him one week, to try and sell the people himself, that the sheriff might not have to sell them to the soul-drivers. I am sure I am sorry for him, as well as for myself; for he has been a good master to us all.

Mr B. Tom, I am sorry for you; but I cannot buy a slave—I cannot give such a sanction to this horrible system. You must get somebody else to buy you : I will hire you, and give the highest wages. I know you are a good hand ; but I cannot hold a slave—it is against my principles.

Tom could not well understand this; but he went to two or three other neighbours without success, and he and his wife were in great trouble.

On Sunday night they were (as usual) called in to family prayers, and it so happened that Mr B., being in the habit of using, on such occasions, Doddridge's Family Expositor, came to that part of the book which contained the precept of our Saviour of doing to others as we would they should do unto us. The exposition of Doddridge is, as we know, very plain and very strong. Tom understood it, and thought it a pity that Mr B.'s *principles* should prevent him from doing the favour he asked. Mr B. was a Christian ; and he felt like a man who has two opposite principles to walk by. He saw it would be a kind thing to buy this poor fellow—that was plain—and that it was just what, in similar circumstances, he should wish done for himself. But slave-holding, he had long settled, was the height of wickedness—and how could he do it? If he could buy him and set him free, then his duty was plain : but this he could not afford to do with justice to his own family. It would leave him without adequate means to hire labour for his farm. Still he was not at ease ; and he arose early in the morning, and called Tom, whom he found taking a sorrowful leave of his wife.

Mr B. Tom, I am sorry I have not the means of buying you and setting you free. If I could afford it, I would gladly do so.

Tom. Master, if you could buy me and let me work for you as long as I live, that would be all I could ask. You would have to run the risk of my dying or running away ; but you would have my labour as long as I worked for you, and this would save you the hire of other hands—so that you might afford to do this, instead of buying me and setting me free for nothing.

Mr B. That is true, and I am not afraid of your running away, Tom ; but I cannot hold a slave—I must not be a slaveholder.

Tom. Master then hold me, not as a slave, but something else—buy me, and you can call me what you please ; you can tell me that I am not a slave and that I may run away when I please—you know I will not.

Mr B. Well, Tom, if I could get around this, I do not see how I can buy you. It would be owning your master's right to you as a slave, and his right to sell you.

Tom. Well, it is very hard. I don't see who has got any right to object to your buying or holding me as a slave, if I am agreed to it. If I ask such a favour, and you grant it, to save me from being sold away, who can complain of you for doing such a kindness—for doing as you would be done by?

Whether this argument succeeded with Mr B., or he was overpowered by the distress of Tom's wife, and the sympathy of his own wife and children, who all came around him, it might be hard to determine; but he told Tom to stay where he was, and he rode over to his master.

Before I conclude what I have to say under this question, permit me again to solicit your attention, and that of your friends, to the present situation of Maryland. This State is a slave State, bordering on a free State. She is changing her condition, as Pennsylvania and other States have done. Her Legislators and citizens very generally avow their determination that she shall be a free State. The free labour of Pennsylvania is flowing over into her, and she can change her labourers; and in many parts of the State bordering on Pennsylvania, there is now scarcely any slavery—certainly none that can be regarded as an evil—for there are no slaves there but such as choose to continue so. Such parts of the State also exhibit a remarkable degree of improvement; so as to convince all that Maryland, in the price, and improvements, and products of her land, in the increase and improvements of her population, and in many other respects, will derive incalculable benefits from the change.

I shall send you some documents and publications upon this subject, which will shew you what the Legislature of that State is doing, and what evident progress is making to accomplish the object of making Maryland a free State.

Thus will soon be worked out this political problem—"A slave State, lying by the side of a free State, will become a free State." I believe this as fully as any demonstration in Euclid.

What a prospect this opens to humane and benevolent men at the North, is obvious—particularly to such as desire to remove this blot from as many of our institutions as possible.

When Virginia becomes the border State she will be brought under the same process. Indeed, in some parts of that State, it is now in operation. Free labour will be brought to her, and she will find that she can change, and change most beneficially, her system. And so will it work on, till the dark line that separates the free from the slave States reaches the southern border of our land.

Thus, and thus only, is the slavery of the southern States to be approached. In many of them, now, it is absurd to propose any scheme of emancipation, or to address their people upon such a question.

But let the work be confined to the border States, and it will go on rapidly and safely.

The slaves of Maryland are diminishing every year, as will appear by the census. They are going off in various ways,—many are sold to the South—many are emancipated—some run away.

Hundreds of masters in Maryland are ready to emancipate their slaves, if they can go away—a condition which they know, from the fullest experience, is beneficial both to themselves and those they liberate. They have already emancipated a great number—some of whom have remained, and others have gone to Africa—and they know how great and obvious have been the advantages of removal.

In some parts of Maryland slave labour is no longer profitable. They cannot be maintained there. Their masters must remove with them, or dispose of them in some way. Humanity to them requires this.

Must they, then, go farther south as slaves? or to Africa as free men?

This is the condition of the coloured population of Maryland—this is the alternative presented for them to the consideration of the benevolent.

I agree that, if removal to Africa is that horrible act of cruelty that it is represented to be—if their condition in the colonies there established is as wretched as is asserted—Humanity may stand still, and be indifferent whether they go south as slaves, or cross the ocean as freemen.

And this brings me to the last topic of your letter—the present condition and prospects of the Colonization scheme. Examine this thoroughly and impartially, and see whether any thing has been done, or can be done, to compare with it, in its beneficial results to the coloured race here and in Africa.

All I need say of this (as I shall send you publications giving you full information on the subject) is, that I think I have seen more indications of the favour of Providence towards this object than any other I have ever considered— that its success is greater than that of any other similar enterprise ever undertaken, and that I have no doubt of its success—that the long-lost children of ill-fated Africa will be restored to their fathers' land, bearing with them the blessings of religion and civilization, and thus

" Vindicate the ways of God to man."

I have no objection to your making use of this communication, and of my name, in any way that you may think will do good.

I am, yours respectfully,

F. S. KEY.

P. S.—I did not observe that I had omitted to answer a part of your last question.

The publications of the society will shew that may of its members have emancipated their slaves, and sent them to Africa, and others have made arrangements for doing so. Mr Murray, of Maryland, sent out all his slaves (upwards of 30) nine or ten years ago ; and he often hears from them, and they speak with great satisfaction of their situation. Mr Fitzhugh, of Virginia, another member of the society, has made provision, by his will, for the removal of all his slaves (I believe about 200) to Africa. Most of those now in Africa have been emancipated with the view to their removal there.   F. S. K.

No. VI.—Referred to on p. 287.

RESOLUTIONS OF THE CLASS WHO ATTENDED THE SECOND COURSE OF LECTURES ON PHRENOLOGY IN NEW YORK.

The average attendance on this course was the following :—subscribers, 139 ; visiters, 35 ; complimentary hearers, 20 ; total average attendance each night, 194.

To George Combe, Esq.

New York, *May* 20. 1839.

Sir,—At a meeting of the class in attendance on your second course of lectures in this city, held on the 18th day of May 1839, the undersigned were appointed a committee to present the accompanying resolutions, which were unanimously adopted by the class, as expressive of their opinions of the truth and importance of Phrenology, of your talents as a lecturer, and of your character as a man.

In fulfilling this pleasurable duty, the undersigned beg to assure you of their hearty concurrence with the opinions and sentiments therein expressed, and of their high personal respect.

Thomas J. Sawyer,
La Roy Sunderland,
E. P. Hurlbut,
Andrew Boardman.

At a meeting of the class in attendance upon Mr George Combe's second course of Lectures, on the 15th day of May 1839, the following gentlemen were appointed a Committee to prepare and report a paper and resolutions expressive of the sentiments of the class, upon the subject of said lectures, and their feelings toward Mr Combe as a lecturer, to-wit : Rev. Mr Sawyer, Mr Boardman, Rev. Mr Sunderland and Mr Hurlbut.

On the 18th day of May instant, Mr Hurlbut, from that Committee, reported the following paper and resolutions, which were adopted unanimously by the class :

The second course of lectures upon Phrenology, delivered in this city by Mr George Combe, of Edinburgh, having closed, the members of his class are desirous of expressing their views of the science which he has taught, and the sentiments entertained by them toward the distinguished lecturer personally.

He has presented to us the wonderful discovery of Dr Gall, and its practical influence upon the character and condition of man. That discovery was characterized by the most minute attention to the laws of our organization—by the most patient observation of facts—and by the deduction of inevitable conclusions from them.

Dr Gall abandoned the school of metaphysical speculation, and taking to the observation of nature, he at length presented to the world his great discovery of the true functions of the brain, and of its various parts.

We now look to nature for the foundation of the science of mental philosophy, and the enlightened mind of the old world and the new is now engaged in illustrating and establishing it.

Our own country has been twice honoured by visits from the earliest and most gifted advocates of this science. The noble and accomplished Spurzheim (a name sacred to every friend of man) fell a victim to disease upon our shores, while just opening the rich fountain of his well-stored intellect to an American audience.

The language of eulogy fails altogether when employed upon so noble a nature as his. But for this we thank him—that he directed the mind of a Combe to the sublime truths he had himself embraced, and allowed his mantle to descend upon the gifted individual to whom we have all listened with intense interest and delight. How nobly has he executed in our coun try the work which his " great and lamented master" had begun !

He came not among us to earn applause, for of that he had already enough ; nor treasure, for we are happy to know of that he had no occasion to go in search. He came not seeking controversy, being no less distinguished for his love of peace than for his devotion to science. But he came as a minister from the enlightened mind of the old world, to treat with the intellect of the new upon matters of the deepest concern to the human race.

His message was of the highest importance to us all. It interested us as students of Nature's laws, as observers of their manifestations, as speculators in mental philosophy, and friends of education. It opened new views of man's moral and intellectual character, and well nigh explained the mystery of *thought*—that most subtle emanation from the divinity of Nature. It taught the discipline of youth : how to inform their intellect, to elevate their sentiments, and to moderate their passions. It pointed the way of happiness to man, by exhibiting the sources of human virtue and its effects ; the causes of vice, and its effects upon his condition in life. It presented the most rational and humane view of moral responsibility, and explained and enforced the whole duty of man ; and, in this his last and crowning lecture, Mr Combe has opened the treasures of his knowledge of the political institutions of the old world—faithfully portrayed their defects, their subversion of human liberty and happiness—and contrasted with them the free institutions of our own country and their happy influences upon the moral and intellectual condition of our citizens.

And now, having attended upon the gifted lecturer through his various illustrations, his well authenticated facts, and heard his sound deductions drawn from them, we hasten to express our profound sense of obligation to him for the instruction he has afforded us, and our high appreciation of the doctrines he has so ably maintained :

Be it therefore—

1. Resolved, That we regard Phrenology as having its foundation in the truths of Nature—and as entitled, in point of dignity and interest, to rank high among the natural sciences.

2. Resolved, That we regard the practical application of Phrenological principles, to physical training, to moral and mental education—to the treatment of the insane, and to criminal legislation—as of the highest importance and utility; and we indulge the hope of witnessing in our own day the beneficial results of such application in the increased happiness of our

homes, in the improved condition of our seminaries of learning, in more enlightened legislation, and in the more benign influences of our civil and religious institutions.

3. Resolved, That the extensive knowledge and sound philosophy which Mr Combe has exhibited in the course of his lectures, have inspired us with a profound respect for his intellectual power and attainments; and, while the simplicity of manner and purity of style with which he has conveyed the most interesting truths, evince a highly cultivated taste, the generous enthusiasm with which he has embarked in the cause of humanity commands our admiration of his sentiments equal to the respect we entertain for his understanding.

4. Resolved, That, entertaining such opinions of the science with which Mr Combe has identified his life and fame, and such sentiments toward him as a lecturer and a man, we beg to tender to him an expression of our heartfelt gratitude for the instruction and delight he has afforded us, and our kindest wishes for his prosperity and happiness through life.

On motion, it was farther resolved, That the gentlemen constituting the Committee who reported the foregoing, be instructed to present the same to Mr Combe.

T. I. SAWYER, Chairman.
ANDW. BOARDMAN, Secretary.

No. VII.—Referred to on p. 321.

(From the Albany Daily Advertiser.)

THE LAW OF THE ROAD.

AN esteemed correspondent sends us the following communication, which is of especial interest to the great moving mass of travellers, who at this season of the year throng our steam-boats, stages, and railroad cars. Most persons attach a vast deal of meaning to the brief notice, " All baggage at the risk of the owner," when in truth it imposes no additional care on the traveller, and certainly relieves of no responsibility the different transportation companies. *Their* duties as *common carriers* are clearly shewn in the annexed communication; and no notice of the above or any other description can free them from the obligations which they assume when they undertake to transport passengers and property.

" ALL BAGGAGE AT THE RISK OF THE OWNER."—Syracuse and Utica Railroad.

" All goods, baggage, freight, specie, bank-bills, or any kind of property taken, shipped, or put on board of these boats must be at the risk of the owners, &c."—New York, Albany, and Troy Steam-boat Line.

" Freight and baggage at the risk of the owners thereof."—Troy and Albany Steam-boats.

" All baggage positively at the risk of the owner. *Way passengers*

will attend personally to the disposition of their baggage at Schenectady."
—Utica and Schenectady Railroad.

" All baggage at the risk of the owners thereof."—Saratoga and Schenectady Railroad, Troy, Ballston, and Saratoga Railroad.

" All baggage at the risk of the owner."—Auburn and Syracuse Railroad.

" All baggage, specie, and freight at the risk of the owners thereof." —New Steam-boat arrangement between Albany and New York.

To the Editor of the Albany Daily Advertiser:

The above notices are taken from advertisements in a single column of the Albany Argus.

As quiet or ignorant people may perhaps be induced to submit to the imposition of a loss of their freight or baggage rather than litigate with a great monopoly, especially when the above notices are thrust in their faces, and they are told *they were bound to take notice of them;* it will perhaps be doing the travelling public a service by referring them to two decisions of the Supreme Court of this State, to-wit: Holister v. Nawlen, 19 Wendell's Reports 234, and Cole v. Goodwin, ibid. 251, both decided at the May term, 1838, in which it is expressly decided, that stage-coach, railroad, and steam-boat proprietors *are common carriers,* and are, like all other common carriers, answerable for the baggage of passengers, that they are regarded as *insurers,* and must answer for any loss not occasioned *by the act of God, or the public enemies.* That the fact that *the owner is present,* or sends his servants to look after the property, does not alter the case. That common carriers cannot restrict their common law liability, by a general notice like that which I have taken above as the text of this article—that a notice, " ALL BAGGAGE AT THE RISK OF THE OWNER," *even if brought home to the knowledge of a passenger* in a stage coach who lost his trunk, was no protection to the proprietors of the coach in an action against them for the loss of the trunk. That *common carriers* are bound to deliver to *each passenger* at the end of *his* journey *his* trunk or baggage. That *the whole duty* in this respect rests upon the carriers. That the exercise of ordinary care in marking the baggage, entering it upon a way-bill, and delivering a check-ticket to the owner, renders easy its discharge. That the *passenger* is not required to expose his person in a crowd, or endanger his safety in the attempt to *designate* or *claim* his property.

What is the reason that the common law will not excuse the carrier unless he shew the act of God, or the enemies of the republic, or the misconduct of the owner? " This," says Lord Holt, in Coggs v. Bernard, 2d Lord Raymond's Reports, 918, " is a politic establishment, contrived by the policy of the law, for the safety of all persons, the necessity of whose affairs requires them to trust these sort of persons *(common carriers)* that they may be safe in their ways of dealing, for else these carriers might have an opportunity of undoing all persons that had any dealings with them, by combining with thieves, &c., and yet doing it in such a clandestine manner as would not be possible to be discovered.

Cowen Justice, in Cole *v.* Goodwin, cited above, says at page 280, " I have said that relaxing the common law rigour opens the high road to fraud, perjury, theft, and robbery. It does more. Looking to the present ordinary, not to say universal means of travel and transportation by coaches, railroads, steam-boats, packets, and merchant vessels, the mere superaddition of negligence, in respect to the safety of passengers and property, would constitute a most fearful item. There is no principle in the law better settled than that whatever has an obvious tendency to encourage guilty negligence, fraud, or crime, is contrary to public policy. Such, in the very nature of things, is the consequence of allowing the common carrier to throw off or in any way restrict his legal liability. The traveller and bailor is under a sort of moral duress, a necessity of employing the common carrier under those legal arrangements, which allow any number of persons to assume that character, and thus discourage and supersede the provision for other modes of conveyance. My conclusion is, that he shall not be allowed, in any form, to higgle with his customer, and extort one exception and another, *not even by express promise, or special acceptance,* any more than by notice. He shall not be privileged to make himself a common carrier for his own benefit, and a mandatary, or less to his employer. He is a public servant with certain duties defined by law ; and he is bound to perform those duties."

No. VIII.—Referred to on p. 324.

The following table will exhibit the relative strength of the different brines from which salt is manufactured in the United States :—

At Nantucket, 350 gallons sea-water give a bushel of Salt.

Boon's Lick (Missouri),	.	450 gallons brine, give	do.
Conemaugh (Penn.),	. .	300 do.	do.
Shawneetown (Illinois),		280 do.	do.
Jackson (Ohio),	. . . .	213 do.	do.
Lockharts (Miss.),	. . .	180 do.	do.
Shawneetown (2d saline),		123 do.	do.
St Catharines (U. C.),	. .	120 do.	do.
Zanesville (Ohio),	. . .	95 do.	do.
Kenawha (Va.),	. . . .	75 do.	do.
Grand River (Arkansas),		80 do.	do.
Illinois River, do.		80 do.	do.
Muskingum (Ohio),	. .	50 do.	do.
Onondaga,* (N. Y.),	.	41 to 45 do.	do.

* This table is chiefly extracted from Dr J. Van Rensselaer's Essay on Salt. The produce of the Kenawha brine, and of the Muskingum saline is added from Hildreth's observations on the saliferous rock-formation in the valley of the Ohio.—Silliman's Journal, No. XXIV. p. 65.

TABLE

SHEWING THE COMPOSITION OF VARIOUS BRINES, FROM ONONDAGA AND CAYUGA COUNTIES, NEW YORK.

LOCALITY OF THE WELL OR SPRING.	Total amount of solid matter in 1000 grains of brine.	Carbonic Acid.	Oxide of Iron and Silica, with a trace of Carbonate of Lime.	Carbonate of Lime.	Sulphate of Lime.	Chloride of Magnesium.	Chloride of Calcium.	Chloride of Sodium, or pure Common Salt.	Water, with a trace of Organic Matter. &c.	Total.
ONONDAGA.										
From the Well at Geddes,	138.55	0.06	0.04	0.10	4.93	0.79	2.03	130.66	861.39	1000
From the Well at Syracuse,	139.53	0.07	0.02	0.14	5.69	0.46	0.83	132.39	860.40	1000
From the Well at Salina,	146.50	0.09	0.04	0.17	4.72	0.51	1.04	140.02	853.41	1000
From the Well at Liverpool,	149.54	0.07	0.03	0.13	4.04	0.77	1.72	142.85	850.39	1000
CAYUGA.										
From a Well at Montezuma.	101.20	0.08	0.02	0.18	5.25	1.00	1.40	93.35	898.72	1000

END OF VOLUME SECOND.